MARTIAL POWER™

ROLEPLAYING GAME SUPPLEMENT

Rob Heinsoo • David Noonan • Chris Sims • Robert J. Schwalb

CREDITS

Design
Rob Heinsoo (lead),
David Noonan, Chris Sims, Robert J. Schwalb

Additional Design
Andy Collins, Nicolas Logue, Rodney Thompson

Development
Stephen Radney-MacFarland (lead),
Stephen Schubert, Peter Schaefer

Editing
Jeremy Crawford (lead),
M. Alexander Jurkat, Gwendolyn F.M. Kestrel

Managing Editing
Kim Mohan

Director of R&D, Roleplaying Games/Book Publishing
Bill Slavicsek

D&D Story Design and Development Manager
Christopher Perkins

D&D System Design and Development Manager
Andy Collins

Art Director
Ryan Sansaver

Special thanks to Brandon Daggerhart, keeper of Shadowfell

Cover Illustration
William O'Connor

Graphic Designer
Emi Tanji

Interior Illustrations
Steve Belledin, Leonardo Borazio, Steve Ellis,
Wayne England, Jason A. Engle, Gonzalo Flores,
Adam Gillespie, Brian Hagan, Jeremy Jarvis, Ron Lemen,
Wes Louie, Howard Lyon, Lee Moyer, Lucio Parrillo,
Jim Pavelec, Steve Prescott, Vincent Proce, Ron Spears,
Ron Spencer, Stephen Tappin, Mark Tedin, Beth Trott,
Ben Wootten

Publishing Production Specialist
Erin Dorries

Prepress Manager
Jefferson Dunlap

Imaging Technician
Sven Bolen

Production Manager
Cynda Callaway

Game rules based on the original DUNGEONS & DRAGONS® rules created by **E. Gary Gygax** and **Dave Arneson**, and the later editions by **David "Zeb" Cook** (2nd Edition); **Jonathan Tweet, Monte Cook, Skip Williams, Richard Baker**, and **Peter Adkison** (3rd Edition); and **Rob Heinsoo, Andy Collins**, and **James Wyatt** (4th Edition).

620-21789720-001 EN
987654321
First Printing: October 2008
ISBN: 978-0-7869-4981-6

U.S., CANADA, ASIA, PACIFIC,
& LATIN AMERICA
Wizards of the Coast, Inc.
P.O. Box 707
Renton WA 98057-0707
+1-800-324-6496

EUROPEAN HEADQUARTERS
Hasbro UK Ltd
Caswell Way
Newport, Gwent NP9 0YH
GREAT BRITAIN
Please keep this address for your records

WIZARDS OF THE COAST, BELGIUM
't Hofveld 6D
1702 Groot-Bijgaarden
Belgium
+32 2 467 3360

VISIT OUR WEBSITE AT WWW.WIZARDS.COM/DND

INTRODUCTION

Armor and shield, blade and bow, stealth and cunning, tactics and command—all of these are the tools of a warrior. One warrior might favor some of these assets over others, depending on training and inclination. All legendary warriors develop martial power to such an extent that their abilities are the equal of magical abilities. Such warriors are always looking for an edge or a technique that exemplifies their manner of fighting.

That's what you'll find in this book.

It's a manual of mighty deeds and wily tricks. In its pages are new ways to build a martial character, along with new options to fill out your role as a fighter, a ranger, a rogue, or a warlord. Members of nonmartial classes might find an appropriate multiclass feat in these pages, but everything else is for martial characters. It is intended to expand your martial horizons in the game.

Using This Book

As you can see by the table of contents, *Martial Power* is organized by class. Whether you have a character of a certain class or you want to make a character of that class, all you have to do is consult the proper chapter for new builds, class features, powers, and paragon paths. The final chapter of the book contains nearly two hundred new feats to hone your martial talents and ten new epic destinies for martial characters.

Use the *Martial Power*™ supplement to start playing a new character with a new build, to pick powers that better define your existing character, or to evolve your character with specific feats, such as those that have racial and class prerequisites. The paragon paths introduced here might allow you to fully express the style you always intended your character to have.

Reimagining Your Character

It happens. You've played your martial character a while, and suddenly *Martial Power* shows up, offering many new possibilities—options you might have picked if you had known about them earlier.

Don't despair; you have a few choices. Retraining rules (see page 28 of the *Player's Handbook*®) make tapping into *Martial Power* easy. If retraining won't do the trick quickly enough, talk to your DM and your fellow players about reworking your character along the lines *Martial Power* provides. Chances are you can overhaul your PC to match your desires without doing any harm to the campaign. Your DM might even have a way to make the change a part of the story. If doing that ultimately proves too difficult, a dramatic exit for the older character could make way for a new one.

CONTENTS

CHAPTER 1

FIGHTER

"Battle line? Formation? Listen—I came here to kill whatever comes at us, not to march in a parade. I'll keep you alive by makin' the bad guys dead. Got me?"

A **FIGHTER** can use training and talent to be a good defender. Doing so is the typical soldier's path. But not all fighters follow that path. Maybe you channel your indignation and bloodlust such that you defy your adversaries despite blows that land solidly. Or maybe you take up two weapons and focus on audacious assaults. In these ways, a good offense makes for solid defense.

Specialized techniques aren't the sole purview of unorthodox fighters, however. Combat systems are as numerous as weapons and the individual warriors who use them. Concentration on a weapon or a style can make your path clear, since certain exploits lend themselves to particular ways of fighting.

Whether you're a scale-clad, sword-and-board trooper; a tattooed, axe-wielding savage; a dual-wielding warrior who moves the battle line from moment to moment; or another sort of fighter, this chapter is for you. It contains the following material.

✦ **New Fighter Builds:** The battlerager and the tempest present different styles of combat that protect your allies while laying your enemies low.

✦ **New Class Features:** Two alternative choices give you the opportunity to focus your fighter even more sharply on one of the new builds.

✦ **New Fighter Powers:** Bring fear of your weapon prowess to your foes in new ways, including exploits that make your basic attacks and charges more dangerous.

✦ **New Paragon Paths:** Your particular road to glory can be represented by one of a dozen new paragon paths, each with its own flair.

GONZALO FLORES

To supplement the fighter builds described in the *Player's Handbook*, this chapter presents two additional groups of fighters who use different styles of melee combat: the battlerager and the tempest.

BATTLERAGER FIGHTER

You're an unpredictable warrior who trusts the adrenaline rush of battle to pull you through as much as heavy armor does. Few aspects of life give you the charge that being in the heat of battle does, and you build up a fury when your enemies manage to hurt you. You thrive on taking it to those foes by wielding highly damaging weapons such as axes, maces, hammers, and picks. Strength is your focus, allowing you to make powerful attacks. You rely on Constitution to give weight to your attacks and to keep you in the fight. Like any other soldier, you count on brutal instinct to help you win the day, so Wisdom is important to you as well. The Battlerager Vigor class feature is designed to complement this build.

Suggested Feat: Power Attack (Human feat: Durable)

Suggested Skills: Athletics, Endurance, Intimidate

Suggested At-Will Powers: *brash strike,* crushing surge**

Suggested Encounter Power: *bell ringer**

Suggested Daily Power: *knee breaker**

*New option presented in this book

TEMPEST FIGHTER

Rather than a shield or a big weapon, you have specialized in fighting using a weapon in each hand. You see it as the best of both worlds—given the right training, you can deliver good damage and make up for the lack of a shield with deft parrying. Strength remains any soldier's bread and butter, and good battlefield awareness—Wisdom—is a must. You also rely on speed, maneuverability, and agility—Dexterity—to get your dirty work done. Constitution is a tertiary ability for you, granting useful staying power against foes not so easily fooled by your fancy footwork and feints. The Tempest Technique class feature is designed to complement this build.

Suggested Feat: Two-Weapon Fighting (Human feat: Human Perseverance)

Suggested Skills: Athletics, Intimidate, Streetwise

Suggested At-Will Powers: *dual strike,* footwork lure**

Suggested Encounter Power: *funneling flurry**

Suggested Daily Power: *tempest dance**

*New option presented in this book

NEW CLASS FEATURES

These fighter class features are available to any fighter who wishes to explore a different area of expertise. You can select one of the following features in place of the Fighter Weapon Talent class feature.

BATTLERAGER VIGOR

Each time an enemy hits you with a melee or a close attack, you gain temporary hit points equal to your Constitution modifier (after the attack is resolved).

When you gain temporary hit points by hitting with an attack that has the invigorating keyword, those temporary hit points stack with any other temporary hit points you already have.

When wearing light armor or chainmail, you gain a +1 bonus to damage rolls with melee and close weapon attacks whenever you have temporary hit points. This bonus increases to +2 if you're wielding an axe, a hammer, a mace, or a pick.

TEMPEST TECHNIQUE

When you wield two melee weapons, you gain a +1 bonus to attack rolls with weapons that have the off-hand property.

You gain Two-Weapon Defense as a bonus feat, even if you don't meet the prerequisites.

When wearing light armor or chainmail, you gain a +1 bonus to damage rolls with melee and close weapon attacks when you are wielding two weapons. This bonus increases to +2 with weapons that have the off-hand property.

NEW FIGHTER POWERS

The tempest fighter and the battlerager fighter center on these powers. Fighters of any stripe can find powers here to their liking, however.

NEW KEYWORDS

Some of the powers in this chapter use these new keywords.

Invigorating: If you are trained in the Endurance skill, you gain temporary hit points equal to your Constitution modifier when you hit with a power that has this keyword. No invigorating power grants temporary hit points more than once per turn, even if you hit more than once with the power or use more than one power with the invigorating keyword in a round.

Rattling: If you are trained in Intimidate and you deal damage with an attack that has this keyword, the target takes a −2 penalty to attack rolls until the end of your next turn. A creature immune to fear is not subject to this penalty.

LEVEL 1 AT-WILL EXPLOITS

Brash Strike	Fighter Attack 1

With a battle cry, you throw your whole body behind your attack.

At-Will ✦ Martial, Weapon
Standard Action   **Melee** weapon
Target: One creature
Attack: Strength + 2 vs. AC
Hit: 1[W] + Strength modifier damage.
Increase damage to 2[W] + Strength modifier at 21st level.
    Weapon: If you're wielding an axe, a hammer, or a mace, the attack deals extra damage equal to your Constitution modifier.
Effect: You grant combat advantage to the target until the start of your next turn.

Crushing Surge	Fighter Attack 1

The feel of your weapon crunching against the enemy puts your heart back in the fight.

At-Will ✦ Invigorating, Martial, Weapon
Standard Action   **Melee** weapon
Target: One creature
Attack: Strength vs. AC
Hit: 1[W] + Strength modifier damage.
Increase damage to 2[W] + Strength modifier at 21st level.

Dual Strike	Fighter Attack 1

You lash out quickly and follow up faster, delivering two small wounds.

At-Will ✦ Martial, Weapon
Standard Action   **Melee** weapon
Requirement: You must be wielding two melee weapons.
Target: One creature
Attack: Strength vs. AC (main weapon and off-hand weapon), two attacks
Hit: 1[W] damage per attack.
Increase damage to 2[W] per attack at 21st level.

Footwork Lure	Fighter Attack 1

You press the attack, engaging your enemy before falling back and drawing him after you.

At-Will ✦ Martial, Weapon
Standard Action   **Melee** weapon
Target: One creature
Attack: Strength vs. AC
Hit: 1[W] + Strength modifier damage. You can shift 1 square and slide the target into the space you left.

LEVEL 1 ENCOUNTER EXPLOITS

Bell Ringer	Fighter Attack 1

You smash your weapon into your enemy, jarring his vitals.

Encounter ✦ Invigorating, Martial, Weapon
Standard Action   **Melee** weapon
Target: One creature
Attack: Strength vs. Fortitude
Hit: The target is dazed until the end of your next turn.
    Weapon: If you're wielding an axe, a hammer, or a mace, the attack deals damage equal to your Constitution modifier.

BUILD AND ATTITUDE

How does your fighter character's build affect his or her personality? It's easy to imagine a guardian fighter as a disciplined soldier, focused on tactics that keep his companions safe. A battlerager fighter, though, might be more like a rampaging juggernaut, rushing at the foe with little thought for anyone's safety. Tempest fighters and great weapon fighters might fall between those two extremes.

Distracting Spate
Fighter Attack 1

Your flurry of feints and strikes leaves your foe's defenses unsteady.

Encounter ✦ Martial, Weapon
Standard Action   Melee weapon
Target: One creature
Attack: Strength vs. AC
Hit: 2[W] + Strength modifier damage, and the target grants combat advantage to you until the end of your next turn.
   Weapon: If you're wielding two melee weapons, the attack deals extra damage equal to your Dexterity modifier.

Funneling Flurry
Fighter Attack 1

With snakelike strikes, you force two of your enemies to move where you want them.

Encounter ✦ Martial, Weapon
Standard Action   Melee weapon
Requirement: You must be wielding two melee weapons.
Targets: Two creatures
Attack: Strength vs. AC (main weapon and off-hand weapon), one attack per target
Hit: 1[W] + Strength modifier damage, and you slide the target 1 square.

Insightful Strike
Fighter Attack 1

Your opponent is showing weakness, and your shrewdness allows you to exploit it.

Encounter ✦ Martial, Weapon
Standard Action   Melee weapon
Target: One creature
Attack: Strength vs. AC
Hit: 2[W] + Strength modifier damage. If the target is bloodied, the attack deals extra damage equal to your Wisdom modifier.

Lunging Strike
Fighter Attack 1

You lunge at a foe that thought it was beyond your reach.

Encounter ✦ Martial, Weapon
Standard Action   Melee weapon + 1 reach
Target: One creature
Attack: Strength - 1 vs. AC
Hit: 2[W] + Strength modifier damage.

DRAGONBORN FIGHTERS

With their naturally high Strength, dragonborn make excellent great weapon fighters or battleragers, putting that physical power to good use with two-handed swords or axes. Like Harann (described in the *Player's Handbook*), many dragonborn fighters strive to achieve mastery of a weapon as they seek the perfection of their spirits. The inner dragon paragon path (page 29) represents a dragonborn fighter who taps into the power of the dragon within.

Shield Bash
Fighter Attack 1

You knock your adversary off balance with your shield and follow up with a strike.

Encounter ✦ Martial
Standard Action   Melee 1
Requirement: You must be using a shield.
Target: One creature
Attack: Strength + 2 vs. Reflex
Hit: 1d10 + Strength modifier damage, and you push the target 1 square and knock it prone.
   Special: If you are a dwarf, the attack deals extra damage equal to your Wisdom modifier.
   Special: When charging, you can use this power in place of a melee basic attack.

LEVEL 1 DAILY EXPLOITS

Flanking Assault
Fighter Attack 1

The presence of so many enemies overwhelms your foe, giving you the opportunity to land a vicious attack.

Daily ✦ Martial, Weapon
Standard Action   Melee weapon
Target: One creature you're flanking
Attack: Strength vs. AC
Hit: 3[W] + Strength modifier damage. For each ally adjacent to the target, the attack deals extra damage equal to your Dexterity modifier.
Miss: Half damage.

Harrier's Ploy
Fighter Attack 1

Your forceful attack promises your foe a pursuit that can end only when one of you is victorious.

Daily ✦ Martial, Weapon
Standard Action   Melee weapon
Target: One creature
Attack: Strength vs. AC
Hit: 3[W] + Strength modifier damage.
Effect: Until the end of the encounter, if the target moves, you can shift a number of squares equal to your Dexterity modifier as an immediate reaction.

DWARF FIGHTERS

Although they're not as strong as dragonborn, dwarves combine high Constitution and high Wisdom to make excellent fighters. Like most dwarves, dwarf fighters favor axes and hammers—partly for cultural reasons and partly because those weapons let them put their Constitution to good use for extra damage. Dwarves have a strong tradition of guardian fighters, and the dwarven defender paragon path (page 27) is the pinnacle of that tradition.

Knee Breaker — Fighter Attack 1

By smashing into your opponent's legs, you make even the thought of moving painful for him.

Daily ✦ Invigorating, Martial, Weapon
Standard Action   **Melee** weapon
Target: One creature
Attack: Strength vs. AC
Hit: 2[W] + Strength modifier damage, and the target is slowed (save ends). If the target is already slowed, it is instead immobilized (save ends).
  Weapon: If you're wielding an axe, a hammer, or a mace, the attack deals extra damage equal to your Constitution modifier.
Miss: Half damage, and the target is not slowed or immobilized.

Lasting Threat — Fighter Attack 1

Following up your challenge with a solid attack, you force your enemy to engage you.

Daily ✦ Martial, Reliable, Weapon
Standard Action   **Melee** weapon
Target: One creature
Attack: Strength vs. AC
Hit: 3[W] + Strength modifier damage, and the target is marked until the end of the encounter or until you are knocked unconscious. No mark can supersede this one.

Tempest Dance — Fighter Attack 1

You lunge from enemy to enemy, giving each a taste of your weapon as you pass.

Daily ✦ Martial, Weapon
Standard Action   **Melee** weapon
Target: One creature
Attack: Strength vs. AC
Hit: 1[W] + Strength modifier damage. If you have combat advantage against the target, the attack deals extra damage equal to your Dexterity modifier.
Effect: You can shift 1 square and repeat the attack against a second target. You can then shift 1 square and repeat the attack against a third target.

LEVEL 2 UTILITY EXPLOITS

Create Opening — Fighter Utility 2

You draw your enemy's attention, allowing an ally to slip away.

Encounter ✦ Martial
Minor Action   **Melee** 1
Target: One creature
Effect: The target is marked until the end of your next turn. The target can then make a melee basic attack against you as a free action, with a -2 penalty to the attack roll. One ally adjacent to the target can shift its speed as a free action.

Defensive Stance — Fighter Utility 2

Dropping into a cautious stance, you maneuver around your opponent's attacks to get into position.

Daily ✦ Martial, Stance
Minor Action   **Personal**
Effect: Until the stance ends, you are slowed and gain a +2 power bonus to AC. Whenever an enemy misses you with a melee attack, you can shift 1 square as an immediate reaction. You can end this stance as a free action.

Pass Forward — Fighter Utility 2

With perfect timing, you slip by your foe without dropping your guard.

At-Will ✦ Martial
Move Action   **Personal**
Effect: You pick an adjacent enemy and move up to your speed. As long as you end this movement in a square adjacent to that enemy, your movement does not provoke opportunity attacks from that enemy.

Shielded Sides — Fighter Utility 2

You whirl with your shield, concentrating on closing any holes in your defenses.

Encounter ✦ Martial
Minor Action   **Personal**
Requirement: You must be using a shield.
Effect: Until the end of your next turn, you gain a +2 power bonus to AC and Reflex and do not grant combat advantage to creatures flanking you.

Shrewd Repositioning — Fighter Utility 2

An enemy's attack lands, but you spot a way to better your tactics.

Encounter ✦ Martial
Immediate Reaction   **Personal**
Trigger: You are hit by an attack
Effect: You can shift a number of squares equal to your Wisdom modifier.

LEVEL 3 ENCOUNTER EXPLOITS

Advance Lunge — Fighter Attack 3

You spring forward to make a quick attack.

Encounter ✦ Martial, Weapon
Standard Action   **Melee** weapon
Effect: Before the attack, you can shift 1 square.
    Weapon: If you're wielding a light blade or a spear, you can either shift 2 squares before the attack or shift 1 square before and 1 square after.
Attack: Strength vs. AC
Hit: 2[W] + Strength modifier damage. If you have combat advantage against the target, the attack deals extra damage equal to your Dexterity modifier.

Blinding Smash — Fighter Attack 3

A sharp blow leaves your enemy seeing only stars.

Encounter ✦ Invigorating, Martial, Weapon
Standard Action   **Melee** weapon
Target: One creature
Attack: Strength vs. Fortitude
Hit: The target is blinded until the end of your next turn.
    Weapon: If you're wielding an axe, a hammer, or a mace, the attack deals damage equal to your Constitution modifier.

Parry and Riposte — Fighter Attack 3

You parry an attack and quickly counter with your own, throwing your foe off balance.

Encounter ✦ Martial, Weapon
Immediate Reaction   **Melee** weapon
Trigger: An enemy misses you or an ally with a melee attack
Target: The triggering enemy
Attack: Strength vs. AC
Hit: 1[W] + Strength modifier damage, and the target grants combat advantage to you and your allies until the end of your next turn.

Probing Attack — Fighter Attack 3

With a careful strike, you find a weak spot in your enemy's defenses.

Encounter ✦ Martial, Weapon
Standard Action   **Melee** weapon
Target: One creature
Attack: Strength vs. Reflex
Hit: 1[W] + Strength modifier damage, and you gain a +4 power bonus to attack rolls against the target until the end of your next turn.
Special: When making an opportunity attack, you can use this power in place of a melee basic attack.

Rhino Strike — Fighter Attack 3

Rushing into the thick of battle, you smash your foes with your eager attack.

Encounter ✦ Martial, Weapon
Standard Action   **Melee** weapon
Requirement: You must charge and use this power in place of a melee basic attack. If you're using a shield, the movement during your charge does not provoke opportunity attacks.
Target: One creature
Attack: Strength vs. AC
Hit: 2[W] + Strength modifier damage.

Shield Slam — Fighter Attack 3

You follow up a successful attack by slamming your shield into the enemy, knocking him aside.

Encounter ✦ Martial
Free Action   **Melee** 1
Trigger: You hit an enemy with a melee attack
Requirement: You must be using a shield.
Target: The triggering enemy
Attack: Strength + 2 vs. Fortitude
Hit: You push the target 1 square and knock it prone.

LEVEL 5 DAILY EXPLOITS

Agonizing Assault — Fighter Attack 5

Your attack hits your adversary in a sensitive area, causing it to reel in pain.

Daily ✦ Martial, Weapon
Standard Action   Melee weapon
Target: One creature
Attack: Strength vs. AC
Hit: 2[W] + Strength modifier damage, and the target is dazed and immobilized (save ends both).
  Weapon: If you're wielding a flail, the attack deals extra damage equal to your Dexterity modifier.
Miss: Half damage, and the target is not dazed or immobilized.

Bedeviling Assault — Fighter Attack 5

While your ally distracts your opponent, you land yet another blow.

Daily ✦ Martial, Weapon
Standard Action   Melee weapon
Target: One creature
Attack: Strength vs. AC
Hit: 2[W] + Strength modifier damage.
Effect: Until the end of the encounter, once per round when an ally hits the target with a melee attack, you can make a melee basic attack with combat advantage against the target as a free action.

Cometfall Charge — Fighter Attack 5

You leap through the air toward your foe, landing with a resounding crunch.

Daily ✦ Martial, Weapon
Standard Action   Melee weapon
Prerequisite: You must be trained in Athletics.
Requirement: You must charge and use this power in place of a melee basic attack.
Target: One creature
Attack: Strength vs. AC
Hit: 3[W] + Strength modifier + Constitution modifier damage.
Miss: Half damage.

Hounding Longarm — Fighter Attack 5

With a sharp jab, you shove your enemy backward, continuing to guard against him with your polearm.

Daily ✦ Martial, Weapon
Standard Action   Melee weapon
Requirement: You must be wielding a reach weapon.
Target: One creature
Attack: Strength vs. Fortitude
Hit: 2[W] + Strength modifier damage, and you push the target 1 square.
  Special: If you are an eladrin, the attack deals extra damage equal to your Dexterity modifier.
Effect: Until the end of the encounter, each time the target shifts or makes an attack that doesn't include you as a target, you can shift 1 square and make a melee basic attack against the target as an immediate interrupt.

Pinning Smash — Fighter Attack 5

You pummel your opponent, knocking him to his knees. You then hold him down.

Daily ✦ Invigorating, Martial, Weapon
Standard Action   Melee 1
Target: One creature
Attack: Strength vs. AC
Hit: 1[W] + Strength modifier damage, and the target is immobilized until you are not adjacent to it.
  Weapon: If you're wielding an axe, a hammer, or a mace, the attack deals extra damage equal to your Constitution modifier.
Miss: Half damage, and the target is immobilized until the end of your next turn.

Subtle Cut — Fighter Attack 5

You deftly maneuver to precisely slash your foe, drawing its blood and slowing it with suffering.

Daily ✦ Martial, Weapon
Standard Action   Melee weapon
Requirement: You must be wielding a light blade.
Target: One creature
Attack: Strength vs. AC
Hit: The target is slowed and takes ongoing damage equal to 10 + your Dexterity modifier (save ends both).
Miss: The target takes ongoing damage equal to your Dexterity modifier (save ends).
Effect: Before and after the attack, you can shift 1 square.

LEVEL 6 UTILITY EXPLOITS

Agile Approach — Fighter Utility 6

You make a quick shift to a better position.

Encounter ✦ Martial
Move Action   Personal
Effect: You can shift 2 squares and must end adjacent to an enemy. If you aren't wearing heavy armor, you can shift 3 squares.

Rock Steady — Fighter Utility 6

You sink your center of gravity into the ground below you and grit your teeth. You are going nowhere.

Daily ✦ Martial, Stance
Minor Action   Personal
Effect: Until the stance ends, you cannot be knocked prone, and if you are subject to a pull, a push, or a slide, you can reduce the forced movement by 1 square.

Settling the Score — Fighter Utility 6

When the attack hits you, you decide then and there to take your enemy out.

Daily ✦ Martial
Immediate Reaction   Personal
Trigger: An enemy hits you with an attack
Effect: You gain a +2 power bonus to attack rolls against the triggering enemy until the end of the encounter.

Strong Focus
Fighter Utility 6

Concentration improves your ability to accomplish feats of strength.

Encounter ✦ Martial
Minor Action   **Personal**
Effect: Until the end of your next turn, you gain a power bonus to Athletics checks and Strength ability checks equal to your Wisdom modifier.

Vigilant Protector
Fighter Utility 6

You sweep your shield out to give your allies protection.

Daily ✦ Martial, Stance
Minor Action   **Personal**
Requirement: You must be using a shield.
Effect: Until the stance ends, you take a -1 penalty to AC and Reflex, but each ally gains a +2 power bonus to AC and Reflex while adjacent to you.
    Special: If you are a dragonborn, your adjacent allies instead gain a +3 power bonus to AC and Reflex.

LEVEL 7 ENCOUNTER EXPLOITS

Hampering Flurry
Fighter Attack 7

Using both weapons, you attack your opponent's legs and hinder him with painful wounds.

Encounter ✦ Martial, Weapon
Standard Action   **Melee** weapon
Requirement: You must be wielding two melee weapons.
Target: One creature
Attack: Strength vs. AC (main weapon and off-hand weapon), two attacks
Hit: 1[W] + Strength modifier damage per attack, and the target is slowed until the end of your next turn. If both attacks hit, the second attack deals extra damage equal to your Dexterity modifier.

Not So Fast
Fighter Attack 7

Your adversary tries to slip away, but you sneak your weapon inside and keep him right where you want him.

Encounter ✦ Martial, Weapon
Immediate Interrupt   **Melee** 1
Trigger: An adjacent enemy moves away from you
Target: The triggering enemy
Attack: Strength vs. AC
Hit: 1[W] + Strength modifier damage, and the target is slowed until the end of its next turn.
    Weapon: If you're wielding a flail or a pick, the target is also immobilized until the end of its next turn.

Savage Parry
Fighter Attack 7

With predatory speed, you violently parry, extorting pain as the penalty for your foe's impudent attack.

Encounter ✦ Invigorating, Martial, Weapon
Immediate Interrupt   **Melee** weapon
Trigger: An enemy hits an ally with a melee attack
Target: The triggering enemy
Attack: Strength vs. AC
Hit: Strength modifier damage, and the ally takes only half damage from the triggering attack.
    Weapon: If you're wielding an axe, a hammer, or a mace, your attack deals extra damage equal to your Constitution modifier.

Stay Down
Fighter Attack 7

You're not above hitting someone who's down.

Encounter ✦ Martial, Weapon
Standard Action   **Melee** weapon
Target: One creature
Attack: Strength vs. AC
Hit: 2[W] + Strength modifier damage. If the target is prone, the attack deals extra damage equal to your Dexterity modifier, and the target can't stand up until the end of your next turn.

Trip Up
Fighter Attack 7

You tangle your enemy's feet with your weapon.

Encounter ✦ Martial, Weapon
Free Action   **Melee** weapon
Trigger: You hit an enemy with a melee basic attack
Target: The triggering enemy
Attack: Strength vs. Reflex
Hit: 1[W] + Strength modifier damage, and the target is slowed until the end of your next turn.
    Weapon: If you're wielding a polearm or a spear, you can knock the target prone instead of slowing it.

Twofold Torment
Fighter Attack 7

Your carefully aimed slashes send two foes reeling away in agony.

Encounter ✦ Martial, Weapon
Standard Action   **Melee** weapon
Requirement: You must be wielding two melee weapons.
Targets: Two creatures
Attack: Strength vs. AC (main weapon and off-hand weapon), one attack per target
Hit: 1[W] + Strength modifier damage, and you push the target a number of squares equal to 1 + your Dexterity modifier. If you have combat advantage against the target, the attack deals extra damage equal to your Dexterity modifier.

ELADRIN FIGHTERS

Eladrin value the skill of swordplay almost as much as the arcane arts, and an eladrin fighter armed with a slim rapier can be a deadly enemy. With their innately high Dexterity, eladrin fighters favor heavy blades, light blades, and, to a lesser extent, spears. Many eladrin fighters learn a scattering of arcane powers with multiclass feats; *thunder wave* is a popular choice because of its ability to mark multiple targets.

LEVEL 9 DAILY EXPLOITS

Fighter's Recovery	Fighter Attack 9

As you swing, you use your momentum to steady and center yourself, gaining vigor for the fight to come.

Daily ✦ Martial, Weapon
Standard Action   **Melee** weapon
Target: One creature
Attack: Strength vs. AC
Hit: 3[W] + Strength modifier damage.
Effect: If you have used all your encounter attack powers, you regain the use of a fighter encounter attack power you have used during this encounter.

Jackal Strike	Fighter Attack 9

Sensing your opponent's flagging strength, you move in for the kill.

Daily ✦ Martial, Reliable, Weapon
Free Action   **Melee** weapon
Trigger: An enemy marked by you becomes bloodied
Target: The triggering enemy
Attack: Strength vs. AC
Hit: 3[W] + Strength modifier damage.

Pestering Wound	Fighter Attack 9

The injury caused by your attack tears open when your foe tries to maneuver.

Daily ✦ Martial, Reliable, Weapon
Standard Action   **Melee** weapon
Target: One creature
Attack: Strength vs. AC
Hit: 3[W] + Strength modifier damage, and if the target moves before the end of your next turn, it takes extra damage equal to your Strength modifier.
  Weapon: If you're wielding a pick, the extra damage instead equals your Strength modifier + your Constitution modifier.

Piquing Dare	Fighter Attack 9

With a precise and provoking blow, you mark your foe and defy him to ignore you on pain of further attack.

Daily ✦ Martial, Weapon
Standard Action   **Melee** weapon
Target: One creature
Attack: Strength vs. AC
Hit: 3[W] + Strength modifier damage. If you have combat advantage against the target, the attack deals extra damage equal to your Dexterity modifier.
Effect: The target is marked (save ends). If the target does not attack you on its turn while it is marked by this power, you can either make a melee basic attack against it or shift 1 square closer to it as a free action.

ELF FIGHTERS

Like eladrin, elf fighters favor heavy blades and light blades to make the best use of their Dexterity. Their high Wisdom also helps them maintain control over their opponents. Many elf fighters learn one or two ranger powers in order to gain effective ranged attacks.

Stop Thrust	Fighter Attack 9

As the enemy moves to attack, you respond by rapidly advancing and striking.

Daily ✦ Martial, Reliable, Weapon
Immediate Reaction   **Melee** weapon
Trigger: An enemy enters a square within 2 squares of you
Target: The triggering enemy
Effect: Before the attack, you can shift 2 squares.
Attack: Strength vs. AC
Hit: 1[W] + Strength modifier damage, and the target is immobilized until the start of your next turn.
Special: If the target moved as part of a charge, it can attack you instead of the original target of its charge.

Terrifying Impact	Fighter Attack 9

Giving an exultant battle cry, you pulverize an opponent and put the fear of impending doom in nearby foes.

Daily ✦ Invigorating, Martial, Weapon
Standard Action   **Melee** weapon
Primary Target: One creature
Primary Attack: Strength vs. AC
Hit: 2[W] + Strength modifier damage.
  Weapon: If you're wielding an axe, a hammer, or a mace, the primary attack deals extra damage equal to our Constitution modifier.
Effect: Make a secondary attack, which has the fear keyword.
  Secondary Target: Each enemy within 3 squares of the primary target
  Secondary Attack: Constitution vs. Will
  Hit: You push the target 1 square.

Level 10 Utility Exploits

Defensive Resurgence — Fighter Utility 10

You buck up under the pressure and redouble your defensive efforts.

Daily ✦ Healing, Martial
Minor Action   **Personal**
Effect: You can spend a healing surge. Until the start of your next turn, you gain a bonus to AC equal to your Dexterity modifier.

Hunker Down — Fighter Utility 10

You drop into a defensive posture, raising your shield to protect yourself.

Daily ✦ Martial, Stance
Minor Action   **Personal**
Requirement: You must be using a shield.
Effect: Until the stance ends, you are slowed, but you gain cover against all attacks. You can end this stance as a free action.

Menacing Stance — Fighter Utility 10

You seem ready to spring at any moment, forcing marked foes to devote more attention to you.

Daily ✦ Martial, Stance
Minor Action   **Personal**
Effect: Until the stance ends, whenever an enemy marked by you makes an attack that doesn't include you as a target, that enemy grants combat advantage to your allies until the start of its next turn.

Shooter's Nemesis — Fighter Utility 10

The fact that your enemy is too cowardly to close to melee swells your confidence.

Daily ✦ Healing, Martial
Immediate Reaction   **Personal**
Trigger: You are hit by a ranged attack
Effect: You spend a healing surge and regain additional hit points equal to twice your Wisdom modifier.

Strength from Pain — Fighter Utility 10

The pain of your wounds opens the floodgates to your inner strength.

Daily ✦ Martial
Minor Action   **Personal**
Requirement: You must be bloodied.
Effect: You gain a +4 power bonus to melee damage rolls, Athletics checks, and Endurance checks until the end of the encounter or until you are no longer bloodied.
Special: If you are a dragonborn, you instead gain a +5 power bonus.

Level 13 Encounter Exploits

Appalling Crunch — Fighter Attack 13

Nearby enemies are so aghast at your remorseless attack that they see you as the most dangerous foe on the field.

Encounter ✦ Invigorating, Martial, Weapon
Standard Action   **Melee** weapon
Target: One creature
Attack: Strength vs. AC
Hit: 3[W] + Strength modifier damage, and enemies adjacent to the target are marked until the end of your next turn.
Weapon: If you're wielding an axe, a hammer, or a mace, enemies within 2 squares of the target are marked until the end of your next turn.

Assured Strike — Fighter Attack 13

You pick out your foe's weak spot and drive your weapon home with surprising force.

Encounter ✦ Martial, Weapon
Standard Action   **Melee** weapon
Target: One creature granting combat advantage to you
Attack: Strength vs. Reflex
Hit: 3[W] + Strength modifier damage.
Weapon: If you're wielding a heavy blade or a light blade, the attack deals extra damage equal to your Dexterity modifier.
Special: If you are a halfling, you don't need combat advantage against the target.

Brutal Rebuke — Fighter Attack 13

By attacking your comrade, your adversary has called down your righteous ire.

Encounter ✦ Martial, Weapon
Standard Action   **Melee** weapon
Target: One creature
Attack: Strength vs. AC. If the target attacked you or an ally since the end of your last turn, you gain a +2 bonus to the attack roll.
Hit: 2[W] + Strength modifier damage.
Weapon: If you're wielding a mace or a pick, the attack deals extra damage equal to your Constitution modifier.
Special: When making an opportunity attack, you can use this power in place of a melee basic attack.

Crumpling Slam — Fighter Attack 13

With a bellow and a mighty wallop, you hurl your foe backward and off her feet.

Encounter ✦ Invigorating, Martial, Weapon
Standard Action   **Melee** weapon
Target: One creature
Attack: Strength vs. AC
Hit: 2[W] + Strength modifier damage, and you push the target 2 squares and knock it prone.
Weapon: If you're wielding an axe, a hammer, or a mace, the attack deals extra damage equal to your Constitution modifier.

Dance of Blades · Fighter Attack 13

You weave between two foes, driving them this way and that with a pair of attacks.

Encounter ✦ Martial, Weapon
Standard Action   Melee weapon
Requirement: You must be wielding two melee weapons.
Primary Target: One creature
Primary Attack: Strength vs. AC (main weapon)
Hit: 1[W] + Strength modifier damage, and you slide the target 2 squares.
    If you have combat advantage against the target, the primary attack deals extra damage equal to your Dexterity modifier.
Effect: You can shift 3 squares and make a secondary attack.
    Secondary Target: One creature other than the primary target
    Secondary Attack: Strength vs. AC (off-hand weapon)
    Hit: 1[W] + Strength modifier damage, and you slide the target 2 squares.
    If you have combat advantage against the secondary target, the secondary attack deals extra damage equal to your Dexterity modifier.

Scattering Swing · Fighter Attack 13

You whip your weapon in a wide arc, and those enemies you don't send staggering must jump out of the way.

Encounter ✦ Martial, Weapon
Standard Action   Close burst 1
Target: Each enemy in burst you can see
Attack: Strength vs. AC
Hit: 2[W] + Strength modifier damage, and you slide the target 1 square.
Miss: You push the target 1 square.

GODS AND FIGHTERS

Bahamut and Kord are popular deities among fighters because of their influence over matters of war, while many fighters turn to Avandra as the god of adventure. Fighters who believe in the virtues of conquest often worship Bane, even if they're not actually evil. Beyond these four gods, all the deities in the pantheon count some fighters among their worshipers. Fighters who view their martial skill as an art form, including many elf and eladrin fighters, worship Corellon. Erathis is a popular civic god, often revered by soldiers. As a god of knowledge, Ioun holds appeal for fighters who study the history of warfare and strategy. Some battlerager fighters seek to mimic the fury of nature that Melora represents. Moradin is commonly revered by dwarves and any fighter who seeks to protect a community. Pelor is popular among good-aligned fighters, while the Raven Queen is a common patron for grim, bitter soldiers and mercenaries. Sehanine's doctrine of seeking one's own destiny appeals to many fighters as well.

LEVEL 15 DAILY EXPLOITS

Boulder Charge · Fighter Attack 15

You and your sweeping weapon become like a stone rolling down a mountain, crushing anyone foolish enough to stay in your path.

Daily ✦ Invigorating, Martial, Weapon
Standard Action   Melee weapon
Requirement: You must charge and use this power in place of a melee basic attack. While charging, you can move through enemies' squares but must end your movement in an unoccupied space.
Targets: One creature and each enemy whose space you move through
Attack: Strength vs. AC, one attack per target
Hit: 2[W] + Strength modifier damage, and you push the target 2 squares and knock it prone.
    Weapon: If you're wielding an axe, a hammer, or a mace, the attack deals extra damage equal to your Constitution modifier.
Miss: You push the target 1 square.

Carve Initials · Fighter Attack 15

You cut deep and leave a meaningful mark.

Daily ✦ Martial, Reliable, Weapon
Standard Action   Melee weapon
Requirement: You must be wielding a light blade.
Target: One creature
Attack: Strength vs. AC
Hit: 4[W] + Strength modifier damage, and the target is marked until the end of the encounter or until you are knocked unconscious. No mark can supersede this one.

Defender's Gambit · Fighter Attack 15

Inviting attack, you lure your enemy into letting its guard down for a counterattack.

Daily ✦ Martial, Weapon
Standard Action   **Melee** weapon
Target: One creature
Primary Attack: Strength vs. Will
Hit: Until the end of your turn, you gain a power bonus to melee attack rolls and melee damage rolls against the target equal to your Wisdom modifier.
Effect: The target can make a basic attack against you as an immediate reaction, and then you make a secondary attack against it as a free action.
    Secondary Attack: Strength vs. AC
    Hit: 5[W] + Strength modifier.
    Miss: Half damage.

Gale of Steel · Fighter Attack 15

You cut through the ranks of your foes like a fierce wind.

Daily ✦ Martial, Weapon
Standard Action   **Close** burst 1
Target: Each enemy in burst you can see
Attack: Strength vs. AC
Hit: 2[W] + Strength modifier damage.
    Weapon: If you're wielding a heavy blade or a light blade, the attack deals extra damage equal to your Dexterity modifier.
Effect: You can shift 1 square and repeat the attack against any enemy you haven't already hit with the attack.

Quicksilver Stance · Fighter Attack 15

Like liquid metal, you flow wherever the gravity of battle carries you.

Daily ✦ Martial, Stance
Minor Action   **Personal**
Effect: Until the stance ends, you can shift 1 square (or 2 squares if you aren't wearing heavy armor) and make a melee basic attack as a move action. If you have combat advantage against the target of the attack and hit, the attack deals extra damage equal to your Wisdom modifier.

FIGHTERS IN THE WORLD

The rank-and-file soldiery of the local barony, the band of mercenaries who sell their services to the duke, the bandits who raid caravans traveling the King's Road, the savages who plunder the outlying farms—these aren't fighters. But fighters do emerge from among these sorts of people. Your fighter character might have served in the military, trained for the knighthood, or fought among bandits or raiders, but you rose from those ranks to become something greater than your colleagues. You're not just a soldier; you're a hero, and that forever sets you above the common folk of the world.

Slayer's Lunge · Fighter Attack 15

Scenting blood, you speed forward to finish your foe.

Daily ✦ Martial, Weapon
Immediate Reaction   **Melee** 1
Trigger: An enemy within 5 squares of you becomes bloodied
Target: The triggering enemy
Effect: Before the attack, you can move your speed.
Attack: Strength vs. AC
Hit: 3[W] + Strength modifier damage, and the target is marked (save ends). If the target is already marked by you when you use this power, the attack deals extra damage equal to your Wisdom modifier.
    Special: If you are an elf, the attack deals extra damage equal to your Dexterity modifier.

LEVEL 16 UTILITY EXPLOITS

Bolstering Stride · Fighter Utility 16

You rush to your friend's side, ready to stand in his defense.

Encounter ✦ Martial
Move Action   **Personal**
Effect: You can move your speed, ending in a space adjacent to an ally. You then gain temporary hit points equal to 2d8 + your Constitution modifier.

Giant's Stride · Fighter 16 Utility

You wade through the chaos of battle like a colossus, heedless of the foes about you.

Daily ✦ Martial
Move Action   **Personal**
Effect: You can shift your speed. You ignore difficult terrain during this shift and can move through occupied squares, as long as you end in an unoccupied space.

Immovable Mountain · Fighter Utility 16

You plant your feet firmly, refusing to move.

Daily ✦ Martial, Stance
Minor Action   **Personal**
Effect: Until the stance ends, if you are subject to a pull, a push, or a slide and you have moved no more than 2 squares since the start of your turn, you can reduce the forced movement by 2 squares.
Special: If you are a dwarf, you can reduce the forced movement by 5 squares.

Marking Stance · Fighter Utility 16

You very presence puts your foes off their guard.

Daily ✦ Martial, Stance
Standard Action   **Personal**
Prerequisite: You must be trained in Intimidate.
Effect: Until the stance ends, any enemy that begins its turn adjacent to you is marked until the start of its next turn.

Regnant Shout
Fighter Utility 16

Your battle cry wracks your enemies' nerves and draws their attention to you.

Daily ✦ Martial
Standard Action   Close burst 3
Target: Each enemy in burst
Effect: You gain a +1 power bonus to attack rolls against the target and it is marked (save ends both).

LEVEL 17 ENCOUNTER EXPLOITS

Boggling Smash
Fighter Attack 17

Your solid blow momentarily costs your enemy its wits.

Encounter ✦ Martial, Weapon
Standard Action   Melee weapon
Target: One creature
Attack: Strength vs. AC
Hit: 3[W] + Strength modifier damage, and the target takes a –2 penalty to attack rolls until the end of your next turn.
   Weapon: If you're wielding a hammer or a mace, the attack deals extra damage equal to your Constitution modifier, and the target is dazed until the end of your next turn.

Buffeting Torque
Fighter Attack 17

Your body and weapon spin as one, and jarring hits knock down those foes who fail to throw themselves out of harm's way.

Encounter ✦ Martial, Weapon
Standard Action   Close burst 1
Requirement: You must be wielding a two-handed weapon.
Target: Each enemy in burst you can see
Attack: Strength vs. AC
Hit: 1[W] + Strength modifier damage, and until the start of your next turn, any enemy that enters a square adjacent to you is marked until the end of your next turn and takes 5 damage.
   Weapon: If you're wielding an axe, a hammer, or a mace, the attack deals extra damage equal to your Constitution modifier.

Driving Flurry
Fighter Attack 17

You force your opponent back with a sustained series of jabs, then use the break in his defenses to slip away.

Encounter ✦ Invigorating, Martial, Weapon
Standard Action   Melee weapon
Target: One creature
Attack: Strength vs. AC
Hit: 2[W] + Strength modifier damage, and you push the target 2 squares. You can then shift 2 squares.
   Weapon: If you're wielding a light blade or a heavy blade, the attack deals extra damage equal to your Dexterity modifier.

Skirmisher Pounce
Fighter Attack 17

You leap forward, skewering one foe and using your momentum to harry another.

Encounter ✦ Martial, Weapon
Standard Action   Melee weapon
Primary Target: One creature
Primary Attack: Strength vs. AC
Hit: 2[W] + Strength modifier damage, and you can shift 2 squares and make a secondary attack.
   If you have combat advantage against the primary target, the primary attack deals extra damage equal to your Dexterity modifier.
Secondary Target: One creature other than the primary target
Secondary Attack: Strength vs. AC
Hit: 1[W] + Strength modifier damage.
   If you have combat advantage against the secondary target, the secondary attack deals extra damage equal to your Dexterity modifier.
Special: When charging, you can use this power in place of a melee basic attack.

Tap and Counterstrike
Fighter Attack 17

You tap your foe, holding back your full strength to keep its attention fixed squarely on you.

Encounter ✦ Martial, Weapon
Standard Action   Melee weapon
Requirement: You must be wielding two melee weapons.
Target: One creature
Primary Attack: Strength vs. Fortitude
Hit: 1[W] + Strength modifier damage. If the target makes an attack that does not include you before the start of your next turn, you can shift 1 square and make a secondary attack against the target with your off-hand weapon as an immediate interrupt.
Secondary Attack: Strength + 2 vs. AC
Hit: 3[W] + Strength modifier damage.

Wild Strike
Fighter Attack 17

Throwing caution to the wind, you lash out desperately at your foe.

Encounter ✦ Martial, Weapon
Standard Action   Melee weapon
Target: One creature
Attack: Strength vs. AC
Hit: 4[W] + Strength modifier damage, and you grant combat advantage to all enemies until the start of your next turn.
   Special: If you are a human, the attack deals extra damage equal to your Wisdom modifier.
   Special: When charging, you can use this power in place of a melee basic attack.

LEVEL 19 DAILY EXPLOITS

Controlling Thrust — Fighter Attack 19

After a vicious stab, you expertly corral your opponent with your polearm.

Daily ✦ Martial, Weapon
Standard Action   **Melee** weapon
Requirement: You must be wielding a polearm or a spear.
Target: One creature
Primary Attack: Strength vs. AC
Hit: 4[W] + Strength modifier damage, and the target is marked (save ends).
Miss: Half damage, and the target is marked until the end of your next turn.
Effect: If the target takes a move action before the end of your next turn and is within your melee reach, you can make a secondary attack against the target as an immediate interrupt.
Secondary Attack: Strength vs. AC
Secondary Damage: 2[W] + Strength modifier damage, and cancel the target's move action.
Special: When charging, you can use this power in place of a melee basic attack.

Protective Sweep — Fighter Attack 19

You swing your weapon around with care, and then take up a defensive posture.

Daily ✦ Martial, Weapon
Standard Action   **Close** burst 1
Target: Each creature in burst you can see
Attack: Strength vs. AC
Hit: 3[W] + Strength modifier damage.
Miss: Half damage.
  Weapon: If you're wielding a flail or a heavy blade, the attack deals extra damage equal to your Dexterity modifier.
Effect: You gain a +4 power bonus to AC until the start of your next turn.

Relentless Assailant — Fighter Attack 19

You get a boost out of pummeling your opponent.

Daily ✦ Healing, Invigorating, Martial, Reliable, Weapon
Standard Action   **Melee** weapon
Target: One creature
Attack: Strength vs. AC
Hit: 4[W] + Strength modifier damage, and you can spend a healing surge.

Smash and Grab — Fighter Attack 19

Your hammering blow distracts your enemy long enough for you to obtain a crushing hold.

Daily ✦ Invigorating, Martial, Reliable, Weapon
Standard Action   **Melee** weapon
Requirement: You must have a hand free.
Target: One creature
Attack: Strength vs. AC
Hit: 3[W] + Strength modifier damage, and you grab the target. Each time you sustain the grab, the target takes 1[W] + Strength modifier damage.
  Weapon: If you're wielding an axe, a hammer, or a mace, the attack deals extra damage equal to your Constitution modifier.

LEVEL 22 UTILITY EXPLOITS

Howl of Defiance — Fighter Utility 22

You respond to pain with a lionhearted shout and wild-eyed watchfulness.

Daily ✦ Fear, Martial
Immediate Reaction   **Close** burst 5
Trigger: An enemy damages you with a melee attack
Target: Each enemy in burst you can see
Effect: The target is marked until the end of the encounter, until you are knocked unconscious, or until another mark supersedes this one. Until this mark ends, the target grants combat advantage to you.

Inspired Resurgence — Fighter Utility 22

Flush with success, you take a deep breath and relocate for your next attack.

Encounter ✦ Healing, Martial
Free Action   **Personal**
Trigger: An enemy marked by you is reduced to 0 hit points
Effect: You can spend a healing surge and shift 3 squares.

Steadfast Stance — Fighter Utility 22

Standing resolutely, you let nothing cause you to falter.

Daily ✦ Martial, Stance
Minor Action   **Personal**
Effect: Until the stance ends, when an attack causes you to take an effect that a save can end, you can make a saving throw against that effect as an immediate reaction.

FIGHTERS AND COMBAT

One might assume that characters who use powers called *brute strike* and *ruthless slaughter* revel in combat, delighting in the violence and mayhem they spread, but that doesn't have to be true of your fighter character. For many of the iconic fighters of literature, war and combat are a burden they hope to be able to lay down someday. These heroes find no joy in killing, just a weariness that grows greater as the cycle of violence expands to swallow more and more of their friends and loved ones. How does your fighter feel about facing combat encounters? The need for violence is plain to see, but do you hope for an end to such violent times? Or are you numb to it—at least until the death of someone you care about awakens you to the grim reality?

LEVEL 23 ENCOUNTER EXPLOITS

Crippling Smash — Fighter Attack 23

You thrash your opponent, leaving him barely able to move.

Encounter ✦ Martial, Weapon
Standard Action   **Melee** weapon
Requirement: You must be wielding a two-handed weapon.
Target: One creature
Attack: Strength vs. AC
Hit: 1[W] + Strength modifier damage, and the target is slowed and weakened until the end of your next turn.
   Weapon: If you're wielding an axe, a hammer, or a mace, the attack deals extra damage equal to your Constitution modifier, and you knock the target prone.

Harrowing Hammer — Fighter Attack 23

Your weapon crashes down on your adversary, forcing nearby enemies to acknowledge the threat you pose.

Encounter ✦ Invigorating, Martial, Weapon
Standard Action   **Melee** weapon
Requirement: You must be wielding a two-handed weapon.
Target: One creature
Attack: Strength vs. AC
Hit: 4[W] + Strength modifier damage, and each enemy adjacent to the target is marked until the start of your next turn.
   Weapon: If you're wielding an axe, a hammer, or a mace, the attack deals extra damage equal to your Constitution modifier.

Meticulous Stab — Fighter Attack 23

Your precision allows you to strike at a tiny hole in your foe's armor.

Encounter ✦ Martial, Weapon
Standard Action   **Melee** weapon
Target: One creature
Attack: Strength vs. Reflex
Hit: 3[W] + Strength modifier damage.
   Weapon: If you're wielding a spear or a light blade, the attack deals extra damage equal to your Dexterity modifier.
Special: When making an opportunity attack, you can use this power in place of a melee basic attack.

Smashing Hammer — Fighter Attack 23

Swinging from high to low, you build momentum as you smash into each foe.

Encounter ✦ Martial, Weapon
Standard Action   **Close** burst 1
Target: Each enemy in burst you can see
Attack: Strength vs. AC. You gain a +1 cumulative bonus to the attack roll against each target after the first.
Hit: 2[W] + Strength modifier damage.
   Weapon: If you're wielding an axe or a hammer, the attack deals extra damage equal to your Constitution modifier.

Unyielding — Fighter Utility 22

Pain just goads you to greater heights of heroism.

Daily ✦ Healing, Martial
Immediate Reaction   Personal
Trigger: You are hit by an attack
Effect: You spend two healing surges and restore your hit points to their maximum value.
Special: If you are a dragonborn, you also gain a +1 power bonus to attack rolls and all defenses until the end of your next turn.

Victor's Stance — Fighter Utility 22

You gain a surge of confidence and vigor each time a foe falls before you.

Daily ✦ Healing, Martial, Stance
Minor Action   Personal
Effect: Until the stance ends, each time you reduce an enemy to 0 hit points, you can use a free action to spend a healing surge, make a saving throw, or both. You gain a bonus to the saving throw equal to your Wisdom modifier.

Turnabout Riposte
Fighter Attack 23

You make a quick parry on your ally's behalf, take a swift jab at his assailant, and then spin into a new position.

Encounter ✦ Martial, Weapon
Immediate Interrupt   Melee 1
Trigger: An enemy adjacent to you hits an ally with a melee attack
Target: The triggering enemy
Attack: Strength vs. AC
Hit: 2[W] + Strength modifier damage, and you can shift 2 squares and must end adjacent to the target.
Effect: The ally takes only half damage from the triggering attack.

Weaponmaster's Lure
Fighter Attack 23

You make a passing attack, throwing your foe off balance. With a shove, you send him stumbling away as you switch positions with him.

Encounter ✦ Martial, Weapon
Standard Action   Melee weapon
Requirement: You must be wielding two melee weapons.
Target: One creature
Attack: Strength vs. AC (main weapon and off-hand weapon), two attacks
Hit: 2[W] + Strength modifier damage per attack. If one attack hits, you can swap places with the target. If both attacks hit, you can swap places with the target and slide it 3 squares. If you have combat advantage against the target, each attack deals extra damage equal to your Dexterity modifier.

LEVEL 25 DAILY EXPLOITS

Ballista Charge
Fighter Attack 25

Like a bolt fired from a ballista, you hurtle forward, transfixing your foe.

Daily ✦ Martial, Reliable, Weapon
Standard Action   Melee weapon
Target: One creature
Primary Attack: Strength vs. AC
Hit: 3[W] + Strength modifier damage, and the target is immobilized (save ends). Make a secondary attack against the target.
  Weapon: If you're wielding a spear, the target is also dazed (save ends).
  Secondary Attack: Dexterity vs. Fortitude
  Hit: 2[W] + Dexterity modifier damage, and you knock the target prone.
Special: When charging, you can use this power in place of a melee basic attack.

HALFLING FIGHTERS

Small but nimble, halfling fighters make up in agility what they might lack in strength. When peaceful halfling communities face danger they can't avoid or deflect, they rely on skilled warriors who use hit-and-run tactics, quick wits, and quicker blades to drive off foes. The halfling bounder paragon path (page 28) is the consummate example of the halfling fighter's tradition.

Earthquake Smash
Fighter Attack 2

With a thunderous blow, you beat your adversary to the ground and send shock waves through the earth. Those waves toss other enemies aside.

Daily ✦ Martial, Reliable, Weapon
Standard Action   Melee weapon
Primary Target: One creature
Primary Attack: Strength vs. AC
Hit: 3[W] + Strength modifier damage, and the target is knocked prone and dazed until the end of your next turn. Make a secondary attack.
  Weapon: If you're wielding an axe, a hammer, or a mace, the primary attack deals extra damage equal to your Constitution modifier.
  Secondary Target: Each enemy within 2 squares of the primary target
  Secondary Attack: Strength vs. Fortitude
  Hit: Strength modifier damage, and you knock the secondary target prone.

Fighter's Resurgence
Fighter Attack 2

You brutalize your enemy and take heart from your prowess.

Daily ✦ Martial, Weapon
Standard Action   Melee weapon
Target: One creature
Attack: Strength + 2 vs. AC
Hit: 5[W] + Strength modifier damage.
Effect: If you have used all your encounter attack powers, you regain the use of a fighter encounter attack power you have used during this encounter.

Marking Barrage
Fighter Attack 25

With a volley of precise attacks, you wound nearby adversaries, showing them that this fight will end badly for them if they fail to take you down quickly.

Daily ✦ Martial, Weapon
Standard Action   Close burst 1
Target: Each enemy in burst you can see
Attack: Strength vs. Reflex
Hit: 4[W] + Strength modifier damage. If you have combat advantage against the target, the attack deals extra damage equal to your Dexterity modifier.
Miss: Half damage.
Effect: The target is marked until the end of the encounter, until you are knocked unconscious, or until another mark supersedes this one.

TIEFLING FIGHTERS

Tiefling is the only race in the *Player's Handbook* that doesn't gain a +2 bonus to one of the ability scores most commonly used by fighters. Even so, tiefling fighters manage to put their innate powers and proclivities to good use as fighters. The tiefling warfiend paragon path (page 35) represents the highest achievements of an infernal tradition dating from ancient Bael Turath, but even tiefling fighters who don't adopt that path channel their *infernal wrath* to good effect on the field of battle.

Ruthless Slaughter — Fighter Attack 25

Without pity, you butcher a foe already at a disadvantage, provoking your other enemies.

Daily ✦ Martial, Reliable, Weapon
Standard Action   **Melee** weapon
Target: One bloodied or prone creature
Attack: Strength + 2 vs. AC
Hit: 6[W] + Strength modifier damage.
Effect: Each enemy within 3 squares of you, other than the target, is marked until the end of your next turn. If the attack reduced the target to 0 hit points, those enemies are instead marked until the end of the encounter, until you are knocked unconscious, or until another mark supersedes this one.

Transfixing Provocation — Fighter Attack 25

Your remorseless and skilled attack wounds flesh and confidence, giving you a lasting edge against your enemy.

Daily ✦ Martial, Weapon
Standard Action   **Melee** weapon
Target: One creature
Attack: Strength vs. AC
Hit: 6[W] + Strength modifier damage.
Miss: Half damage.
Effect: The target is marked until the end of the encounter, until you are knocked unconscious, or until another mark supersedes this one. Until this mark ends, the target grants combat advantage to you.

SIGNATURE WEAPON

Great fighters are often known by the weapons they wield. Your fighter character might use many different weapons over the course of his or her adventuring career, but there's no reason any of those weapons has to be just a mundane *+3 flaming greatsword*. From the first weapon you use at the start of the campaign to the mighty +6 artifact that deals the death blow to the campaign's ultimate villain, each weapon can be the stuff of legends.

Special weapons are often distinguished by their makers. A blade crafted in the infernal forges of Bael Turath, a spear hardened with white dragon breath by the smiths of Arkhosia, or a hammer crafted by an exarch of Moradin in the vaults of Celestia are weapons worthy of a hero. A weapon that you made yourself might be the greatest of all.

Other weapons are noteworthy because other heroes—or villains—wielded them in the past. Did your sword belong to an eladrin general of Cendriane? Was your axe used to hew the head of the mighty fire titan Kurthmaug from his shoulders? Was your flail the favored weapon of a gnoll chieftain you killed?

Finally, a weapon's construction or appearance can make it distinctive. Perhaps your sword is crafted from a single piece of strange metal, carved rather than forged, but still terribly effective. Your spear might be tipped with the tooth or claw of an ancient dragon. Or the haft of your mace might be the bone of a giant, bound with silver bands engraved with Dwarven script.

BRIAN HAGAN

LEVEL 27 ENCOUNTER EXPLOITS

Blood Rush — Fighter Attack 27

Filled with bloodlust, you leap into the thick of battle.

Encounter ✦ Invigorating, Martial, Weapon
Standard Action   **Melee** weapon
Target: One creature
Attack: Strength vs. AC
Hit: 4[W] + Strength modifier damage. If the target is bloodied when you make the attack, the attack deals extra damage equal to your Constitution modifier.
Special: When charging, you can use this power in place of a melee basic attack.

Coward's Reward — Fighter Attack 27

You fling your weapon at the retreating foe, hobbling him as he tries to get away.

Encounter ✦ Martial, Weapon
Immediate Reaction   **Ranged** 5
Trigger: An enemy marked by you leaves an adjacent square
Requirement: You must be wielding a melee weapon.
Target: The triggering enemy
Attack: Strength vs. AC
Hit: 2[W] + Strength modifier damage, and the target is immobilized until the end of your next turn. Your weapon falls into a square of your choice adjacent to the target.

Desperate Strike — Fighter Attack 27

You strike wildly, frantic to finish off your opponent.

Encounter ✦ Martial, Weapon
Standard Action   **Melee** weapon
Target: One creature
Attack: Strength vs. AC
Hit: 5[W] + Strength modifier damage, and you take a –2 penalty to attack rolls until the end of your next turn.
    Special: If you are a human, the attack deals extra damage equal to your Wisdom modifier.

Dual-Weapon Supremacy — Fighter Attack 27

You land two vicious blows on your enemy, gaining a rush of confidence from the proof of your style's superiority.

Encounter ✦ Martial, Weapon
Standard Action   **Melee** weapon
Requirement: You must be wielding two melee weapons.
Target: One creature
Attack: Strength vs. AC (main weapon and off-hand weapon), two attacks
Hit: 2[W] + Strength modifier damage per attack. If both attacks hit, the target grants combat advantage to you for the first attack you make against it before the end of your next turn.

Spinning Death Strike — Fighter Attack 27

You slash forward, and then bring your weapon around in a deadly arc.

Encounter ✦ Martial, Weapon
Standard Action   **Melee** weapon
Requirement: You must be wielding a two-handed weapon.
Primary Target: One creature
Primary Attack: Strength vs. AC
Hit: 2[W] + Strength modifier damage. Make a secondary attack.
    Secondary Target: Each enemy within 1 square of you
    Secondary Attack: Strength vs. AC
    Hit: 1[W] + Strength modifier + Dexterity modifier damage.

Stabbing Torrent — Fighter Attack 27

You roil like a storm cloud, raining sharp blows on all enemies foolish enough to stand in your shadow.

Encounter ✦ Martial, Weapon
Standard Action   **Close** burst 1
Requirement: You must be wielding a light blade.
Target: Each enemy in burst you can see
Attack: Strength vs. AC. If you're wielding two melee weapons, you can attack each target with both your main weapon and your off-hand weapon.
Hit: 1[W] + Strength modifier damage. If you have combat advantage against the target, the attack deals extra damage equal to your Dexterity modifier.

LAST STAND

Brandis stood in the doorway and waited. A slow breath did nothing to calm his pounding heart, and he emptied his lungs with a whispered prayer to the Raven Queen: "Not today, Dark Lady. Please."

He listened to the pounding of the demon's hooves drawing near and to the frantic rhythm of his companions' feet as they fled behind him. If he could buy them a little time, maybe they could get to safety. Maybe Verna wouldn't die.

The demon rounded the corner and bellowed in triumph. Its roar assaulted his ears, shook the stone beneath his feet, and blasted at his face, but Brandis held his ground. Lowering its head, the demon charged.

With a roar of his own, Brandis ran to meet the onrushing demon. He let his fury and his despair carry him forward like a crashing wave of steel. He threw himself down under the demon's curving horn, then with all his strength brought his blade over his head to slash across its neck. Acrid blood sprayed over him, but the demon didn't fall. Howling, it swatted at Brandis with a massive fist, sending him staggering backward.

"At least I know I got your attention," Brandis muttered, gripping his sword more tightly. He couldn't hear his friends anymore, just the pounding of blood in his ears.

LEVEL 29 DAILY EXPLOITS

Avalanche of Steel Fighter Attack 29

You crash forward with the unrelenting fury of a landslide, letting your weapon be your guide and having no concern other than burying your foe.

Daily ✦ Invigorating, Martial, Weapon
Standard Action   Melee weapon
Requirement: You must be wielding a two-handed weapon.
Target: One creature
Attack: Strength vs. AC
Hit: 8[W] + Strength modifier damage.
Miss: Half damage.
Effect: You grant combat advantage to all enemies until the start of your next turn.
Special: When charging, you can use this power in place of a melee basic attack.

Blade Storm Fighter Attack 29

You weave through your foes, your weapon flashing as you strike through their ranks.

Daily ✦ Martial, Weapon
Standard Action   Melee weapon
Target: One creature
Attack: Strength vs. Reflex
Hit: 3[W] + Strength modifier + Dexterity modifier damage, and the target is dazed (save ends).
Miss: Half damage, and the target is not dazed.
Effect: You can shift 3 squares and repeat the attack against a second target. You can then shift 3 squares and repeat the attack against a third target.

Cascading Catapult Slam Fighter Attack 29

The brunt of your mighty swing sends your enemy bowling into another foe.

Daily ✦ Martial, Weapon
Standard Action   Melee weapon
Requirement: You must be wielding a two-handed weapon.
Primary Target: One creature
Primary Attack: Strength vs. Fortitude
Hit: 4[W] + Strength modifier damage, and you push the target a number of squares equal to 1 + your Constitution modifier and knock it prone. Then make a secondary attack.
   Secondary Target: One creature adjacent to the primary target
   Secondary Attack: Strength vs. Fortitude
Hit: 1d10 + Strength modifier damage, and you push the secondary target 2 squares and knock it prone. Then repeat the secondary attack against a creature adjacent to the secondary target.
Miss: Half damage, you push the target 1 square, and no secondary attack.

Catastrophic Flurry Fighter Attack 29

You become a tempest of violence, launching a barrage of lightning-fast attacks.

Daily ✦ Martial, Weapon
Standard Action   Melee weapon
Target: One creature
Attack: Strength vs. AC, three attacks
Hit: 2[W] + Strength modifier damage per attack. If you hit twice, you deal 1d10 extra damage to the target. If you hit three times, you instead deal 2d10 extra damage to the target.
Miss: Half damage per attack.

Mortal Wound Fighter Attack 29

You open your up foe, unleashing a fountain of vitality from the wound.

Daily ✦ Martial, Reliable, Weapon
Standard Action   Melee weapon
Target: One creature
Attack: Strength vs. AC
Hit: 3[W] + Strength modifier damage, and ongoing 20 damage (save ends). Until the target saves against this ongoing damage, the target has a -2 penalty to saving throws.

Titan's Hammer Fighter Attack 29

Your blow hits with ungodly force, knocking the sense out of your foe.

Daily ✦ Martial, Weapon
Standard Action   Melee weapon
Target: One creature
Attack: Strength vs. Fortitude
Hit: 3[W] + Strength modifier damage, and the target is stunned (save ends).
   Weapon: If you're wielding a hammer, the attack deals extra damage equal to your Constitution modifier.
Miss: Half damage, and the target is dazed (save ends).
Special: When charging, you can use this power in place of a melee basic attack.

Note: The giantslayer, a paragon path open to fighters as well as rangers, is described on page 62.

AVENGING SLAYER

"Justice is hard to come by. I'm here to make sure you pay for your crimes!"

Prerequisite: Fighter

Beyond a few safe havens, the world is an unforgiving land filled with cruelty, terror, and profound evil. The blameless are slaughtered and the works of civilization are torn down, sometimes in a bid for conquest, but just as often out of sheer brutality. Destructive monsters regularly leave behind survivors, and a few of these take up the sword or the axe. These brave souls seek not to put past wrongs right, but to prevent others from suffering as they have, and to slake a thirst for vengeance. In this way, heroism is often forged in darkness.

At some point in your life, your course was set, your path laid before you. Maybe your career as a grim hero began the moment you or those close to you fell victim to a fate you were powerless to prevent—your life forever changed by one act of depravity. Perhaps instead, as you have adventured, you've witnessed too many appalling acts, seen too many innocents buried, or found wickedness in too many shadows. Whatever the case, you now see yourself as the only one who can stand between the helpless few and the predatory hordes. You know no respite exists for those who would protect the weak. Even so, you willingly take on that task.

As an avenging slayer, your brutal efficiency makes you a menacing figure no enemy can safely ignore. You strike fear into your enemies to protect your allies and those who have less power than you. You punish corruption with merciless retribution, defining yourself as a righteous executioner.

AVENGING SLAYER PATH FEATURES

Slayer's Action (11th level): When you spend an action point to take an extra action, you gain combat advantage against an enemy marked by you until the end of your next turn.

Bloodied Edge (11th level): When you have combat advantage against a bloodied enemy, you gain a bonus to weapon damage rolls equal to your Charisma modifier.

Brutal Justice (16th level): When you reduce a target marked by you to 0 hit points, you gain a +2 bonus to attack rolls until the end of your next turn.

AVENGING SLAYER EXPLOITS

Comeuppance Strike	Avenging Slayer Attack 11

With an indignant roar and a brutal hit, you wound your enemy and force others to cower before your might.

Encounter ✦ Martial, Rattling, Weapon
Standard Action   **Melee** weapon
Primary Target: One creature
Primary Attack: Strength vs. AC
Hit: 2[W] + Strength modifier damage. Make a secondary attack.
   Secondary Target: Each bloodied enemy within 2 squares of the primary target
   Secondary Attack: Strength vs. Will
   Hit: The target takes a -2 penalty to all defenses until the end of your next turn.

Looming Justice	Avenging Slayer Utility 12

You take on an aspect of menace, forcing your enemies where you want them with a fierce look.

Daily ✦ Fear, Martial, Stance
Minor Action   **Personal**
Effect: Until the stance ends, whenever an enemy marked by you makes an attack that doesn't include you as a target, you can slide the enemy 1 square as an immediate reaction.

Ruthless Outburst	Avenging Slayer Attack 20

You lay about with pitiless blows, leaving those you strike bleeding and traumatized.

Daily ✦ Martial, Rattling, Weapon
Standard Action   **Close** burst 1
Target: Each enemy in burst you can see
Attack: Strength vs. AC
Hit: 3[W] + Strength modifier damage, and ongoing 5 damage (save ends). If the target is bloodied by this attack, the target takes a -2 penalty to attack rolls (save ends).
Miss: Half damage, and no ongoing damage or penalty to attack rolls.

DREADNOUGHT

"You can't slow me down, much less stop me."

Prerequisite: Fighter

World-shaking battles were fought between the tieflings of Bael Turath and the dragonborn of Arkhosia. The deeds and exploits of those conflicts resound still in epic story and song. One such anthem is *Lament of the Dreadnought,* a somber song that recounts the final march of Jagannash the Unstoppable, a great dragonborn hero.

A doughty warrior famed for his ability to fight on no matter the injuries he sustained, Jagannash accumulated a number of legends. He withstood the full fury of an angry blue dragon, shrugged off the lashes of a pit fiend's whip, and even killed a tiefling warlock who had hurled him through Hell. The *Lament,* though, speaks of his final battle and all he achieved in the last offensive against the tiefling empire. Jagannash felled a full legion of devils, strangled their succubus sorceress commander with his bare hands, and hammered his way through the walls of a fortress. He was climbing the tower that housed the tiefling war room when the earth rebelled and swallowed the citadel and all within it. It is whispered that Jagannash fights there still, despite the centuries. Such is his resilience.

It is from Jagannash's example that other fighters who follow a similar creed take inspiration. The mind-body practices of these warriors are kept and taught by a few masters, dragonborn and otherwise. Some even develop these talents without formal training.

As a dreadnought, you are an inexorable force of destruction. You turn aside weapons with nothing more than your force of will. Fire cannot touch you; lightning cannot blind you. The core of your might grows from your ability to detach your mind from your body, to disassociate yourself from the pain of your wounds and press onward to keep fighting when others would succumb. You attain this state through discipline and a commitment. All who attempt to stand against you are bound to fall.

DREADNOUGHT PATH FEATURES

Dreadnought Action (11th level): When you spend an action point to make an attack, you gain resist 10 to all damage until the start of your next turn.

Unfailing Resources (11th level): Your maximum hit point value increases by 10.

As a free action, you can take 10 damage to save automatically against an effect that a save can end. You must have at least 10 hit points to use this ability, and you can't reduce this damage by any means.

Critical Hardening (16th): When you score a critical hit with a weapon, you gain resist 10 to all damage until the end of your next turn.

DREADNOUGHT EXPLOITS

Inexorable Advance	Dreadnought Attack 11

You relentlessly pound through and past your foes.

Encounter ✦ Invigorating, Martial, Weapon
Standard Action   Melee weapon
Targets: One or two creatures
Effect: You can shift 1 square before each attack.
Attack: Strength vs. AC, two attacks
Hit: 1[W] + Strength modifier damage per attack.
　Weapon: If you're wielding an axe, a hammer, or a mace, the attacks deal extra damage equal to your Constitution modifier.

Blood Iron	Dreadnought Utility 12

Detaching your mind from your injuries, you ignore minor wounds for the rest of the battle.

Daily ✦ Martial
Immediate Reaction   **Personal**
Trigger: You become bloodied
Effect: You gain resist 5 to all damage until the end of the encounter.

Line-Breaker Assault	Dreadnought Attack 20

Your hammering strike knocks your foe where you want it and leaves it staggering.

Daily ✦ Martial, Reliable, Weapon
Standard Action   Melee weapon
Target: One creature
Attack: Strength vs. Fortitude
Hit: 3[W] + Strength modifier damage, and you slide the target to an adjacent space. The target is dazed (save ends).
Effect: You gain resist 5 to all damage until the start of your next turn.

HOWARD LYON

DREAD REAPER

"All things die, friend. It's my job to make sure you do, too."

Prerequisite: Fighter

Countless fighting styles issue from dedicated masters—unimpeachable figures who devote their lives to perfecting combat maneuvers that are carried onto the battlefield by their disciples. But not all techniques evolve from the teachings of these paragons of the warrior's art. Some methods come from origins far less noble. The path of the dread reaper is one such shadowy road.

According to legend, the first dread reaper was Gulkanon, a human paladin of the Raven Queen, stripped of his station and power for offending his god. Even without the connection to the deity he had long revered, Gulkanon was unwilling surrender his place as her champion. He turned to a new avenue of military study, building upon the techniques of savage and fell races in the world—orcs, goblins, ogres, and trolls. He took the crude strokes of these brutish creatures and refined them, developing a range of exploits that focused his strength into a vehicle of appalling carnage. As he grew more confident in his newfound skills, he took the title "dread reaper." He set out to send souls to his estranged patron in hopes of rekindling the bond that had been broken. Whether he succeeded is lost to time, but his legacy remains.

Some dread reapers serve the Raven Queen, and small cults of such warriors can be found who are willing to train promising candidates. Others who have this training, however, lack the will or discipline to find true favor with the god. A few stretch her tenets to accommodate their own excesses. The Raven Queen's vigilant servants have been known to hunt and slay the worst of those offenders.

Whether you had an affinity for death-dealing or found inspiration in the actions of another, you turned to the techniques of the dread reaper. The training offers you a special array of fighting maneuvers that emphasize your already impressive proficiency with two-handed weapons. Your training transformed you from a competent warrior to a terrifying force of destruction. Rather than minding your defenses, you favor wreaking havoc in combat. Enemies can't help but notice your destructive potential and ignore you at their peril. You can perform astonishing attacks, sweeping through your foes and laying them open with your steel.

DREAD REAPER PATH FEATURES

Reaper's Action (11th level): When you spend an action point to make an attack with a two-handed weapon, each enemy adjacent to you takes damage equal to your Strength modifier.

Impending Slaughter (11th level): If your opportunity attack bloodies an enemy marked by you, you can knock the enemy prone.

Reaping Cleave (16th level): When you hit with a melee basic attack using a two-handed weapon, an enemy adjacent to you takes damage equal to your Strength modifier. When you hit with the *cleave* power, all enemies adjacent to you take damage equal to your Strength modifier.

DREAD REAPER EXPLOITS

Reaping Lunge	Dread Reaper Attack 11

You make a long swing at your adversary, and your solid attack sends a clear message about the threat you represent.

Encounter ✦ Martial, Weapon
Standard Action   **Melee** weapon + 1 reach
Target: One creature
Attack: Strength vs. AC
Hit: 2[W] + Strength modifier damage. Until the start of your next turn, if the target makes an attack that doesn't include you as a target, you can shift 1 square and make a melee basic attack against the target as an immediate interrupt.
  Weapon: If you're wielding a two-handed weapon, the attack and the melee basic attack both deal extra damage equal to your Constitution modifier.

Reaper's Warning	Dread Reaper Utility 12

Sweeping your weapon in a threatening arc, you force your foes to reassess their tactics.

Encounter ✦ Martial
Minor Action   **Close** burst 2
Target: Each enemy in burst you can see
Effect: The target is marked until the end of the encounter, until you are knocked unconscious, or until another mark supersedes this one.

Blood Harvest	Dread Reaper Attack 20

Your series of vicious swipes leaves your enemies bleeding and in a bad spot.

Daily ✦ Martial, Weapon
Standard Action   **Close** burst 1
Target: Each enemy in burst you can see
Attack: Strength vs. AC
Hit: 3[W] + Strength modifier damage, and the target takes ongoing 5 damage (save ends). If the target moves on its turn, it cannot make a saving throw against the ongoing damage.
  Weapon: If you're wielding a two-handed weapon, the target instead takes ongoing 10 damage (save ends).
Miss: Half damage, and no ongoing damage.

Dwarven Defender

"The wrath of Hell can't move me, but I can hammer you into place!"

Prerequisites: Dwarf, fighter

Your people defied the titans and giants. Unity has sustained them, and tenaciousness has upheld them; traditions preserving these values serve them well. They stand unmoved and unconquered, like the mountains, against orcs and goblins and dragons.

Dwarf soldiers are unmatched in their fighting prowess and loyalty to one another. War stories hold that a single dwarf foot soldier is the match of any two warriors of another race and the same skill. Two such soldiers are worth five similarly skilled enemies. When the enemy forces are composed of little more than savages, dwarven armies break them like stone channels water.

All the institutions of dwarven society have soldiers loyal to the cause. Doughty fighters serve king or lord, guild or business, deity or church, or a simple creed. A few serve the almighty coin, selling their time and axes for wealth. Time-honored fighting techniques teach a dwarf warrior to use his or her racial abilities to the fullest and to use fine weapons and heavy armor. When the dogs of war are loosed, dwarf soldiers hold the line.

You are a master of dwarven fighting arts, relying on loyal allies as much as your own courage and resilience. Your expertise lies in defensive maneuvers and battle-line tactics. You know how to take advantage of holes in enemy lines. Allies come to rely on you as the center of the squad. They take heart in your steadfastness and your ability to break the defenses of your enemies.

Dwarven Defender Features

Defensive Action (11th level): Whenever you spend an action point to take an extra action, you gain a +2 bonus to your AC and Fortitude until the end of your next turn.

Stalwart Defender (11th level): Whenever you are adjacent to at least one ally, you and adjacent allies gain a +1 bonus to AC, and all adjacent allies can reduce the distance they are moved by any pull, push, or slide by 1 square.

Roots of the Earth (16th level): The Stand Your Ground racial trait can reduce the distance you are moved by 5 squares.

Dwarven Defender Exploits

Press Forward — Dwarven Defender Attack 11

Knocking your enemies back, you step into the gap.

Encounter ✦ Martial, Weapon
Standard Action   **Close** burst 1
Target: Each enemy in burst you can see
Attack: Strength vs. AC
Hit: 1[W] + Strength modifier damage, and you slide the target 1 square. You can then shift 1 square into the space that the target occupied.
  Weapon: If you're wielding an axe, a hammer, or a pick, the attack deals extra damage equal to your Constitution modifier.

Forge-Fire Heart — Dwarven Defender Utility 12

By looking to your own defense, you instill adjacent allies with courage.

Encounter ✦ Martial
Minor Action   **Personal**
Effect: Until the end of your next turn, you gain a +4 power bonus to all defenses, and any ally adjacent to you gains a +2 power bonus to Will.

Keystone Collapse — Dwarven Defender Attack 20

Your strike hammers your foe and causes him to flail about, toppling nearby adversaries in the confusion.

Daily ✦ Martial, Weapon
Standard Action   **Melee** weapon
Target: One creature
Attack: Strength vs. AC
Hit: 4[W] + Strength modifier damage, and you push enemies adjacent to the target 1 square and knock them prone.
  Weapon: If you're wielding an axe, a hammer, or a pick, the attack deals extra damage equal to your Constitution modifier.
Miss: Half damage, and you push enemies adjacent to the target 1 square.

HALFLING BOUNDER

"Let my size fool you, and that'll be your last mistake."

Prerequisites: Halfling, fighter

The world is wide and wild, and the nomadic halflings are small folk. Deftness and quick wits have allowed them to survive nonetheless. As they have done so, they have come to rely on wily and daring warriors to protect them. Even settled halflings maintain a soldierly class to see to their interests among other, and larger, civilized folk.

The fighting tradition of the halfling bounder favors halfling traits. Bounders are practiced in hit-and-run strategies and pack tactics. They spring about the battlefield, avoiding the attacks of their bigger enemies, striking from unexpected angles, and making harrying assaults. Bounders willingly lay down their lives to allow those they care for to survive and escape danger.

Most wandering halfling clans have a number of bounders who serve as scouts. These warriors help keep the traveling band carefree—they put down dangers before the threat becomes dire. Able and willing halflings can easily learn the techniques of the bounder. More than a few put this expertise to use outside halfling communities, satisfying their natural curiosity while protecting friends and common folk.

You are one such champion of the halfling people. A flashing blade in hand, you leap about, laughing as bumbling, oversized fools trip over themselves trying to stop you. You've learned to use your small size to see the battle from a different angle, enabling you to easily spot openings others miss, hounding your enemies and taking every advantage the battle offers. If your skill comes up short for some reason, your luck more than makes up for it.

HALFLING BOUNDER FEATURES

Shifty Action (11th level): You can spend an action point to shift a number of squares equal to your Dexterity modifier, instead of taking an extra action.

Chance Retaliation (11th level): If you use your *second chance* racial power and the result of the second roll is a miss, you can make a melee basic attack against the attacker as a free action.

Move the Battle (16th level): Whenever you make an attack because of the Combat Challenge class feature and hit, you can slide the target 1 square and then shift 1 square.

HALFLING BOUNDER POWERS

Too Close for Comfort — Halfling Bounder Attack 11

You and your biting blade stay on your enemy's heels.

Encounter ✦ Martial, Weapon
Standard Action — Melee weapon
Target: One creature
Attack: Strength vs. AC
Hit: 2[W] + Strength modifier damage. Until the end of your next turn, if the target moves, you can move up to your speed as a free action, ending your movement adjacent to the target.

Switching Leap — Halfling Bounder Utility 12

You throw your body in front of an incoming attack, knocking your ally out of the way.

Daily ✦ Martial, Weapon
Immediate Interrupt — Melee 1
Trigger: An adjacent ally is hit by a melee attack
Target: The triggering ally
Effect: You slide the target 2 squares and can shift into the space the target occupied. You become the target of the triggering attack.

Quicksilver Lunge — Halfling Bounder Attack 20

Spotting a weak point, you quickly lunge and strike.

Daily ✦ Martial, Weapon
Standard Action — Melee weapon
Target: One creature
Attack: Strength vs. Reflex
Hit: 4[W] + Strength modifier damage.
Miss: Half damage.
Special: When charging, you can use this power in place of a melee basic attack.

INNER DRAGON

"The fury of the dragon seethes in my blood!"

Prerequisites: Dragonborn, fighter

Dragonborn issue from the same spiritual line as mighty dragons. Since the earliest days, dragonborn have nurtured their raw fury into a fighting spirit and a proud martial tradition. The empire of Arkhosia formed from these roots, and it expanded at times based as much on the power of its military force as on its civilizing influence.

In Arkhosia, dragonborn served dragons in numerous capacities, from vizier to archmage, oracle to valet. The most important roles performed by dragonborn, however, were as agents in a dangerous world or as defenders of the homeland. Soldierly ways passed through the generations, as did the ability to tap one's inner draconic nature.

Particular dragonborn masters hone body, mind, and spirit through martial practice to perfectly tap into the inner dragon. Some come to this knowledge on their own; others gain it from teachers eager to train younger dragonborn in ancient traditions. Only a few master the techniques well enough to become legendary heroes or villains.

Whatever your personal history, the untamed blood of dragons flows in your veins. Your veneration of your warrior ancestors has manifested as a supernatural tie to this heritage. You hear the call of the dragon within. Its ferocity courses through you. Woe to those who harm you, for the shedding of your blood rouses the ire of your draconic heart.

INNER DRAGON FEATURES

Breath Action (11th level): When you spend an action point to take an extra action while you are bloodied, you can use your *dragon breath* racial power as a free action, even if you've already used it during this encounter.

Dragonborn Fury (11th level): While you are bloodied, your racial bonus to attack rolls is +2, instead of +1.

Eternal Breath (16th level): Whenever you hit a target with *dragon breath*, the target takes ongoing 5 damage (save ends). The ongoing damage is the same damage type as your *dragon breath*.

INNER DRAGON EXPLOITS

Dragon Blast	Inner Dragon Attack 11

As a wound opens, your boiling blood blinds nearby enemies.

Encounter ✦ Martial
Immediate Reaction   **Close** blast 3
Trigger: An attack damages you
Target: Each creature in blast
Attack: Constitution + 4 vs. Reflex
  Increase to Constitution + 6 vs. Reflex at 21st level.
Hit: 2d6 + Constitution modifier damage, and the target is blinded until the end of your next turn.

Ancestral Manifestation	Inner Dragon Utility 12

Drawing vitality from your draconic legacy, you channel the blood rage of your ancestors.

Daily ✦ Martial
Minor Action   **Personal**
Requirement: You must not be bloodied.
Effect: Your hit points fall to your bloodied value, and you gain temporary hit points equal to the hit points you lost by using this power. Until you have no temporary hit points, you gain resistance to all damage equal to your Constitution modifier.

Dragonbreath Strike	Inner Dragon Attack 20

Each time you swing your weapon, you release a blast of your dragon breath.

Daily ✦ Martial, Stance
Minor Action   **Personal**
Effect: Until the stance ends, when you deal damage with a melee attack against an adjacent enemy, the attack deals extra damage equal to your Constitution modifier. The extra damage is the same damage type as your *dragon breath*.

BRIAN HAGAN

KNIGHT PROTECTOR

"Nerath might have fallen, but the need for just warriors who abide by a code of honor remains still."

Prerequisite: Fighter

In this age of darkness, covered by the shadow of fallen empires, never has there been a greater need for those who champion the causes of the innocent. Not since the fall of Nerath has a coherent force of warriors been guided by honor and justice in all that they do. Bold knights who fought for King Elidyr of Nerath are long lost, and the honor code to which they adhered is a curiosity of history to most. However, some see the need for such nobility today, and they try to live up to the standards set by righteous soldiers long dead. These modern fighters name themselves the knight protectors.

Some of those who call themselves knights could equal Nerath's storied fighters in might and zeal. Without a code, though, who can say with certainty if the new knights can match bygone honor? Without a fellowship, how can like-minded individuals work toward similar ends and police their own? Indeed, a number of those who claim to be knights—and even a few who call themselves knight protectors—are anything but counterparts to the admirable warriors of old. Far too many use their self-claimed title for profligate or brutal gain.

A loose confederation of knight protectors acts as an organization for those who claim this path. Its members are pledged to look out for one another and to keep the principles of the order. Courage, industriousness, respect, courtesy, and the glory of battle are all guiding principles. Those who fail to uphold these standards quickly find themselves at odds with other knight protectors.

Taking up the sword and cloak of a knight protector, you see it as your task to emulate the knights of old. A warrior and something of a leader, you abide by the knight protector code for personal glory and out of respect for the past. In life, you strive to be noble, honest, and fair. When you and your comrades come under attack, you are at the forefront, testing and displaying your courage. Even if smaller minds mock you as an idealist, you know you fight with dignity and purpose.

KNIGHT PROTECTOR PATH FEATURES

Protector's Action (11th level): When you spend an action point to take an extra action, one ally within 5 squares of you gains a +4 bonus to AC until the end of your next turn.

Devoted Protector (11th level): When an enemy marked by you attacks an ally adjacent to you, you can slide the ally 1 square as an immediate interrupt.

Knight's Focus (16th level): When you can make an attack because of the Combat Challenge class feature or an opportunity attack, you can instead grant adjacent allies a +2 bonus to AC until the start of your next turn as an immediate interrupt.

KNIGHT PROTECTOR EXPLOITS

Protector's Strike	Knight Protector Attack 11

You smite your chosen opponent, wreaking vengeance for its attack on an ally.

Encounter ✦ Martial, Weapon
Standard Action · · · Melee weapon
Target: One creature marked by you
Attack: Strength vs. AC
Hit: 3[W] + Strength modifier damage. If the target attacked any of your allies since the end of your last turn, the attack deals extra damage equal to your Wisdom modifier, and the target is dazed until the end of your next turn.

Knightly Bulwark	Knight Protector Utility 12

At your beckoning, an ally uses you as a shield against danger.

Encounter ✦ Martial
Minor Action · · · Close burst 5
Target: One ally in burst you can see
Effect: The target can shift into a square adjacent to you as a free action and gains a +2 power bonus to AC until the start of your next turn.

Blood Justice	Knight Protector Attack 20

Your foe sends an ally staggering, and you instantly drive that enemy back with a devastating smite.

Daily ✦ Martial, Weapon
Immediate Reaction · · · Melee weapon
Trigger: An adjacent enemy bloodies an ally with a melee attack
Target: The triggering enemy
Attack: Strength vs. AC
Hit: 5[W] + Strength modifier damage, and you slide the target 1 square. You can shift into the space it occupied.
Miss: Half damage, and no slide.
Effect: The ally gains a +2 power bonus to AC until the start of your next turn.

POLEARM MASTER

"Victory is easier to achieve when your reach is longer."

Prerequisite: Fighter

The versatile polearm is easier to manufacture than a sword, and often easier to use effectively. In its simplest form, the polearm is a longspear—a short blade on the end of a long shaft. Since reach is an advantage, even the humble longspear is an effective weapon in unpracticed hands. In the hands of a master, its deadliness can be unparalleled.

More complex polearms offer even greater rewards on the battlefield and off. They combine the best aspects of spear and blade or axe, allowing the user control and damage unmatched by other weapons. It's little wonder that whole units of soldiers use polearms in war, and that city watches use these weapons to protect citizens, as well as keep them in line.

Because polearms are so common and easily crafted, learning to use one is part of most basic military instruction. Advanced skill isn't so easy to obtain, but the trials of regular combat serve as well as, if not better than, the training ground. The ability to use a polearm against a variety of foes can seldom be learned through the rigors of soldierly education.

Through your adventures, you have mastered the polearm. You prefer a weapon that extends your options and your reach, understanding that it's better to keep monsters at a distance. With such a weapon at your disposal, you not only deal wounding blows to your adversaries and cut wide arcs through multiple foes, you also better protect your allies by commanding more of your surroundings.

POLEARM MASTER FEATURES

Lunging Action (11th level): You can spend an action point to increase the reach of your reach weapons by 1 square until the start of your next turn, instead of taking an extra action.

Forceful Reach (11th level): If you use a reach weapon to deliver a weapon power that pushes, pulls, or slides a target, you increase the distance of the forced movement by 1 square.

Longarm Grasp (16th level): If you're wielding a reach weapon, whenever an enemy within 2 squares of you and marked by you shifts or makes an attack that doesn't include you as a target, you can make a melee basic attack against that enemy as an immediate interrupt.

POLEARM MASTER EXPLOITS

Leveraging Strike	Polearm Master Attack 11

You use your weapon to move your target where you want.

Encounter ✦ Martial, Weapon
Standard Action   **Melee** weapon
Requirement: You must be wielding a two-handed reach weapon.
Target: One creature
Attack: Strength vs. AC
Hit: 2[W] + Strength modifier damage, and you slide the target a number of squares equal to your Wisdom modifier.
Miss: Half damage, and no slide.

Reaching Stance	Polearm Master Utility 12

You take a wide stance that allows you to lunge at careless foes.

Daily ✦ Martial, Stance, Weapon
Minor Action   **Personal**
Requirement: You must be wielding a two-handed reach weapon.
Effect: Until the stance ends, you can make opportunity attacks against enemies within your weapon's reach.

Polearm Sweep	Polearm Master Attack 20

Whirling your weapon, you strike all foes within your reach.

Daily ✦ Martial, Weapon
Standard Action   **Close** burst 2
Requirement: You must be wielding a two-handed reach weapon.
Target: Each enemy in burst you can see
Attack: Strength vs. AC
Hit: 3[W] + Strength modifier damage.
Miss: Half damage.

RAVAGER

"For Kord!"

Prerequisites: Fighter, Battlerager Vigor class feature

A ravager is the quintessential battlerager, a savage and fearless fighter. Such a warrior thrives on rage and bloodlust, literally chewing on a shield's rim or weapon's haft to diffuse wild energy when a promised clash is too long in coming. When combat is joined, a ravager rushes headlong into the fray, leaving a trail of bleeding foes and twitching corpses behind.

You scoff at disciplined practice, romantic devotion to a code, and effete arms such as rapiers. A dedicated killer, you rely on the force of your weapon and the rush that battle gives you. Some might describe you as an uncultured lout, but you laugh at them as well. When they cower before the horrors of the night and the wild places, you stand fast, ready to whet your weapon on your enemies.

Being a ravager means that every skirmish is a chance for blood and glory. It's an opportunity to win fame, the favor of the gods, and maybe more than one form of immortality. You throw yourself into every fight as if it were your last, leaping fearlessly among your foes where you can wreak the most havoc. With your reckless bravery, you bring fame and honor to yourself, your people, your ancestors, and the gods who watch over you. And if the gods can't be bothered—to Hell with them too.

RAVAGER PATH FEATURES

Ravaging Action (11th): You can spend an action point to make a melee basic attack against each adjacent enemy, instead of taking an extra action. You gain a bonus to each damage roll equal to your Constitution modifier.

Strive to Slay (11th): Each time you reduce an enemy to 0 hit points, you gain a +2 bonus to the next melee attack roll you make before the end of your next turn.

Marauding Fury (16th): Once per round, when you miss with a melee attack while you are bloodied, you can make a melee basic attack against the same target as a free action.

RAVAGER EXPLOITS

Driven Before You	Ravager Attack 11

The savagery of your attack makes your enemies recoil.

Encounter ✦ Invigorating, Martial, Weapon
Standard Action   **Melee** weapon
Target: One creature
Attack: Strength vs. AC
Hit: 2[W] + Strength modifier damage, and you push each enemy within 3 squares of you, other than the target, 1 square.

Blood-Soaked Fury	Ravager Utility 12

You pause, wipe the blood from your lips, and rush headlong back into the fight.

Daily ✦ Healing, Martial, Stance
Immediate Reaction   **Personal**
Trigger: An enemy bloodies you with a melee attack
Effect: Until the stance ends, you take a -2 penalty to all defenses, but you gain a +2 power bonus to melee attack rolls. Whenever you reduce an enemy to 0 hit points, you regain hit points equal to your Constitution modifier.

Marked Savagery	Ravager Attack 20

Your vicious attack opens a gaping wound, and your focus on the enemy prevents him from tending to it.

Daily ✦ Invigorating, Martial, Reliable, Weapon
Standard Action   **Melee** weapon
Target: One creature
Attack: Strength vs. AC
Hit: 2[W] + Strength modifier damage, and ongoing 15 damage (save ends). Until the target is not marked by you, it takes a -2 penalty to saving throws against the ongoing damage.

SHIELD ADEPT

"The shield in my left hand speaks of my survival. With my sword, it whispers of your defeat."

Prerequisite: Fighter

Storied history follows the shield, a warrior's best friend and an implement of honor and identity in a fighter's panoply. A stout shield can turn aside mundane swords and arrows, as well as monstrous venom sprays and dragon fire. Only a steadfast ally is better for covering the flank while you're taking it to the enemy. Nothing is better to protect that ally.

Throughout time, the use of the shield has defined military tactics. In phalanx formations, common among many folk, one soldier stands alongside another, each relying on a comrade's shield for added protection. During a charge, a shield aids in pushing the enemy back or even down. Warriors in a unit of skilled shield bearers can place their shields together in an overarching arrangement, completely protecting all within the shield shell from outside attack. This is said to have originally been a dwarven trick, a "boulder formation."

The Arkhosian warrior-philosopher Khomagar said, "The shield is the law of the battlefield, protecting the soldier as lordly and righteous edicts protect the empire." Phalanx fighters from many cultures suffer dishonor or worse for losing their shields in battle, since such a loss weakens the unit as a whole. Numerous peoples maintain a tradition of bringing dead warriors home on their shields, and burying a shield with its owner. Especially among dwarves, a broken shield is seen as a symbol of loss or corruption.

The shield is even more important to a small-unit fighter who relies upon it to protect his or her few allies. To the wise soldier who fulfills such duties, a shield is as much a weapon as a defensive item.

You know these facts well. Through your countless skirmishes, you have mastered the use of your one-handed weapon and shield. Such is your skill that those who pay too much attention to one of your armaments inevitably suffer punishment from the other.

SHIELD ADEPT FEATURES

Covering Action (11th level): While using a shield, you can spend an action point to gain superior cover against ranged and area attacks until the end of your next turn, instead of gaining an extra action.

Shield Bearer's Payback (11th level): Each time an enemy adjacent to you attacks an ally with a melee attack, you gain a cumulative +2 bonus to your next melee damage roll.

Shielded Stamina (16th level): While using a shield, you add its shield bonus to your Fortitude defense.

SHIELD ADEPT EXPLOITS

Sudden Shield Bash — Shield Adept Attack 11

Your foe chooses to ignore you, receiving a solid blow from your shield as thanks.

Encounter ✦ Martial
Immediate Interrupt   Melee 1
Trigger: An adjacent enemy marked by you shifts or makes an attack that doesn't include you as a target
Requirement: You must be using a shield.
Target: The triggering enemy
Attack: Strength + 4 vs. Fortitude
　Increase to Strength + 6 vs. Fortitude at 21st level.
Hit: The target is stunned until the end of your next turn.

Shield Wall — Shield Adept Utility 12

Readying your shield, you prepare to defend yourself and nearby allies from incoming fire.

Daily ✦ Martial, Stance
Minor Action   Personal
Requirement: You must be using a shield.
Effect: Until the stance ends, you and allies adjacent to you gain cover against ranged and area attacks.

Reverberating Shield — Shield Adept Attack 20

You turn and shove your shield into your foe's attack, causing a numbing vibration.

Daily ✦ Martial
Immediate Reaction   Melee 1
Trigger: An adjacent enemy misses you or an ally with a melee attack
Requirement: You must be using a shield.
Target: The triggering enemy
Effect: The target is dazed and weakened (save ends both).

Shock Trooper

"Move fast, people! And hit them hard!"

Prerequisite: Fighter

Nerath was a just nation, it is said, but it would be a lie to say that it was built solely through negotiation, the spread of knowledge, and cultural influence. No, as any historian can tell you, Nerath rose on the splintered shields and shattered blades of its soldiers. When an object of conquest doesn't bend, it must be made to bow.

That was the job of Nerath's legions. Those armies consisted primarily of highly trained heavy infantry supplemented by heavy cavalry—the famed knight protectors. Nerath's military traditions were derived from older sources. In what any dragonborn would claim to be fine dragonborn style, a special auxiliary force of devastating light infantry led many of Nerath's assaults. These were the empire's shock troopers. Military historians liken them to similar troops among other cultures and peoples, especially elves and dragonborn.

The typical shock trooper wore chainmail over leather, and carried a longsword and short sword, or dual short swords. The trooper was trained to break the line of an enemy force, moving quickly to kill and wound as many enemy soldiers as possible. If a trooper broke through the enemy line, the job then became direct assault on enemy command positions.

Although Nerath no longer exists as an empire, more than a few of its traditions linger. Numerous fighters and schools of soldiery carry on shock trooper traditions. This is to say nothing of the similar soldiers among other peoples, such as dwarf assault fighters. Any warrior who wants training in this brutal and mobile assault style can readily find it.

You are part of this sudden strike tradition of fighting. Unlike those warriors who form battle lines, you move among your enemies, defying them to strike you down and forcing them to pursue you. Your daring onslaughts confuse and astonish your adversaries. Even so, your guard is never down, especially in your favorite place: the center of a throng of foes.

Shock Trooper Path Features

Footwork Action (11th level): When you spend an action point to take an extra action, you gain a +2 bonus to AC and Reflex until the end of your next turn. If a melee attack misses you while this bonus applies, you can shift 1 square as a free action.

Deadly Soldier (11th level): When you wield an off-hand weapon, increase the weapon's damage die by one size.

Quicker Death (16th level): Once per round, when you have combat advantage against a target, you can add your Dexterity modifier to a melee damage roll against that target.

Shock Trooper Exploits

Shocking Twister	Shock Trooper Attack 11

Slipping around your enemy, you deliver a series of exact stabs, leaving the foe reeling from three wounds.

Encounter ✦ Martial, Weapon
Standard Action   Melee weapon
Requirement: You must be wielding two melee weapons.
Target: One creature
Primary Attack: Strength + 2 vs. AC (main weapon)
Hit: 1[W] + Strength modifier damage. Make a secondary attack against the target.
Secondary Attack: Strength vs. AC (off-hand weapon)
Hit: 1[W] + Strength modifier damage, and you can shift 1 square. Make a tertiary attack against the target.
Tertiary Attack: Strength vs. AC (main or off-hand weapon)
Hit: 1[W] + Strength modifier damage, you can shift 1 square, and the target is dazed until the end of your next turn.

Assault Footwork	Shock Trooper Utility 12

With the poise of a seasoned sailor on a storm-tossed deck, you hold your weapons ready to parry, while remaining coiled to dodge.

Daily ✦ Martial, Stance
Minor Action   Personal
Effect: Until the stance ends, once during each of your turns when you miss with a melee attack, you can either shift 1 square or gain a +1 power bonus to AC until the end of your next turn.

Shocking Skewer	Shock Trooper Attack 20

You grab your foe and yank her toward you, driving your waiting blade in the opposite direction.

Daily ✦ Martial, Reliable, Weapon
Standard Action   Melee weapon
Requirement: You must be wielding an off-hand weapon and have a hand free.
Target: One creature
Primary Attack: Strength + 5 vs. Fortitude
Hit: You grab the target. Make a secondary attack against it.
Secondary Attack: Strength vs. Reflex
Hit: 3[W] + Strength modifier + Dexterity modifier damage, and the target is dazed (save ends).

TIEFLING WARFIEND

"My rage might be justified, but it still burns within the heart of a devil."

Prerequisites: Tiefling, fighter

The mixing of devils and mortals created the tieflings, infusing them forever with tainted fiendish blood. But in that corruption is power. Like any power, it can be tapped for good or ill.

Long have tieflings used the devilish energy burning in their spirits. In its most basic form, this infernal might allows the tiefling to channel anger and a desire for vengeance into attacks more vehement than normal. In ages past, however, tiefling warriors learned to channel their negative emotions into tools for war.

Fallen Bael Turath had whole cadres of mighty fighters who could funnel fiendish fury into their military maneuvers. Despite the loss of the empire, some of these devilish fighters survived. Their fighting customs were passed on, lasting through the centuries. Today, a few tiefling soldiers offer training that allows would-be warfiends to control the devil inside. Others, who must do without such guidance, find that the inner fiend is best directed into violence lest it pollute other aspects of life.

So many of your kind fear the taint lurking in their soul, but you realize it is merely a tool at your disposal. Without needing to embrace evil, you nurtured your infernal aspect and mastered it. You've coupled deadly skill at arms with the dread power of your heritage, helping you to defend your allies and to make your foes pay for daring to stand against you. Now the corruption within you serves your aims, coating your weapon in baleful fire and allowing you to consume the fleeting energy of dying foes.

TIEFLING WARFIEND FEATURES

Infernal Action (11th level): When you spend an action point to take an extra action, you regain the use of the *infernal wrath* racial power if you have used it during this encounter.

Hellfire Retribution (11th level): Whenever an enemy marked by you makes an attack that doesn't include you as a target, that enemy takes fire damage equal to 3 + your Constitution modifier.

Burning Opportunism (16th level): Whenever you make an attack because of the Combat Challenge class feature or an opportunity attack, you deal fire damage equal to 3 + your Constitution modifier if you hit.

TIEFLING WARFIEND EXPLOITS

Hellfire Reprisal — Tiefling Warfiend Attack 11

As you strike, your anger at your foe's attack on an ally manifests as baleful fire on your weapon.

Encounter ✦ Fire, Martial, Weapon
Standard Action   **Melee** weapon
Target: One creature
Attack: Strength vs. AC
Hit: 2[W] + Strength modifier damage. If the target has hit an ally with an attack during this encounter, the attack deals fire damage equal to 3 + your Constitution modifier.

Infernal Resurgence — Tiefling Warfiend Utility 12

You revitalize yourself with the shreds of a defeated foe's spirit.

Daily ✦ Healing, Martial
Free Action   **Personal**
Trigger: You reduce an enemy to 0 hit points
Effect: You regain hit points as if you had spent a healing surge.

Burning Wrath Smite — Tiefling Warfiend Attack 20

You pour all your hate and anger into a single attack, leaving your stricken opponent aflame.

Daily ✦ Fire, Martial, Reliable, Weapon
Standard Action   **Melee** weapon
Target: One creature
Attack: Strength vs. AC
Hit: 3[W] + Strength modifier damage, and ongoing 10 fire damage (save ends).

RANGER

"Keeping a pet lets me bring the wild with me wherever I go. I like it. Keeps me warm inside. Oh, and the wild packs one hell of a bite."

RANGERS ARE people of the wild frontier. They are bold wanderers who face the dangers that keep common folk living within walled cities and traveling along well-used roads. Every ranger is also a killer who uses terrain, keen senses, and hunt-honed strikes to end threats quickly. Where rangers differ is in their execution.

Blade and bow are typical ranger tools, but a few rangers forge a deeper alliance with the wilderness. Such a ranger calls a beast as a friend and a weapon. The affinity for a beast might grow from one of many roots. Legend speaks of those raised among wild animals, as well as of those with a supernatural affinity for wild creatures. For enigmatic reasons, Melora blesses a few with such a connection to animals. More often, however, a young would-be ranger befriends a beast or raises it from pup to warrior.

This chapter presents and supports such rangers. It also provides other sorts of rangers with ways to shape their capabilities. In it, you'll find the following:

✦ **New Ranger Build:** The beastmaster ranger build lets you bring to life the fantasy archetype of hero and pet as a fighting unit.

✦ **New Class Feature:** Every beastmaster needs, well, a beast to master, and that's what the Beast Mastery class feature is all about. You can choose a beast companion from one of eight categories designed to fit the style of your character.

✦ **New Ranger Powers:** With a specialized build such as the beastmaster, a whole new assortment of exploits is required. Rangers who favor the blade or the bow have new power options in this chapter, too.

✦ **New Paragon Paths:** Focus your training in one of a dozen ways, even shoring up quirky ranger techniques such as throwing or using a crossbow. Focus on slaying a particular sort of enemy, absorb the magic of the lands you walk, or run with the pack.

GONZALO FLORES

To supplement the ranger builds described in the *Player's Handbook,* this chapter presents one new ranger build: the beastmaster.

BEASTMASTER RANGER

A deadly hunter, you specialize in double-teaming your enemies with the aid of a beast companion. Your beast is an extension of you, and thereby it is an invaluable member of your group. No other is needed to help you flank your quarry. Melee combat with the aid of your beast is your focus, so you favor Strength. You count on Dexterity for your AC and occasional ranged attacks, so your secondary focus is on that ability score. Wisdom, your tertiary ability score, makes you better at the Perception skill and gives you an edge with many ranger powers. The Beast Mastery class feature is designed to complement this build.

Suggested Feat: Lethal Hunter (Human feat: Improved Initiative)

Suggested Skills: Athletics, Heal, Nature, Perception, Stealth

Suggested At-Will Powers: *circling strike,* predator strike**

Suggested Encounter Power: *synchronized strike**

Suggested Daily Power: *partnered savaging**

*New option presented in this book

NEW CLASS FEATURE

The Beast Mastery class feature is available to any ranger who wishes to gain a loyal beast companion. To select this class feature, you must give up the Prime Shot class feature, and you do not select either the Archer Fighting Style or the Two-Blade Fighting Style.

Beast Mastery: You gain a beast companion, chosen from one of these categories: bear, boar, cat, lizard, raptor, serpent, spider, or wolf. These cat-

CHAPTER 2 | *Ranger*

egories do not describe specific animals, but rather groups of similarly themed creatures in the D&D world. You decide the creature's relevant details—its species, physical details, and so forth—making sure they are appropriate for its category and the campaign.

For example, if your character hails from a swampy region, your lizard companion might be a crocodile. The lizard companion of a ranger from a different region might be a giant monitor lizard or a drake. A beast companion's species doesn't affect its game statistics, which are based on its category and level.

You and your beast companion work so well together that the creature is almost an extension of you. Using your actions in combat, you control your beast companion by issuing it commands (see "Commanding a Beast Companion," page 41).

Beast Mastery also alters your Hunter's Quarry class feature. When you use Hunter's Quarry, your quarry can be either the enemy nearest to you that you can see or the enemy nearest to your beast companion that you can see. You or your beast companion can deal the extra damage from Hunter's Quarry, but only one of you can deal this extra damage per round.

Your beast companion is considered a creature and an ally and can be affected by powers. A cleric can heal it with *healing word*, a warlord can give it a melee basic attack with *commander's strike*, and so forth. You and your beast companion are treated as separate creatures.

You can have only one beast companion at a time. You can dismiss your beast companion at any time, but gaining a new one isn't a simple task (see "Gaining a New Companion," page 42). The link between a ranger and his or her beast companion is not one of master and servant but of two close friends.

As part of the training you underwent that allowed you to form a close bond with a beast, you learned the Raise Beast Companion ritual, which allows you to raise your companion from the dead, even if you are otherwise unable to master and perform rituals. (This ritual is described on page 41.)

BEAST COMPANION STATISTICS

A beast companion's category determines most of its game statistics, although all beast companions share a few characteristics.

Level: Your beast companion's level is always equal to yours. The beast's defenses, hit points, and attack bonus improve with level.

Ability Scores: Your beast companion's category determines its ability scores, which go up with level.

Add 1 to two of your beast companion's ability scores at 4th, 8th, 14th, 18th, 24th, and 28th level. All of your beast companion's ability scores improve by 1 at 11th and 21st level.

Healing Surges: Your beast companion has two healing surges. The beast's healing surge value is equal to a quarter of its maximum hit points, as normal.

Vision: Your beast companion has low-light vision.

BEAST CATEGORIES

Choose one of the following categories for your beast companion. Once you choose a category, such as wolf, you can then describe the beast's appearance, such as timber wolf, mastiff, or hyena.

BEAR

Brown bears and similar creatures fall into this category. Bears are tougher and deadlier than other beast companions, but they are a little slower.

> **BEAR STATISTICS**
> **Ability Scores:** Strength 16, Constitution 14, Dexterity 12, Intelligence 6, Wisdom 12, Charisma 6
> **Size:** Medium
> **Speed:** 5 squares
> **Defenses:** AC 12 + level, Fortitude 14 + level, Reflex 10 + level, Will 12 + level
> **Hit Points:** 16 + 10 per level
> **Attack Bonus:** Level + 2
> **Damage:** 1d12
> **Melee Basic Attack:** Claw; level + 2 vs. AC; 1d12 + Strength modifier damage.
> **Trained Skills:** Athletics, Endurance

BOAR

Boars are tough, resilient, and ferocious companions.

> **BOAR STATISTICS**
> **Ability Scores:** Strength 16, Constitution 16, Dexterity 14, Intelligence 6, Wisdom 12, Charisma 6
> **Size:** Medium
> **Speed:** 6 squares, 8 squares when charging
> **Defenses:** AC 14 + level, Fortitude 12 + level, Reflex 10 + level, Will 12 + level
> **Hit Points:** 14 + 8 per level
> **Attack Bonus:** Level + 4
> **Damage:** 1d8
> **Melee Basic Attack:** Gore; level + 4 vs. AC; 1d8 + Strength modifier damage.
> **Charge:** When charging, a boar gains a +2 bonus to its damage roll.
> **Trained Skill:** Endurance

CAT

Cats include lions, tigers, cougars, and similar predators. Their natural agility and stealth allow them to excel on scouting missions.

CAT STATISTICS

Ability Scores: Strength 14, Constitution 12, Dexterity 16, Intelligence 6, Wisdom 14, Charisma 6
Size: Medium
Speed: 7 squares
Defenses: AC 14 + level, Fortitude 11 + level, Reflex 13 + level, Will 12 + level
Hit Points: 14 + 8 per level
Attack Bonus: Level + 4
Damage: 1d8
Melee Basic Attack: Claw; level + 4 vs. AC; 1d8 + Dexterity modifier damage.
Trained Skills: Athletics, Stealth

LIZARD

The lizard category includes crocodiles and drakes. These thick-skinned beasts are tough combatants.

LIZARD STATISTICS

Ability Scores: Strength 16, Constitution 14, Dexterity 16, Intelligence 6, Wisdom 12, Charisma 6
Size: Medium
Speed: 6 squares
Defenses: AC 15 + level, Fortitude 12 + level, Reflex 12 + level, Will 10 + level
Hit Points: 14 + 8 per level
Attack Bonus: Level + 4
Damage: 1d8
Melee Basic Attack: Bite or claw; level + 4 vs. AC; 1d8 + Strength modifier damage.
Opportunity Attacks: A lizard gains a +2 bonus to the attack roll when making an opportunity attack.
Trained Skills: Athletics, Endurance

RAPTOR

The raptor category includes eagles, falcons, hawks, and other birds of prey. They are mobile and agile but not as ferocious as other beast companions.

RAPTOR STATISTICS

Ability Scores: Strength 12, Constitution 12, Dexterity 18, Intelligence 6, Wisdom 12, Charisma 6
Size: Small
Speed: 2 squares, fly 7 squares (hover)
Defenses: AC 14 + level, Fortitude 10 + level, Reflex 14 + level, Will 12 + level
Hit Points: 12 + 6 per level
Attack Bonus: Level + 5
Damage: 1d6
Melee Basic Attack: Claw; level + 5 vs. AC; 1d6 + Dexterity modifier damage.
Trained Skill: Perception

SERPENT

The serpent category includes massive constrictors and other hunting snakes. These beasts are common in tropical environments.

SERPENT STATISTICS

Ability Scores: Strength 14, Constitution 14, Dexterity 16, Intelligence 6, Wisdom 12, Charisma 6
Size: Medium
Speed: 5 squares, swim 5 squares
Defenses: AC 14 + level, Fortitude 12 + level, Reflex 13 + level, Will 12 + level
Hit Points: 14 + 8 per level
Attack Bonus: Level + 4
Damage: 1d8
Melee Basic Attack: Bite; level + 4 vs. AC; 1d8 + Dexterity modifier damage.
Opportunity Attacks: A serpent gains a bonus to opportunity attack damage rolls equal to its Strength modifier.
Trained Skill: Stealth

GAINING A BEAST COMPANION

How did you acquire your beast companion? What accounts for the special bond you share? You might consider one of these possibilities, or invent a background story of your own:

✦ You rescued the animal from a cruel trap or a menagerie and nursed it back to health.
✦ You captured the beast when it was young and trained it rigorously as it grew.
✦ You retreated into the wilderness, fasting and praying to Melora, until she found you worthy and sent you a companion.

✦ You performed a secret ritual to bind your spirit with your companion's.
✦ You were raised as part of a pack of these animals, and your companion is almost like a brother or sister to you.
✦ When you were nearly killed in a wilderness ambush, the animal found you and cared for you.
✦ The animal attacked you in the wilderness, and you wrestled with it until it agreed to become your companion.

SPIDER

In the Underdark and in primeval forests, goblins and many fey creatures train hunting spiders.

SPIDER STATISTICS

Ability Scores: Strength 14, Constitution 12, Dexterity 16, Intelligence 6, Wisdom 12, Charisma 6

Size: Medium

Speed: 6 squares, climb 6 squares (spider climb)

Defenses: AC 14 + level, Fortitude 11 + level, Reflex 12 + level, Will 12 + level

Hit Points: 14 + 8 per level

Attack Bonus: Level + 4

Damage: 1d8

Melee Basic Attack: Bite; level + 4 vs. AC; 1d8 + Dexterity modifier damage.

Trained Skills: Athletics, Stealth

WOLF

The wolf category includes predatory canines and dog-like creatures, from mastiffs to timber wolves to jackals.

WOLF STATISTICS

Ability Scores: Strength 14, Constitution 14, Dexterity 14, Intelligence 6, Wisdom 14, Charisma 6

Size: Medium

Speed: 7 squares

Defenses: AC 14 + level, Fortitude 12 + level, Reflex 12 + level, Will 13 + level

Hit Points: 14 + 8 per level

Attack Bonus: Level + 4

Damage: 1d8

Melee Basic Attack: Bite; level + 4 vs. AC; 1d8 + Strength modifier damage.

Combat Advantage: When a wolf has combat advantage against a target, the wolf gains a bonus to damage rolls against the target equal to the wolf's Wisdom modifier.

Trained Skills: Endurance, Perception

GODS AND RANGERS

Melora, the god of the wilderness, is revered by many rangers, as are Kord and the Raven Queen, who both hold some influence over the field of battle where rangers demonstrate their prowess. As a patron of adventurers and travelers, Avandra is revered by many rangers as well.

A significant number of rangers don't worship any gods, or revere them while also offering sacrifices to and striving to live their lives in harmony with the primal spirits of nature. Some of these rangers believe that the gods are interlopers in the world, which properly belongs to these primal spirits. Some of them even multiclass into primal classes such as druid or barbarian (described in *Player's Handbook 2*), calling on nature spirits to enhance their martial prowess.

RAISE BEAST COMPANION

You call out to your beast companion. Though death separates you, the ties of faith and friendship between you can cross any gulf.

Level: 1
Category: Restoration
Time: 4 hours
Duration: Instantaneous

Component Cost: 50 gp
Market Price: None
Key Skill: Nature (no check)

This ritual allows you to restore life to your slain beast companion. This ritual works only for rangers who have the Beast Mastery class feature.

The ritual functions as the Raise Dead ritual, with the following exceptions:

✦ You need not have any part of your beast companion's corpse.

✦ The death penalty lasts until you have reached three milestones.

✦ A paragon tier beast companion costs 500 gp to raise, and an epic tier beast companion costs 5,000 gp to raise.

COMMANDING A BEAST COMPANION

Your beast companion doesn't usually take its own actions during combat. It acts on your turn as you direct it, using the options below. To command your beast companion, you take the action specified for a command, and the beast must be able to see or hear you. If you don't command your beast companion, it remains where it is, as long as you are conscious and present in the encounter. If you are unconscious or aren't present, your beast companion can act independently (see "Beast Companion Independent Actions" below).

Attack (Standard Action): Your beast companion makes a melee basic attack against an enemy of your choice.

Defend (Standard Action): Your beast companion or both of you go on total defense. If you are adjacent to each other, the bonus to defenses is +3 rather than +2.

Move (Move Action): Your beast companion or both of you take a move action. The move actions need not be the same.

Opportunity Attack (Immediate Interrupt): When a creature provokes an opportunity attack from your beast companion, you spend an immediate interrupt to command the beast to make the attack.

Other Action: For any other action, you spend the required action and your beast companion completes it. For example, picking up an object requires a minor action, so you can spend a minor action to order your beast companion to grab a bag of coins in its jaws.

If your beast companion is incapable of completing an action, your action is wasted and the beast does nothing. Your beast companion cannot use your powers, and the DM is the final judge on whether a beast is capable of completing an action.

Beast Companion Independent Actions

In situations where you can't command your beast companion, it can act independently. For example, if you're unconscious or dead or if you aren't present in an encounter, your beast companion doesn't necessarily sit around waiting for you to show up, unless that's what you want it to do.

A beast companion acting independently can take a standard action, a move action, and a minor action on each of its turns, as a character can. You choose the beast's actions, with one restriction: If your character is present in the encounter but incapable of commanding the beast, it must move as far as it can toward you each round on its turn, choosing the safest route possible. Once adjacent to you, the beast companion can act in any manner you wish.

Beast Companions and Healing

Your beast companion can spend healing surges as any character can, and it can receive the benefits of healing abilities, such as a cleric's *healing word*.

Second Wind: When you use your second wind, your beast companion can use second wind as well.

Other Healing: When you are adjacent to your beast companion, you can spend a minor action and one of your healing surges to heal the beast companion as if it had spent a healing surge.

Death and Dying: A beast companion follows the same rules as a character for death and dying (*Player's Handbook*, page 295). If your beast companion dies, you can use the Raise Beast Companion ritual to restore it to life.

Gaining a New Companion

If you wish to switch to a new beast companion, you can use the retraining rules in the *Player's Handbook* (page 28) to select a different beast when you level up. Instead of changing a feat, a power, or a skill selection when you retrain, you can change your beast companion selection.

You keep your current beast companion until you have the opportunity to spend a few hours seeking its replacement in an environment where the new beast can be found. If your beast companion dies and you choose to replace it rather than raise it, you follow the same rules.

The DM can choose to run a short adventure that involves you finding a companion, perhaps rescuing it from captivity or overcoming a foe together. Otherwise, the DM can allow you to create the story of how you found your new companion.

NEW RANGER POWERS

A ranger exists at a nexus of disparate capabilities, all embodying the bold tracker and fearless hunter. As a beastmaster ranger, you have exploits that allow you to expertly guide and work with your beast companion. In many ways, the beast is like a weapon under your skilled control. Such specialty means that you favor powers that other rangers can't even use, and you often eschew exploits other rangers prefer. Those other rangers are far from forgotten. Even if you aren't a beastmaster ranger, you'll still find powers in this chapter that are to your taste.

Some powers in this chapter use the new beast keyword, while others use a special range or damage notation.

Beast

A power that has this keyword can be used only while your beast companion is conscious and present in an encounter.

Range

The following range designations appear in some powers.

Melee beast 1: The attack's target must be adjacent to your beast companion.

Melee weapon (beast 1): The attack's target must be within the reach of the weapon you're wielding and must be adjacent to your beast companion.

Close burst (beast): The burst originates from your beast companion.

Beast Attacks and Damage Notation

Powers that rely on your beast companion to attack use the beast's attack bonus and use [B] to denote the beast's damage die. A number before [B] tells you the number of times you roll the die. For example, a wolf companion's damage die is 1d8. If you use *partnered savaging*, which deals 2[B] + beast's Strength modifier damage, a wolf companion would deal 2d8 + its Strength modifier damage.

Level 1 At-Will Exploits

Circling Strike — Ranger Attack 1

Using the distraction your attack provides, your beast companion finds a better position.

At-Will ✦ Beast, Martial, Weapon
Standard Action   Melee weapon
Target: One creature
Attack: Strength vs. AC
Hit: 1[W] + Strength modifier damage.
   Increase damage to 2[W] + Strength modifier at 21st level.
Effect: Before or after the attack, your beast companion can shift 1 square.

Predator Strike — Ranger Attack 1

Your enemy focuses its attention on you, allowing your beast to attack.

At-Will ✦ Beast, Martial
Standard Action   Melee beast 1
Target: One creature adjacent to you
Attack: Beast's attack bonus vs. AC
Hit: 1[B] + beast's Strength modifier + your Wisdom modifier damage.
   Increase damage to 2[B] + beast's Strength modifier + your Wisdom modifier at 21st level.

Level 1 Encounter Exploits

Enclose the Prey — Ranger Attack 1

Your beast companion circles your quarry, gaining a better position just before you strike.

Encounter ✦ Beast, Martial, Weapon
Standard Action   Melee weapon (beast 1)
Target: One creature designated as your quarry
Effect: Before the attack, both you and your beast companion can shift 2 squares.
Attack: Strength vs. AC
Hit: 2[W] + Strength modifier damage.
   Beast: If your companion is a cat, a spider, or a wolf, the attack deals extra damage equal to your Wisdom modifier.

Hunting-Partner Strike — Ranger Attack 1

Working with an ally allows you that extra edge.

Encounter ✦ Martial, Weapon
Standard Action   Melee weapon
Target: One creature
Attack: Strength vs. AC
Hit: 2[W] + Strength modifier damage. If you're flanking the target, the attack deals extra damage equal to your Wisdom modifier.

Off-Hand Strike — Ranger Attack 1

A weapon in your off-hand allows for a quick attack.

Encounter ✦ Martial, Weapon
Minor Action   Melee weapon
Requirement: You must be wielding two melee weapons.
Target: One creature
Attack: Strength vs. AC (off-hand weapon)
Hit: 1[W] + Strength modifier damage (off-hand weapon).

Rapid Volley — Ranger Attack 1

With amazing speed, you unleash a pair of arrows at your enemies.

Encounter ✦ Martial, Weapon
Standard Action   Ranged weapon
Targets: One or two creatures
Attack: Dexterity vs. AC, one attack per target. If you target one creature, you gain a +2 bonus to the damage roll. If you target two creatures, you take a –2 penalty to both attack rolls.
Hit: 1[W] + Dexterity modifier damage.

Singular Shot — Ranger Attack 1

You single out a foe for a deadly attack.

Encounter ✦ Martial, Weapon
Standard Action   Ranged weapon
Target: One creature
Attack: Dexterity vs. AC
Hit: 2[W] + Dexterity modifier damage. If no creatures are adjacent to the target, the attack deals extra damage equal to your Wisdom modifier.

Synchronized Strike — Ranger Attack 1

You command your beast companion to tear into your opponent, opening a gap for you to exploit.

Encounter ✦ Beast, Martial, Weapon
Standard Action   Melee weapon (beast 1)
Target: One creature
Primary Attack: Beast's attack bonus vs. AC
Hit: 1[B] + beast's Strength modifier damage.
Effect: You make a secondary attack against the target.
   Secondary Attack: Strength vs. Reflex
   Hit: 1[W] + Strength modifier damage.
   Beast: If your companion is a bear, a boar, a lizard, a raptor, or a snake, the secondary attack deals extra damage equal to your Wisdom modifier.

LEVEL 1 DAILY EXPLOITS

Boar Assault — Ranger Attack 1

Each successful attack against your foe increases your tenacity.

Daily ✦ Martial, Weapon
Standard Action   **Melee** or **Ranged** weapon
Target: One creature
Attack: Strength vs. AC (melee) or Dexterity vs. AC (ranged)
Hit: 2[W] + Strength modifier damage (melee) or 2[W] + Dexterity modifier damage (ranged), and you gain temporary hit points equal to your Wisdom modifier.
Miss: Half damage.
Effect: Until the target is reduced to 0 hit points, you gain temporary hit points equal to your Wisdom modifier each time you hit the target.

ELADRIN RANGERS

Because of their naturally high Dexterity, eladrin are fine archer rangers, and the mobility provided by their *fey step* power serves them well in that role. As a race, they also have a long tradition of melee-focused rangers, who wield twin longswords in a deadly keening dance of steel. The pinnacle of this tradition is the blade banshee paragon path (page 59). Eladrin beastmaster rangers naturally choose beast companions of fey origin and learn to teleport side by side with their companions (see the Feyborn Companion feat, page 136).

Driving the Quarry — Ranger Attack 1

You fiercely assault your quarry, and your beast companion compels that same foe forward.

Daily ✦ Beast, Martial, Weapon
Standard Action   **Melee** weapon (beast 1)
Target: One creature
Attack: Strength vs. AC
Hit: 2[W] + Strength modifier damage.
Miss: Half damage.
Effect: If the target is your quarry, you slide it 2 squares and slide your beast companion 2 squares, ending its movement adjacent to the target. If the target is your quarry and is also bloodied, you instead slide the beast 4 squares.
    Beast: If your companion is a cat, a raptor, a spider, or a wolf, you can slide it to any square adjacent to the target.

Hunt's End — Ranger Attack 1

You carefully focus to make your attack spell your target's end.

Daily ✦ Martial, Weapon
Standard Action   **Melee** or **Ranged** weapon
Target: One bloodied creature
Attack: Strength vs. AC (melee) or Dexterity vs. AC (ranged). If the target is your quarry, the attack can score a critical hit on a roll of 19–20.
Hit: 3[W] + Strength modifier damage (melee) or 3[W] + Dexterity modifier damage (ranged).
Miss: Half damage.

Off-Hand Parry — Ranger Attack 1

You ready your off-hand weapon to deflect incoming attacks.

Daily ✦ Martial, Weapon
Standard Action   **Melee** weapon
Requirement: You must be wielding two melee weapons.
Target: One creature
Attack: Strength vs. AC (main weapon)
Hit: 2[W] + Strength modifier damage (main weapon).
Effect: You gain a power bonus to AC equal to your Wisdom modifier until the end of your next turn or until you attack with your off-hand weapon.

Partnered Savaging — Ranger Attack 1

Your beast companion brutalizes the enemy as you slip in for a quick strike.

Daily ✦ Beast, Martial
Standard Action   **Melee** beast 1
Target: One creature
Attack: Beast's attack bonus vs. AC
Hit: 2[B] + beast's Strength modifier damage.
Miss: Half damage.
Effect: If the target is your quarry, you can shift 3 squares and make a basic attack against it.

Level 2 Utility Exploits

Ferret an Opening — Ranger Utility 2

With a keen eye, you use one moment of advantage to create another.

Encounter ✦ Martial
Minor Action   **Personal**
Requirement: You must be flanking an enemy.
Effect: You gain combat advantage against the flanked enemy until the end of your next turn.

Fox Shift — Ranger Utility 2

Distracted by your ally, your foe can't respond effectively to your sly maneuvering.

Encounter ✦ Martial
Free Action   **Personal**
Trigger: You hit a target with a melee attack and the target is marked by an ally
Effect: You can shift 1 square, and you gain a +2 power bonus to all defenses against your target's attacks until the end of your next turn.

ELF RANGERS

Elf heroes combine high Dexterity and high Wisdom to become excellent archer rangers. Their high speed and Wild Step ability grant them excellent mobility, making them hard to outrun or pin down, and their keen senses help them thrive in the wild. The sylvan archer paragon path (page 68) reflects the spiritual union of an elf ranger and a bow. The Elven Beast Mastery feat (page 135) allows an elf beastmaster ranger to share both mobility and accuracy with a beast companion.

Hearten the Beast — Ranger Utility 2

With an encouraging shout, you give your beast companion the desire to fight harder.

At-Will ✦ Beast, Martial
Standard Action   **Close** burst 20
Target: Your beast companion in burst
Effect: The target makes a saving throw.
     Beast: If the target is a bear or a boar, it gains a bonus to the saving throw equal to your Wisdom modifier.

Hunter's Privilege — Ranger Utility 2

Your keen senses and uncanny instincts give you an edge over your quarry.

Daily ✦ Martial, Stance
No Action   **Personal**
Trigger: You make an initiative check at the beginning of an encounter and your check result is higher than any other combatant's
Effect: Until the stance ends, you add 3 to the extra damage you deal with Hunter's Quarry.

Pack Alertness — Ranger Utility 2

Through subtle communications, you and your beast companion act almost as if you share senses.

At-Will ✦ Beast, Martial
Minor Action   **Close** burst 10
Targets: You and your beast companion in burst
Effect: The targets each make a Perception check and share the better result. Also, if your beast companion becomes aware of a target, you do as well, and vice versa.
     Beast: If your companion is a cat, a raptor, or a wolf, the targets gain a +2 bonus to the Perception checks.

Level 3 Encounter Exploits

Beast Latch — Ranger Attack 3

Your attack diverts your foe's attention long enough for your beast companion to take hold, hampering your foe and allowing the beast to easily follow.

Encounter ✦ Beast, Martial, Weapon
Standard Action   **Melee** weapon (beast 1)
Target: One creature
Attack: Strength vs. AC
Hit: 2[W] + Strength modifier damage.
     Beast: If your companion is a bear, a cat, a raptor, a spider, or a snake, the attack deals extra damage equal to your Wisdom modifier.
Effect: If the target moves during its next turn, your beast companion can shift to any square adjacent to the target's new location as a free action. If the target is your quarry, it is slowed until the end of your next turn.

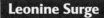

Leonine Surge — Ranger Attack 3

Like a hunting lion, you throw yourself at your enemy in an attempt to land two blows and put your victim down.

Encounter ✦ Martial, Weapon
Standard Action   **Melee** weapon
Requirement: You must be wielding two melee weapons.
Target: One creature
Attack: Strength vs. AC, two attacks
Hit: 1[W] + Strength modifier damage per attack. If both attacks hit, the target is knocked prone and takes extra damage equal to your Wisdom modifier. If both attacks miss, you grant combat advantage to all enemies until the start of your next turn.

Paired Predators — Ranger Attack 3

Coupling attacks, you and your beast efficiently take it to your enemies.

Encounter ✦ Beast, Martial, Weapon
Standard Action   **Melee** weapon
Target: One creature
Attack: Strength vs. AC
Hit: 2[W] + Strength modifier damage.
Effect: Your beast companion can make a melee basic attack against a target within its reach as a free action.
    Beast: If your companion is a boar, a lizard, or a wolf, the attacks deal extra damage equal to your Wisdom modifier.

Ruffling Sting — Ranger Attack 3

With a scorpion-like jab, you unsettle your opponent enough to gain a momentary advantage.

Encounter ✦ Martial, Weapon
Minor Action   **Melee** weapon
Requirement: You must be wielding two melee weapons.
Target: One creature
Attack: Strength vs. AC (off-hand weapon)
Hit: 1[W] + Strength modifier damage (off-hand weapon). Until the end of your turn, the target grants combat advantage to you for your next melee attack against it.

Scattering Volley — Ranger Attack 3

Your hail of shots causes your foes to dive for cover, clearing a path for your allies.

Encounter ✦ Martial, Weapon
Standard Action   **Ranged** weapon
Targets: One or two creatures
Attack: Dexterity vs. AC, one attack per target. If you target one creature, you gain a +2 bonus to the damage roll. If you target two creatures, you take a -2 penalty to both attack rolls.
Hit: 1[W] + Dexterity modifier damage, and you slide the target 1 square.

Thwarting Shot — Ranger Attack 3

Your cutting projectile discombobulates your adversary for a moment.

Encounter ✦ Martial, Weapon
Standard Action   **Ranged** weapon
Target: One creature
Attack: Dexterity vs. Fortitude
Hit: 1[W] + Dexterity modifier damage, and the target is slowed and takes a –2 penalty to attack rolls until the end of your next turn.

LEVEL 5 DAILY EXPLOITS

Adaptive Assault — Ranger Attack 5

Your quick attacks might have different results.

Daily ✦ Martial, Weapon
Standard Action   **Melee** or **Ranged** weapon
Requirement: You must be wielding two melee weapons or a ranged weapon.
Targets: One or two creatures
Attack: Strength vs. AC (melee; main weapon and off-hand weapon) or Dexterity vs. AC (ranged), two attacks
Hit: 1[W] + Strength modifier damage (melee) or 1[W] + Dexterity modifier damage (ranged) per attack. If both attacks hit the same target, the target either takes ongoing 5 damage or is dazed (save ends either).
Miss: Half damage per attack.

Bloodied Frenzy — Ranger Attack 5

Injury, whether yours or your beast companion's, provokes an instant assault from the beast that leaves your adversary momentarily hobbled.

Daily ✦ Beast, Martial
Immediate Reaction   **Melee** beast 1
Trigger: An enemy bloodies you or your beast companion
Target: The triggering enemy
Effect: Before the attack, your beast companion can shift 5 squares.
Attack: Beast's attack bonus vs. AC
Hit: 2[B] + beast's Strength modifier damage, and the target is immobilized (save ends).
Miss: Half damage.

Close-Combat Shot — Ranger Attack 5

You punish your enemy for closing with you.

Daily ✦ Martial, Weapon
Immediate Reaction   **Ranged** weapon
Trigger: An enemy enters a square adjacent to you
Target: The triggering enemy
Attack: Dexterity vs. AC
Hit: 3[W] + Dexterity modifier damage.
Miss: Half damage.
Special: Using this power doesn't provoke an opportunity attack from the target.

Lacerating Maul — Ranger Attack

Opening your quarry up with a decisive attack, you allow your beast companion to tear a wound. The scent of blood eggs the beast on.

Daily ✦ Beast, Martial, Weapon
Standard Action   **Melee** weapon
Target: One creature
Attack: Strength vs. AC
Hit: 2[W] + Strength modifier damage.
  Beast: If your companion is a bear, a boar, or a lizard, the attack deals extra damage equal to your Wisdom modifier.
Miss: Half damage.
Effect: If the target is your quarry and your beast companion is adjacent to it, the target takes ongoing 5 damage (save ends). Until the ongoing damage ends, the target grants combat advantage to the beast.

Spitting-Cobra Stance — Ranger Attack

You stand ready to launch a quick attack against any foe that menaces you.

Daily ✦ Martial, Stance, Weapon
Minor Action   **Personal**
Effect: Until the stance ends, you can make a ranged basic attack as an opportunity action against any enemy within 5 squares of you that moves closer to you.

HUNTER'S QUARRY

Stripped to its core, your Hunter's Quarry class feature is nothing more than a way to designate a single target and let you do massive amounts of damage to that target. It represents your focus on that target and your single-minded dedication to getting rid of that foe. But what do you do when you use Hunter's Quarry?

Take a moment, a focusing breath, and study your foe—the way it moves, its speed, its patterns. When you understand how it moves, you can predict where it will be when your sword or arrow reaches it.

Search out its weaknesses: Where does its armor not protect it? Where are the scales of its hide not as thick? How might an eye or a mouth offer access to its vulnerable organs?

Put yourself in its place. What does it see? How does it defend itself? Who does it attack, and why? What surprises it? Hunter and prey are one, linked in the cycles of nature.

Find your range. Learn exactly how far you must pull back the string, how much to angle your bow, exactly how to line up your shot against this particular target. Feel it in your muscles, force them to remember, and duplicate the perfect shot time after time.

Tag the Prey — Ranger Attack 5

Your keen hunter's instinct picks out this foe from the rest.

Daily ✦ Martial, Weapon
Standard Action   **Ranged** weapon
Target: One creature
Attack: Dexterity vs. AC. This attack ignores the target's cover but not superior cover.
Hit: 2[W] + Dexterity modifier damage, and you designate the target as your quarry until the end of your next turn. If the target was already your quarry, the attack deals 1[W] extra damage.
Miss: Half damage, and you do not designate the target as your quarry.

Level 6 Utility Exploits

Battle Runner — Ranger Utility 6

You move with astonishing speed, making it hard for your foes to track your movement.

Daily ✦ Martial, Stance
Minor Action   **Personal**
Effect: Until the stance ends, you can run a number of squares equal to your speed + 4, instead of your speed + 2, and you do not grant combat advantage from running.

Boundless Energy — Ranger Utility 6

You call upon your inner strength to persevere.

Encounter ✦ Martial
Free Action   **Personal**
Trigger: You roll an Endurance check and dislike the result
Prerequisite: You must be trained in Endurance.
Effect: Reroll the Endurance check. You decide whether to make the reroll before the DM announces the result.

Defensive Posture — Ranger Utility 6

Puffing up defensively, your beast rolls with a blow.

Encounter ✦ Beast, Martial
Immediate Interrupt   **Close** burst 20
Trigger: Your beast companion is hit by an attack within 20 squares of you
Target: Your beast companion in burst
Effect: The target gains a +4 power bonus to the defense targeted by the attack.
    Beast: If your companion is a bear, a spider, or a snake, the bonus lasts until the start of your next turn.

Invigorate the Beast — Ranger Utility 6

Your urging pushes your beast companion onward, despite fatigue and injury.

Daily ✦ Beast, Healing, Martial
Minor Action   **Melee** 1
Target: Your beast companion
Effect: The target regains hit points as if it had spent a healing surge.
    Beast: If your companion is a boar or a lizard, it regains additional hit points equal to your Wisdom modifier.

Serpentine Dodge — Ranger Utility 6

You snake past your enemies, weaving so that they have a hard time making a follow-up attack against you.

Encounter ✦ Martial
Move Action   **Personal**
Requirement: You must be within 2 squares of at least two enemies.
Effect: You can shift a number of squares equal to 1 + your Wisdom modifier. Until the end of your next turn, you gain a power bonus to all defenses equal to the number of enemies you were adjacent to at any time during this shift.

Level 7 Encounter Exploits

Beast Rush — Ranger Attack 7

You designate an enemy to your beast companion, and the beast moves toward that enemy as you strike.

Encounter ✦ Beast, Martial, Weapon
Standard Action   **Melee** weapon (beast 1)
Target: One creature
Effect: Before the primary attack, your beast companion can shift a number of squares equal to your Wisdom modifier.
Primary Attack: Beast's attack bonus vs. AC
Hit: 1[B] + beast's Strength modifier damage.
    Beast: If your companion is a boar, a cat, a raptor, or a wolf, the primary attack deals extra damage equal to your Wisdom modifier.
Effect: You make a secondary attack against the target.
    Secondary Attack: Strength vs. AC
    Hit: 1[W] + Strength modifier damage.

Biting Volley — Ranger Attack 7

Two lucky shots find chinks in your target's armor.

Encounter ✦ Martial, Weapon
Standard Action   **Ranged** weapon
Targets: One or two creatures
Attack: Dexterity vs. Reflex, two attacks. Each attack can score a critical hit on a roll of 18–20.
Hit: 1[W] + Dexterity modifier damage per attack.

Harried Quarry — Ranger Attack 7

Your attack, coupled with the threat of your beast companion, throws your quarry off balance.

Encounter ✦ Beast, Martial, Weapon
Standard Action   **Melee** weapon (beast 1)
Target: One creature
Attack: Strength vs. AC
Hit: 2[W] + Strength modifier damage.
Effect: If the target is your quarry, it grants combat advantage to you and your allies until the end of your next turn.
    Beast: If your companion is a bear, a lizard, a spider, or a snake, your attacks against the target deal extra damage equal to your Wisdom modifier until the end of your next turn.

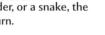

Hunter's Shot · Ranger Attack 7

You draw a bead on your chosen opponent and take the shot.

Encounter ✦ Martial, Weapon
Standard Action   **Ranged** weapon
Target: One creature
Attack: Dexterity vs. AC. If the target is your quarry, the attack hits if the attack roll hits the target's AC or Reflex.
Hit: 2[W] + Dexterity modifier damage.

Jackal Ploy · Ranger Attack 7

Twin strikes harass your enemy, opening a gap for an ally's attack as you slip away.

Encounter ✦ Martial, Weapon
Standard Action   **Melee** weapon
Requirement: You must be wielding two melee weapons.
Target: One creature
Attack: Strength vs. Reflex (main weapon and off-hand weapon). Make two attack rolls—one with each weapon—and use the higher result.
Hit: 1[W] + Strength modifier damage, and the target grants combat advantage to an ally of your choice until the start of your next turn. You can then shift a number of squares equal to your Wisdom modifier.

Twofold Flinch · Ranger Attack 7

You feint with both weapons, taking your adversary aback.

Encounter ✦ Martial, Weapon
Minor Action   **Melee** weapon
Requirement: You must be wielding two melee weapons.
Target: One creature
Attack: Strength vs. Reflex (main weapon and off-hand weapon), two attacks
Hit: The target takes a -2 penalty to attack rolls against you until the start of your next turn. If both attacks hit, the penalty is -4.

Level 9 Daily Exploits

Caging Strike · Ranger Attack 9

You box your foe in with one weapon and then open a wound with the other.

Daily ✦ Martial, Weapon
Standard Action   **Melee** weapon
Requirement: You must be wielding two melee weapons.
Target: One creature
Attack: Strength vs. AC
Hit: 2[W] + Strength modifier damage, and ongoing 5 damage (save ends). If the target is your quarry, it instead takes ongoing 10 damage (save ends).
Miss: Half damage, and no ongoing damage.

Jarring Salvo · Ranger Attack 9

Each shot that hits your enemy knocks it backward.

Daily ✦ Martial, Weapon
Standard Action   **Ranged** weapon
Target: One creature
Attack: Dexterity vs. Fortitude, three attacks
Hit: 1[W] damage per attack, and you push the target 1 square.
Miss: Half damage per attack, and no push.

Menacing Cry · Ranger Attack 9

Your beast companion issues a piercing cry, chilling the blood of nearby enemies.

Daily✦ Beast, Fear, Martial
Standard Action   **Close** burst 2 (beast)
Target: Each enemy in burst
Attack: Beast's attack bonus vs. Will
Hit: 1d8 + beast's Wisdom modifier psychic damage, and the target is immobilized (save ends).
  Beast: If your companion is a bear, a cat, a raptor, or a wolf, the attack deals extra damage equal to your Wisdom modifier.
Miss: Half damage, and the target is not immobilized.

MELEE OR RANGED?

More than perhaps any other class, the different builds of the ranger play very differently. The two-blade ranger is a melee-focused character who is similar in many ways to a rogue, relying on high mobility and devastating melee attacks to face foes in direct combat without the high defenses or hit points of a defender class. The archer ranger is more like a warlock, attacking from a relatively safe distance while circling around the thick of melee to get the best shots. The beastmaster build is a different approach to building a melee-focused ranger, one that stands out from other classes of any role as something unique.

Passing Ambush | Ranger Attack 9

You appear as if from nowhere, skewer your adversary, and then fade away.

Daily ✦ Martial, Weapon
Standard Action   **Melee** or **Ranged** weapon
Target: One creature that is surprised or unaware of your presence
Attack: Strength vs. AC (melee) or Dexterity vs. AC (ranged)
Hit: 3[W] + Strength modifier + Wisdom modifier damage (melee) or 3[W] + Dexterity modifier + Wisdom modifier damage (ranged), and you can shift 2 squares. If you were hidden from the target when you made the attack, you remain hidden if you have any cover or concealment.
Miss: Half damage, and you can shift 1 square. If you were hidden from the target when you made the attack, you can make a Stealth check with a +2 bonus to remain hidden if you have any cover or concealment.

Ranger's Recovery | Ranger Attack 9

After taking a moment to make a measuring strike and move into a better position, you're ready for action again.

Daily ✦ Martial, Weapon
Standard Action   **Melee** or **Ranged** weapon
Target: One creature
Attack: Strength vs. AC (melee) or Dexterity vs. AC (ranged)
Hit: 2[W] + Strength modifier damage (melee) or 2[W] + Dexterity modifier damage (ranged).
Effect: Before or after the attack, you can shift half your speed. If you have used all your encounter attack powers, you regain the use of a ranger encounter attack power you have used during this encounter. Or if you hit your quarry with this attack, you can instead choose to deal 2[W] extra damage.

Level 10 Utility Exploits

Companion Emplacement | Ranger Utility 10

You move into position, and you order your beast companion to warily do the same.

Encounter ✦ Beast, Martial
Move Action   **Close** burst 20
Targets: You and your beast companion in burst
Effect: You can move your speed, and your beast companion can shift its speed.
  Beast: If your companion is a raptor or a wolf, you can move 1 extra square, and it can shift 1 extra square.

Hunting Party | Ranger Utility 10

You're not about to give up with a simple miss.

Daily ✦ Martial, Stance
Minor Action   **Personal**
Effect: Until the stance ends, each time you miss your quarry with an attack, you can choose an ally within 5 squares of the quarry. If that ally hits the quarry before the start of your next turn, the ally's attack deals extra damage equal to your Hunter's Quarry damage.

Prime Shift | Ranger Utility 10

Always in motion, you dart in for the shot before spinning away.

Daily ✦ Martial, Stance
Minor Action   **Personal**
Effect: Until the stance ends, you can shift a number of squares equal to your Wisdom modifier as a move action whenever you hit an enemy with a ranged attack that has the bonus from the Prime Shot class feature.

Quick Recovery | Ranger Utility 10

Your quick command allows your beast companion to recover from an ill effect.

At-Will ✦ Beast, Martial
Immediate Reaction   **Close** burst 20
Trigger: Your beast companion receives an effect that a save can end within 20 squares of you
Target: Your beast companion in burst
Effect: The target makes a saving throw against the effect, with a bonus to the saving throw equal to your Wisdom modifier.

Shed the Mark | Ranger Utility 10

Your enemies can't keep track of your fast movements.

At-Will ✦ Martial
Move Action   **Personal**
Requirement: You must be marked.
Effect: The marked condition ends, and you can shift 1 square.

Level 13 Encounter Exploits

Bloodlust Strike | Ranger Attack 13

You aim for where the blood already flows.

Encounter ✦ Martial, Weapon
Standard Action   **Melee** or **Ranged** weapon
Target: One bloodied creature
Attack: Strength vs. AC (melee) or Dexterity vs. AC (ranged)
Hit: 3[W] + Strength modifier + Wisdom modifier damage (melee) or 3[W] + Dexterity modifier + Wisdom modifier damage (ranged).

Hammering Volley | Ranger Attack 13

Pulling back on your bow with great effort, you unleash a pair of arrows that slam your foes into the ground.

Encounter ✦ Martial, Weapon
Standard Action   **Ranged** weapon
Targets: One or two creatures
Attack: Dexterity vs. Fortitude, one attack per target. If you target one creature, you gain a +2 bonus to the damage roll. If you target two creatures, you take a -2 penalty to both attack rolls.
Hit: 2[W] + Dexterity modifier damage, and you knock the target prone.

Herd the Prey — Ranger Attack 13

Nipping at an adversary, your beast forces that foe toward your waiting weapon.

Encounter ✦ Beast, Martial, Weapon
Standard Action   Melee beast 1
Target: One creature
Attack: Beast's attack bonus vs. Fortitude
Hit: 1[B] + beast's Strength modifier damage, and your beast companion can shift 2 squares toward you and then pull the target 2 squares. The target grants combat advantage to you until the end of your next turn.
    Beast: If your companion is a lizard, a snake, a spider, or a wolf, the attack deals extra damage equal to your Wisdom modifier.

Knockdown Pounce — Ranger Attack 13

Your beast companion hurls itself at your quarry as you make a forceful attack. The combination sends your foe sprawling.

Encounter ✦ Beast, Martial, Weapon
Standard Action   Melee weapon (beast 1)
Target: One creature designated as your quarry
Effect: Before the attack, your beast companion can shift its speed.
Attack: Strength vs. AC
Hit: 2[W] + Strength modifier damage, and you push the target 1 square and knock it prone.
    Beast: If your companion is a bear, a boar, a cat, or a raptor, you instead push the target 2 squares.

Off-Hand Diversion — Ranger Attack 13

Your quick off-hand strike leaves your foe open to attacks.

Encounter ✦ Martial, Weapon
Minor Action   Melee weapon
Requirement: You must be wielding two melee weapons.
Target: One creature
Attack: Strength vs. AC (off-hand weapon)
Hit: 1[W] + Strength modifier damage (off-hand weapon), and the target grants combat advantage to you and your allies until the start of your next turn.

LEVEL 15 DAILY EXPLOITS

Armor-Piercing Shot — Ranger Attack 15

You take careful aim at your target's weak point before unleashing a deadly shot.

Daily ✦ Reliable, Weapon
Standard Action   Ranged weapon
Target: One creature
Attack: Dexterity vs. Reflex
Hit: 3[W] + Dexterity modifier damage.

Arterial Strike — Ranger Attack 15

The wound you leave seems small, but it bleeds freely.

Daily ✦ Martial, Reliable, Weapon
Standard Action   Melee or Ranged weapon
Target: One creature
Attack: Strength vs. AC (melee) or Dexterity vs. AC (ranged)
Hit: 2[W] + Strength modifier damage (melee) or 2[W] + Dexterity modifier damage (ranged), and ongoing 10 damage (save ends).
    Aftereffect: Ongoing 5 damage (save ends).

Blood Frenzy — Ranger Attack 15

Your attack unleashes a torrent of blood, and your beast companion goes into a frenzy.

Daily ✦ Beast, Martial, Weapon
Standard Action   Melee weapon
Target: One creature
Attack: Strength vs. AC
Hit: 3[W] + Strength modifier damage.
Miss: Half damage.
Effect: Until the end of the encounter, your beast companion gains a +2 power bonus to attack rolls and damage rolls. In addition, the beast gains 10 temporary hit points.
    Beast: If your companion is a boar, a lizard, or a spider, it instead gains 20 temporary hit points.

Scent of Fear — Ranger Attack 15

Once your beast companion senses weakness in an opponent, it attacks with ruthless intensity.

Daily ✦ Beast, Martial
Standard Action   Melee beast 1
Target: One creature
Attack: Beast's attack bonus vs. AC
Hit: 3[B] + beast's Strength modifier damage.
Effect: Until the end of the encounter, the target grants combat advantage to your beast companion, and on each of your turns, you can take a minor action to command the beast to make a melee basic attack against the target as a free action.

Steeling Flurry — Ranger Attack 15

You whip your weapons around you before dropping back into a defensive posture.

Daily ✦ Martial, Weapon
Standard Action   Close burst 1
Requirement: You must be wielding two melee weapons.
Target: Each enemy in burst you can see
Attack: Strength vs. AC (main) and Strength vs. AC (off-hand), two attacks per target
Hit: 1[W] + Strength modifier damage per attack. If you hit at least twice, you gain a +2 bonus to AC until the start of your next turn.
Miss: Half damage per attack.

Tracking Shot
Ranger Attack 15

You use this shot to size up your enemy, gaining insight you need for further attacks.

Daily ✦ Martial, Weapon
Standard Action   **Ranged** weapon
Target: One creature
Attack: Dexterity vs. AC
Hit: 3[W] + Dexterity modifier damage.
Effect: Until you hit the target again or until the end of the encounter, you gain a power bonus to attack rolls against the target equal to your Wisdom modifier.

LEVEL 16 UTILITY EXPLOITS

Curving Shot
Ranger Utility 16

For a moment, it looked like you were going to miss.

Daily ✦ Martial
Free Action   **Personal**
Trigger: You miss with a ranged at-will attack
Effect: You reroll the attack.

Pack Stealth
Ranger Utility 16

Moving as one, you and your beast companion disappear into the mist.

Encounter ✦ Beast, Martial
Minor Action   **Close** burst 2
Prerequisite: You must be trained in Stealth.
Requirement: You and your beast companion must have cover or concealment.
Targets: You and your beast companion in burst
Effect: The targets become hidden from any enemy that they have cover or concealment against.
     Beast: If your companion is a cat, a spider, or a snake, it can be within 5 squares of you when you use this power.

Shared Healing
Ranger Utility 16

You and your beast companion draw strength from each other, restoring your vitality.

Daily ✦ Beast, Healing, Martial
Minor Action   **Close** burst 5
Targets: You and your beast companion in burst
Effect: Each target regains hit points as if spending a healing surge.

Stalker's Senses
Ranger Utility 16

Your prey can't hide from you.

Daily ✦ Martial, Stance
Minor Action   **Personal**
Effect: Until the stance ends, you take no attack roll penalty because of concealment or total concealment when you attack your quarry.

Wary Shooter
Ranger Utility 16

Your agile shooting style keeps you safe from enemy attacks.

Encounter ✦ Martial
Minor Action   **Personal**
Effect: Until the end of your next turn, any ranged attack you make does not provoke opportunity attacks.

LEVEL 17 ENCOUNTER EXPLOITS

Blade and Fang
Ranger Attack 17

Attacking as one, you and your beast companion tear into an opponent.

Encounter ✦ Beast, Martial, Weapon
Standard Action   **Melee** weapon (beast 1)
Target: One creature
Primary Attack: Strength vs. AC
Hit: 2[W] + Strength modifier damage.
Effect: Your beast companion makes a secondary attack against the target.
     Secondary Attack: Beast's attack bonus vs. AC
     Hit: 1[B] + beast's Strength modifier damage.
     Beast: If your companion is a bear, a boar, a lizard, or a snake, the secondary attack deals extra damage equal to your Wisdom modifier.

Blow-Through Assault — Ranger Attack 17

Your attack flies through the ranks of closely clustered foes, hurting them all.

Encounter ✦ Martial, Weapon
Standard Action   **Melee** or **Ranged** weapon
Requirement: You must be wielding two melee weapons or a ranged weapon.
Targets: One creature
Attack: Strength vs. AC (melee) or Dexterity vs. AC (ranged)
Hit: 3[W] + Strength modifier damage (melee) or 3[W] + Dexterity modifier damage (ranged), and each enemy adjacent to the target takes damage equal to your Wisdom modifier.

Hounding Beast — Ranger Attack 17

Your beast companion darts around an opponent, leaving it hopelessly sidetracked.

Encounter ✦ Beast, Martial, Weapon
Standard Action   **Melee** weapon (beast 1)
Target: One creature
Attack: Strength vs. AC
Hit: 2[W] + Strength modifier damage, and the target provokes opportunity attacks from you if it shifts or attacks on its next turn.
Effect: Before or after the attack, your beast companion can shift 1 square. If the beast shifts, the target grants combat advantage to you for other attacks until the end of your next turn.
Beast: If your companion is a cat, a raptor, a spider, or a wolf, it can shift 1 square both before and after the attack.

Pounding Barrage — Ranger Attack 17

You pepper your enemy with a flurry of projectiles, leaving it tottering and unable to move.

Encounter ✦ Martial, Weapon
Standard Action   **Ranged** weapon
Target: One creature
Attack: Dexterity vs. AC, three attacks
Hit: 1[W] + Dexterity modifier damage per attack. If two of the attacks hit, the target takes 1d6 extra damage. If three of the attacks hit, the target is also immobilized until the end of your next turn.

Untamed Outburst — Ranger Attack 17

You lash out with your weapons, surprising your enemy with your wildness.

Encounter ✦ Martial, Weapon
Standard Action   **Melee** weapon
Requirement: You must be wielding two melee weapons.
Target: One creature
Attack: Strength + 2 vs. AC (main weapon and off-hand weapon), two attacks
Hit: 2[W] + Strength modifier damage per attack. If both attacks hit, the target is dazed until the end of your next turn.

LEVEL 19 DAILY EXPLOITS

Claim the Prize — Ranger Attack 19

Taking advantage of your foe's weakness, you try to land a finishing blow.

Daily ✦ Martial, Reliable, Weapon
Standard Action   **Melee** or **Ranged** weapon
Target: One bloodied creature designated as your quarry
Attack: Strength vs. AC (melee) or Dexterity vs. AC (ranged)
Hit: 5[W] + Strength modifier damage (melee) or 4[W] + Dexterity modifier damage (ranged).

Dead Stop — Ranger Attack 19

With a well-timed shot, you bring down a charging adversary, which skids to a halt at your feet.

Daily ✦ Martial, Weapon
Immediate Interrupt   **Ranged** weapon
Trigger: An enemy makes a charge attack against you
Target: The triggering enemy
Attack: Dexterity vs. Reflex
Hit: 3[W] + Dexterity modifier damage, and you knock the target prone.
Miss: Half damage, and you don't knock the target prone.
Special: Using this power doesn't provoke an opportunity attack from the target.

Driving Offensive — Ranger Attack 19

An initial strike hurls your opponent away from you, and as it stumbles, you heave a sense-rattling chaser after it.

Daily ✦ Martial, Weapon
Standard Action   **Melee** weapon
Requirement: You must be wielding two melee weapons.
Target: One creature
Primary Attack: Strength vs. AC (main weapon)
Hit: 3[W] + Strength modifier damage, and you push the target 3 squares.
Miss: Half damage, and you push the target 1 square.
Effect: Make a ranged secondary attack against the target.
  Secondary Attack: Strength vs. AC (off-hand weapon)
  Hit: 1[W] + Strength modifier damage, and the target is dazed (save ends).
  Miss: Half damage, and the target is not dazed.

Ferocious Roar — Ranger Attack 19

With a terrifying vocalization, your beast sends nearby enemies lurching in panic.

Daily✦ Beast, Fear, Martial
Standard Action   **Close** burst 2 (beast)
Target: Each enemy in burst
Attack: Beast's attack bonus vs. Will
Hit: 2d8 + Wisdom modifier psychic damage, and the target is pushed 1 square and dazed (save ends).
  Beast: If your companion is a bear, a cat, a snake, or a wolf, the attack deals extra damage equal to your Wisdom modifier.
Miss: Half damage, the target is pushed 1 square, and the target is not dazed.

Gnawing Assault — Ranger Attack 19

Your beast companion clamps down on a foe and rends its flesh.

Daily ✦ Beast, Martial
Standard Action   **Melee** beast 1
Target: One creature
Attack: Beast's attack bonus vs. AC
Hit: 2[B] + beast's Strength modifier damage, and the target is immobilized (save ends).
Miss: Half damage, and the target is immobilized until the end of its next turn.
Effect: If the target was already immobilized and your beast companion began the turn adjacent to it, the target takes ongoing 10 damage (save ends).

Threefold Assault — Ranger Attack 19

In a wild onslaught, you unleash three attacks with escalating potential.

Daily ✦ Martial, Weapon
Standard Action   **Melee** or **Ranged** weapon
Requirement: You must be wielding two melee weapons.
Targets: One, two, or three creatures
Attack: Strength vs. AC, three attacks (at least one attack with each weapon)
Hit: 1[W] + Strength modifier damage per attack. If you hit a target twice, you push it a number of squares equal to your Wisdom modifier. If you hit a target three times, it is also dazed until the end of your next turn.
Miss: Half damage per attack.
Special: If you use this power as a ranged attack, it doesn't provoke opportunity attacks.

LEVEL 22 UTILITY EXPLOITS

Adamant Recovery — Ranger Utility 22

You stay up despite all odds, showing what you're really made of.

Daily ✦ Healing, Martial
Immediate Interrupt   Personal
Trigger: You are reduced to 0 hit points or fewer
Effect: You spend a healing surge and can shift 1 square.

Hunt the Herd — Ranger Utility 22

You make prey out of all nearby foes.

Daily ✦ Martial
Minor Action   **Close** burst 1
Target: Each enemy in burst you can see
Effect: Until the end of your next turn, you designate each target as your quarry and can deal your Hunter's Quarry damage against each one you hit.

Preternatural Senses — Ranger Utility 22

Employing all your senses, you are aware of the unseen and the silent.

Daily ✦ Martial, Stance
Minor Action   **Personal**
Prerequisite: You must be trained in Perception.
Effect: Until the stance ends, you gain blindsight 5 and a +5 power bonus to Perception checks.

Selfless Sacrifice — Ranger Utility 22

You or your beast companion steps in front of an incoming attack meant for the other.

Daily ✦ Beast, Martial
Immediate Interrupt   Close burst 1
Trigger: You or your adjacent beast companion is damaged by an attack
Targets: You and your beast companion in burst
Effect: The target damaged by the triggering attack takes only half of the damage, and the other target takes the remainder. (If both targets were damaged by the triggering attack, one target can take half of the other's damage.) The target taking the remainder of the other's damage gains temporary hit points equal to your level.

Wild Dash — Ranger Utility 22

Your beast companion rushes forward to intercept a threat, or perhaps to flee an attacker.

Daily ✦ Beast, Martial
Immediate Reaction   Personal
Trigger: Your beast companion is hit by an attack or an enemy enters a square within 5 squares of you
Effect: Your beast companion can shift its speed.

LEVEL 23 ENCOUNTER EXPLOITS

Chase Down
Ranger Attack 23

You knock your adversary to one side, and your beast companion pursues.

Encounter ✦ Beast, Martial, Weapon
Standard Action   Melee weapon (beast 1)
Target: One creature
Attack: Strength vs. AC
Hit: 3[W] + Strength modifier damage, and you slide the target 2 squares. Your beast companion can shift 4 squares and must end adjacent to the target.
    Beast: If your companion is a bear, a cat, a raptor, a spider, or a wolf, it can instead shift its speed.

Dazing Volley
Ranger Attack 23

You shoot quickly enough to get off one shot with accuracy or two with haste. Either way, you leave struck foes in momentary shock.

Encounter ✦ Martial, Weapon
Standard Action   Ranged weapon
Targets: One or two creatures
Attack: Dexterity vs. AC, one attack per target. If you target one creature, you gain a +2 bonus to the damage roll. If you target two creatures, you take a –2 penalty to both attack rolls.
Hit: 3[W] + Dexterity modifier damage, and the target is dazed until the end of your next turn.

Hobbling Shot
Ranger Attack 23

The enemy wobbles from your shot and can move only poorly for a moment.

Encounter ✦ Martial, Weapon
Standard Action   Ranged weapon
Target: One creature
Attack: Dexterity vs. AC
Hit: 4[W] + Dexterity modifier damage, and the target is slowed until the start of your next turn. If the target is your quarry, it is instead immobilized until the start of your next turn.

Nonchalant Collapse
Ranger Attack 23

With your off-hand weapon, you casually send a foe to the floor.

Encounter ✦ Martial, Weapon
Minor Action   Melee weapon
Requirement: You must be wielding two melee weapons.
Target: One creature
Attack: Strength vs. Fortitude (off-hand weapon)
Hit: 2[W] + Strength modifier damage, and you knock the target prone.

Overwhelming Fury
Ranger Attack 23

You throw yourself at the enemy, distracting it while your beast companion moves to strike.

Encounter ✦ Beast, Martial, Weapon
Standard Action   Melee weapon (beast 1)
Target: One creature
Primary Attack: Strength vs. AC
Hit: 1[W] + Strength modifier damage, and the target grants combat advantage to your beast companion until the end of your next turn.
Effect: Your beast companion makes a secondary attack against the target.
    Secondary Attack: Beast's attack bonus vs. AC
    Hit: 3[B] + beast's Strength modifier damage.
    Beast: If your companion is a boar, a lizard, or a snake, the secondary attack deals extra damage equal to your Wisdom modifier.

LEVEL 25 DAILY EXPLOITS

Ambusher's Reaping
Ranger Attack 25

You leap from the shadows, cut down two foes, and then disappear from view.

Daily ✦ Martial, Weapon
Standard Action   Melee or Ranged weapon
Targets: One or two creatures that are surprised or that you are hidden from
Attack: Strength vs. AC (melee) or Dexterity vs. AC (ranged), one attack per target
Hit: 5[W] + Strength modifier + Wisdom modifier damage (melee) or 5[W] + Dexterity modifier + Wisdom modifier damage (ranged), and you can shift your speed. If you are hidden from the target when you make the attack, you remain hidden If you have any cover or concealment.
Miss: Half damage, and you can shift 1 square. You can make a Stealth check with a +2 bonus to remain hidden if you have any cover or concealment.

Primal Rampage
Ranger Attack 25

In a blur, you and your beast companion leap forward, knocking your foe down.

Daily ✦ Beast, Martial, Weapon
Standard Action   Melee weapon (beast 1)
Requirement: You and your beast companion must charge and use this power in place of a melee basic attack.
Target: One creature
Primary Attack: Beast's attack bonus vs. AC
Hit: 2[B] damage, and the target is knocked prone.
    Beast: If your companion is a boar, a cat, a raptor, a lizard, or a spider, the primary attack deals extra damage equal to your Wisdom modifier.
Effect: Your beast companion can shift 1 square, and you make a secondary attack against the target.
    Secondary Attack: Strength vs. AC
    Hit: 3[W] + Strength modifier damage, and the target is dazed (save ends).
    Miss: Half damage.

Pursuit of the Wild Hunt — Ranger Attack 25

You nail your adversary and your beast companion follows the scent of faltering prey.

Daily ✦ Beast, Martial, Weapon
Standard Action   **Melee** weapon (beast 1)
Target: One creature
Attack: Strength vs. AC
Hit: 4[W] + Strength modifier damage.
Miss: Half damage.
Effect: Until the end of the encounter, before you take any actions on each of your turns, you can take a free action to command your beast companion to shift its speed to a space closer or adjacent to the target. In addition, the target provokes an opportunity attack from your beast companion whenever the target shifts or makes an attack that doesn't include the beast as a target.

Ranger's Resurgence — Ranger Attack 25

With the grace of immortals, you move where you will and strike hard, leaving yourself prepared to make another assault.

Daily ✦ Martial, Weapon
Standard Action   **Melee** or **Ranged** weapon
Target: One creature
Attack: Strength vs. AC (melee) or Dexterity vs. AC (ranged)
Hit: 4[W] + Strength modifier damage (melee) or 4[W] + Dexterity modifier damage (ranged).
Effect: Before or after the attack, you can shift your speed. If you have expended all your encounter attack powers, you regain the use of a ranger encounter attack power you have used during this encounter. Or if you hit your quarry with this attack, you can instead choose to deal 4[W] extra damage.

True-Eye Shot — Ranger Attack 25

You can sometimes hit any target you can see.

Daily ✦ Martial, Reliable, Weapon
Standard Action   **Ranged** sight
Target: One creature
Attack: Dexterity - 2 vs. AC
Hit: 5[W] + Dexterity modifier damage.

LEVEL 27 ENCOUNTER EXPLOITS

Beastly Vise — Ranger Attack 27

Your attack leaves your foe with no idea how to escape its position between you and your beast.

Encounter ✦ Beast, Martial, Weapon
Standard Action   **Melee** weapon (beast 1)
Target: One creature
Attack: Strength vs. AC
Hit: 3[W] + Strength modifier damage. If you and your beast companion are both flanking the target, the target is immobilized until the start of your next turn.
  Beast: If your companion is a boar, a cat, a raptor, a spider, or a wolf, the attack deals extra damage equal to your Wisdom modifier.

Catch and Drop — Ranger Attack 27

A quick strike from your beast companion sends your opponent stumbling to the ground, and you have no qualms about hitting a downed foe.

Encounter ✦ Beast, Martial, Weapon
Standard Action   **Melee** weapon (beast 1)
Target: One creature
Primary Attack: Beast's attack bonus vs. Reflex
Hit: 1[B] + beast's Strength modifier damage, and the target is knocked prone.
  Beast: If your companion is a bear, a lizard, or a snake, it slides the target 1 square.
Effect: You make a secondary attack against the target.
  Secondary Attack: Strength vs. AC
  Hit: 2[W] + Strength modifier damage.

Unstable Gash — Ranger Attack 27

You leave a wound ready to tear open at the slightest strain.

Encounter ✦ Martial, Weapon
Standard Action   **Melee** weapon
Target: One creature
Attack: Strength vs. Fortitude
Hit: 2[W] + Strength modifier damage. If the target attacks or moves more than 1 square before the start of your next turn, it takes 4[W] extra damage.

NIGHT WATCH

Varis settled into place on the thick branch, and his panther, Shara, settled beside him. Together they watched the road below, claws and fingers clutching bark. Only their eyes moved, scanning the forest, catching every movement—every autumn leaf drifting to the ground, every squirrel scurrying across the forest floor or among the branches around them.

As the sun's last light drained from the sky and Varis's friends drifted to sleep beneath him, he closed his eyes and drank in the forest's sounds: the lonely call of an owl, the chirping of crickets and tiny tree frogs, the distant rustling of a bear in the fallen leaves. He could hear the bear snuffling as it rooted through the leaves for food.

He felt Shara stiffen ever so slightly, and he opened his eyes. The moon bathed the trees in silver light, enough for his elf eyes to see. He glanced at Shara and followed her gaze, then saw what had alarmed her: a dark shape flitting between the shadows of the trees, stalking toward the camp. He saw a second one, then a third, then beyond them a great many more, creeping in perfect silence, trusting in the cover of the dark.

Shara's breath was almost a growl, and he lifted a finger to silence her. Whether it was his movement or the panther's sound, the nearest creature below held up a hand and froze. Varis could just make out beady goblin eyes searching the forest. It was too late. Roaring as one, Varis and Shara leaped from the tree, and the goblin was dead before their feet touched the ground.

LEVEL 29 DAILY EXPLOITS

Five-Missile Dance
Ranger Attack 29

Moving warily, you launch five projectiles at your opponents, each shot more capable than the last of felling a target.

Daily ✦ Martial, Weapon
Standard Action   **Ranged** weapon
Targets: One, two, three, four, or five creatures
Attack: Dexterity vs. AC, five attacks
Hit: 2[W] + Dexterity modifier damage per attack. If you hit a target at least twice, you push it 1 square. If you hit a target at least four times, you also knock it prone. If you hit a target five times, it is also immobilized (save ends).
Miss: Half damage per attack.
Effect: You can shift 1 square after each attack.

Huntmaster's Bloodbath
Ranger Attack 29

Your horrific attack strikes a vital center, rapidly spilling your adversary's life force.

Daily ✦ Martial, Weapon
Standard Action   **Melee** or **Ranged** weapon
Target: One creature
Attack: Strength vs. Fortitude (melee) or Dexterity vs. Fortitude (ranged)
Hit: 4[W] + Strength modifier damage or 4[W] + Dexterity modifier damage, and ongoing 20 damage (save ends).
Miss: Half damage, and ongoing 10 damage (save ends).

Huntmaster's Mauling
Ranger Attack 29

You slice the flesh, and your beast companion tears it open.

Daily ✦ Beast, Martial, Weapon
Standard Action   **Melee** weapon (beast 1)
Target: One creature
Primary Attack: Strength vs. AC
Hit: 2[W] + Strength modifier damage.
Miss: Half damage.
Effect: Your beast companion makes a secondary attack against the target. If the primary attack bloodied the target, the beast gains combat advantage for the secondary attack.
Secondary Attack: Beast's attack bonus vs. AC
Hit: 5[B] + beast's Strength modifier damage.
Miss: Half damage.
Beast: If your companion is a bear, a snake, or a wolf, the secondary attack deals extra damage equal to your Wisdom modifier.

Suffering's End
Ranger Attack 29

Intending to slay your foe one way or another, you strike with deadly force.

Daily ✦ Martial, Weapon
Standard Action   **Melee** weapon
Target: One bloodied creature
Effect: Before the attack, you can shift a number of squares equal to your Wisdom modifier.
Attack: Strength vs. AC
Hit: 8[W] + Strength modifier damage.
Miss: 5[W] + Strength modifier damage.

Twin-Strike Tornado
Ranger Attack 29

You move and strike with such speed that your wounded foes are the only proof you moved at all.

Daily ✦ Martial, Weapon
Standard Action   **Close** burst 2
Requirement: You must be wielding two melee weapons.
Target: Each enemy in burst you can see
Attack: Strength vs. AC
Hit: 5[W] + Strength modifier damage.
Miss: Half damage.

RANGERS OF MANY RACES

Their high Strength makes dragonborn excellent two-blade or beastmaster rangers. Dragonborn rangers commonly have drake beast companions.

Dwarf rangers aren't particularly common, but their high Wisdom and their natural tenacity lead some dwarf heroes to become rangers. Most dwarf rangers choose the two-blade fighting style and wield twin axes, picks, or hammers.

Halfling rangers are rare. Because their size prevents them from using longbows, most halfling rangers choose

beast mastery rather than a fighting style, with a preference for raptor companions.

Not many tiefling heroes become rangers, but those who do generally favor wielding two sharp blades in melee combat. A few tiefling rangers learn ancient infernal secrets to imbue their attacks with hellfire—see the hellborn shadow paragon path (page 63).

See also "Eladrin Rangers" and "Elf Rangers," page 44.

JIM PAVELEC

Note: The borderlands marshal, a paragon path described on page 119, is open to a character who is both a ranger and a warlord (having multiclassed into the second class).

Avalanche Hurler

"Go ahead, keep making fun of me. I don't need a bow to hit you from down here."

Prerequisite: Ranger

The first avalanche hurlers were dwarf slaves in the ancient realms of the giants. Tempered by suffering and endless labor, and without access to soldierly methods, these dwarves tailored their ways of fighting to their work tools. They developed martial techniques that allowed them to be flexible in combat. A rebel needs ranged capability to kill in ambushes and slay retreating adversaries. Skill in melee is required to stand up to larger and quicker foes.

Revolutionary dwarves took up their hammers and axes. They threw these tools into the faces of their oppressors. Then, hammering and hewing from underfoot, the first avalanche hurlers brought their outsized masters down and escaped to the wilderness. They settled in underground halls they cut for themselves, places too small for their enemies to invade. Dwarves then made war on giants in Moradin's name.

Dwarf clans have maintained the avalanche hurler fighting style across the generations. They preserve their earliest original combat style, but they never held it so sacred that they failed to give it to allies among all sorts of folk. Further, the avalanche hurler might have been originally recorded in dwarven folklore, but other races developed similar military methods independently.

As an ever resourceful avalanche hurler, you are effective both in close combat and at range. Rather than mastering one ranger fighting style, you embrace both, using thrown melee weapons as your chosen instruments of death. What you lose in range and damage, you make up for with your versatility, being able to make attacks against adjacent enemies and then send your weapons flying against those beyond your reach.

Avalanche Hurler Path Features

Throwing Action (11th level): When you spend an action point to take an extra action, you can make a ranged basic attack with a light thrown weapon or a heavy thrown weapon as a free action. This ranged attack does not provoke opportunity attacks. You can then take an extra action.

Throwing Master (11th level): When you use a light thrown weapon or a heavy thrown weapon as a ranged weapon, increase the weapon's damage die by one size.

Uncanny Thrower (16th level): You take no penalty to attack rolls when using a light thrown weapon or a heavy thrown weapon against a target at long range.

Avalanche Hurler Exploits

Landslide Strike · Avalanche Hurler Attack 11

You hurtle forward, lashing out with your weapons at the end of your advance.

Encounter ✦ Martial, Weapon
Standard Action   Melee or **Ranged** weapon
Requirement: You must be wielding two melee weapons.
Targets: One or two creatures
Effect: Before the attack, you can shift 2 squares.
Attack: Strength vs. AC (melee; main weapon and off-hand weapon) or Dexterity vs. AC (ranged), one attack per target
Hit: 2[W] + Strength modifier + Dexterity modifier damage.

Quick-Draw Trick · Avalanche Hurler Utility 12

You draw and stow your weapons with dazzling speed.

At Will ✦ Martial
Free Action   Personal
Effect: You draw or stow one or two weapons.

Eruption of Steel · Avalanche Hurler Attack 20

After attacking with each of your weapons, you pause just long enough to find new targets for your furious assault.

Daily ✦ Martial, Weapon
Standard Action   Melee or **Ranged** weapon
Requirement: You must be wielding two melee weapons.
Primary Target: One creature
Primary Attack: Strength vs. AC (melee; main weapon and off-hand weapon) or Dexterity vs. AC (ranged), two attacks
Hit: 2[W] + Strength modifier + Dexterity modifier damage per attack.
Miss: Half damage per attack.
Effect: Make a secondary attack.
  Secondary Targets: One or two creatures other than the primary target
  Secondary Attack: Strength vs. AC (melee; main weapon and off-hand weapon) or Dexterity vs. AC (ranged), one attack per target
  Hit: 1[W] + Strength modifier + Dexterity modifier damage.
  Miss: Half damage.

Blade Banshee

"That hum is the sound of your death approaching."

Prerequisites: Eladrin, ranger

The Feywild sings with eldritch energy. It is infused with magic from its twilight sky to its sparkling depths. Fey creatures, its children, are bathed in its supernatural flow. Even the simplest among them have powers beyond those of worldly mortals, bestowing simple tasks with an other-worldly enchantment.

Eladrin are among the heritors of the Feywild's nature. As humans and other races tamed portions of the world, so too did the eladrin subdue parts of the Feywild according to their fey temperament. They evolved a complex society, rich in crafts and traditions that also sing in concordance with the Feywild. As followers of mores inspired in elder days by the god Corellon, eladrin treat life and all its aspects as an art. Everything they do, wonderful or wicked, reflects this ideal.

Like their counterparts in the world, eladrin have had to fight and die to defend their way of life. Each eladrin learns to wield the longsword, the traditional weapon of the eladrin people. They have martial disciplines that teach an eladrin to channel the innate magic in his or her spirit, as well as that stored within the elements.

A blade from the Feywild or crafted by eladrin hands has a special beauty. The metal vibrates with bizarre potential. Some eladrin learn to make steel shaped into such a blade sing its heart's song. That song is a fey cry that portends loss of life, and those who wield it are known across the cosmos as blade banshees.

Over the years, you've developed a terrifying synergy with your blades. You understand the secret heart of fey-crafted steel. Its unmistakable, dread voice announces your displeasure. As you fight, your blades buzz and keen, unleashing rending vibrations against your foes. But when your soul is bent to friendship or mercy, your swords hum with your own gentleness, briefly bringing a bit of peace to others before shrieking into battle once again.

Blade Banshee Path Features

Banshee's Action (11th level): When you spend an action point to take an extra action while wielding two melee weapons, any enemy adjacent to you takes thunder damage equal to your Wisdom modifier.

Bladed Disruption (11th level): While you're wielding two melee weapons, any creature you hit with more than one of your melee attacks during your turn takes a –2 penalty to attack rolls until the start of your next turn.

Shrieking Blades (16th level): While you're wielding two melee weapons, your melee attacks deal extra thunder damage equal to your Wisdom modifier.

Blade Banshee Exploits

Steel Scream	Blade Banshee Attack 11

You clash your blades together, unleashing a mind-numbing screech.

Encounter ✦ Martial, Thunder, Weapon
Standard Action   **Close** burst 1
Requirement: You must be wielding a longsword and another melee weapon.
Target: Each creature in burst
Attack: Strength vs. Will
Hit: 1[W] + Strength modifier thunder damage, and the target is dazed until the end of your next turn.

Soothing Reverberation	Blade Banshee Utility 12

With a soft sweep, your blades purr, reaching out to the minds of nearby allies and revitalizing them.

Daily ✦ Healing, Martial, Weapon
Minor Action   **Close** burst 3
Requirement: You must be wielding a longsword and another melee weapon.
Target: Each ally in burst
Effect: Each target can spend a healing surge either to regain hit points or to negate being dazed or stunned.

Mind-Bending Blades	Blade Banshee Attack 20

You use your blades to set up a fey harmonic pattern, allowing you to control your target until you unleash the sound in a disruptive wail.

Daily ✦ Charm, Martial, Reliable, Weapon
Standard Action   **Melee** weapon
Requirement: You must be wielding a longsword and another melee weapon.
Target: One creature
Attack: Strength vs. Fortitude
Hit: 1[W] + Strength modifier damage, and the target is dominated (save ends). As a standard action, you can end the dominated effect and deal 5d6 thunder damage to the target and each creature adjacent to it.

BLADE DANCER

"Clashing blades create the rhythm for our final dance."

Prerequisite: Ranger

Halflings have long used music and a sense of fun to enliven physical labor and various dull tasks. When the race was young, they created dancelike movements that mimicked martial skills—and translated into deadliness in melee. Halflings learned that bladed weapons lent themselves easily to such a refined use. As their battle dances evolved, halflings began to consider the nimble use of a pair of bladed weapons a refinement of the style.

Halflings came to call skilled practitioners of this dual-weapon method blade dancers. The mingling of itinerant halflings with other peoples eventually made the blade dance famous. The blade-dancer way spread far and wide, and other folk adapted it to new weapon types. Today, numerous people know and teach the essentials of the method. The strictest masters require the student to show proficiency in combat as well as a love of life and wandering like that of halflings.

Halfling or not, you have put your body through a grueling regimen to attain mastery of the blade dance. Twin blades twirl about you like deadly veils. Intricate footwork allows you to dance in and out of danger with ease. Your weapons, like good dance partners, know where you want them to go almost before you do. One day, you and your weapons might dance your way into legend.

BLADE DANCER PATH FEATURES

Dual-Blade Action (11th level): You can spend an action point to make one melee basic attack with your primary weapon and another one with your off-hand weapon, instead of taking an extra action. You gain a bonus to the damage rolls equal to your Wisdom modifier.

Dancing Defense (11th level): If you're wielding two melee weapons and hit with at least two melee attacks on your turn, you gain a +2 bonus to AC and Reflex until the start of your next turn.

Cutting Steps (16th level): While wielding two melee weapons, you gain a +1 bonus to melee damage rolls and AC.

BLADE DANCER EXPLOITS

Cross-Body Parry — Blade Dancer Attack 11

As your foe swings, you quickly cross your blades to parry, then scissor those blades brutally into your attacker.

Encounter ✦ Martial, Weapon
Immediate Interrupt   Melee weapon
Trigger: An enemy makes a melee attack against you
Requirement: You must be wielding two melee weapons.
Target: The triggering enemy
Attack: Strength vs. Reflex (main weapon and off-hand weapon), two attacks
Hit: 1[W] damage per attack. If both attacks hit, the target is weakened until the end of your next turn.
    Weapon: If you're wielding two light blades, two heavy blades, or a heavy blade and a light blade, each attack deals extra damage equal to your Dexterity modifier.

Misleading Bladework — Blade Dancer Utility 12

Whirling your blades, you dance in and out of your enemies' reach, knocking weapons aside and leaving foes off balance.

Daily ✦ Martial, Weapon
Move Action   Personal
Requirement: You must be wielding two melee weapons.
Effect: You shift a number of squares equal to your Dexterity modifier. Throughout the shift, each adjacent enemy takes a -2 penalty to attack rolls and grants combat advantage to your allies until the start of your next turn.

Blade Dance — Blade Dancer Attack 20

For a moment, you transform into a deadly storm of blades.

Daily ✦ Martial, Weapon
Standard Action   Melee weapon
Requirement: You must be wielding two melee weapons.
Target: One creature
Attack: Strength vs. AC
Hit: 2[W] + Strength modifier damage.
Miss: Half damage.
Effect: You can shift 3 squares and repeat the attack against a second target. You can then shift 3 squares and repeat the attack against a third target.
    Weapon: If you're wielding two light blades, two heavy blades, or a heavy blade and a light blade, the attack deals extra damage equal to your Dexterity modifier.

Feral Spirit

*"He doesn't like you. I don't like you either. Watch yourself—
we both bite."*

Prerequisites: Ranger, Beast Mastery class feature

To most mortals, an animal is a pet or a tool, a companion or a means to an end. Such creatures provide food, labor, protection, and even company. Only in rare cases does the relationship between master and beast transcend these mundane trappings. Every beastmaster is an exception to this generality, learning to become one formidable unit with an animal that is at once a friend, a guardian, and a weapon. Beastmasters know that, after the bond is formed, the capabilities and fate of master and beast are linked.

Beastmasters among many races have nurtured the mystical connection between master and pet. They cultivated communication that transcends speech and approaches telepathy. As such a beastmaster grew in power, the magic of the world infused the relationship. It bound the animal and mortal closer together, driven to do so by the devotion, ritual connection, and common cause the two shared. Contact among peoples spread this technique, which some claim originated with elves.

Elf or not, you've managed to foster such a transcendent relationship with your beast companion. Although each of you is fiercely independent and deadly, you share emotions and thoughts. Each knows when the other is in need. You work in unison to fell your foes, and even your allies swear you act to support each other more quickly than any communication could possibly allow. In time, you might grow

so close as to seem like one incredible being sharing two bodies (see the Beastlord epic destiny, page 151).

Feral Spirit Path Features

Fearsome Partnership (11th level): While you are within 10 squares of your beast companion, it gains a +2 bonus to damage rolls.

Feral Action (11th level): When you spend an action point to take an extra action, your beast companion also gains a +4 bonus to attack rolls until the start of your next turn.

Spirit Link (16th level): When your beast companion uses second wind, you can choose to spend one of your own healing surges rather than one of the beast's healing surges.

Feral Spirit Exploits

Feral Diversion — Feral Spirit Attack 11

Your companion draws a foe's attention, allowing you to slip safely away.

Encounter ✦ Beast, Martial
Standard Action   **Melee** beast 1
Target: One creature adjacent to you
Effect: Before the attack, your beast companion can shift 3 squares.
Attack: Beast's attack bonus vs. AC
Hit: 2[B] + Strength modifier + Dexterity modifier damage, and you can shift 3 squares away from the target as a free action.

Swiftness of Spirit — Feral Spirit Utility 12

At your signal, your beast companion is poised for action.

Encounter ✦ Beast, Martial
Minor Action   **Close** burst 5
Target: Your beast companion in burst
Effect: The target takes a move action or gains a +2 bonus to its next attack roll during this encounter.

Twin-Soul Strike — Feral Spirit Attack 20

Whether attacking together or apart, you coordinate your strike with the attack of your beast companion to maximize devastation.

Daily ✦ Beast, Martial, Weapon
Standard Action   **Melee** weapon (beast 1)
Primary Target: One creature
Primary Attack: Strength vs. AC
Hit: 3[W] + Strength modifier damage.
Miss: Half damage.
Effect: Your beast companion gains combat advantage against the primary target for the next attack the beast makes against it before the end of your next turn. Then the beast makes a secondary attack.
Secondary Target: The primary target or another creature
Secondary Attack: Beast's attack bonus vs. AC
Hit: 2[B] + Strength modifier + Dexterity modifier damage.
Effect: If the secondary target is different from the primary target, you gain combat advantage against the secondary target for the next attack you make against it before the end of your next turn.

Giantslayer

"Don't like being hit in the shins? Then bring your face down here!"

Prerequisite: Fighter or ranger

When the deities first called upon their mortal followers to take up arms against the primordials, the first giantslayers were among the heroes who joined the angelic legions. Not all who fought giants were deemed slayers, but a tough corps of warriors faced giants successfully time and again, thus earning the moniker their descendants use with pride to this day. They developed a battle style that proved effective against creatures larger than human size, as numerous monstrous beings are.

The giantslayer is, then, an intrepid warrior prepared to face enormous foes. Although plenty of other martial paths have more mundane applications, only the gutsy and the venturesome bother to train as giantslayers. Skill in a broad range of weaponry makes taking out big foes easier. Ranged attacks can hit the eyes or other hard-to-reach areas; melee weapons can be used to take out the legs, cutting a gigantic creature down to manageable size. Such a warrior is ever resourceful.

A giantslayer must also acknowledge that gruesome death is a possible end to his or her vocation. This fact, combined with the sheer audacity required for the job, means that most giantslayers are larger-than-life figures. Those who claim the title of giantslayer have a reputation for fighting hard and playing hard. Those who share the calling respect each other. Legitimate slayers police the ranks for charlatans, following up on rumors of fake giantslayers.

When it comes to being a giantslayer, you are the genuine article. Maybe you learned the trade from a mentor. Although some military organizations incorporate such techniques, no formalized tradition of giant slaying exists. The lessons learned on your past adventures might have been all the instruction you need. Fast, tough, and courageous, you know what it takes to cut down big opponents—even if that means going for a ride on one.

Giantslayer Path Features

Giant-Slaying Action (11th level): When you spend an action point to take an extra action, you gain a +2 bonus to attack rolls and AC until the start of your next turn. Against Large or larger enemies, the bonus to AC is +4.

Through the Fingers (11th level): If a creature grabs you, you can make a melee basic attack against it as an opportunity action. If this attack hits, you can make an escape attempt as a free action, with a bonus to the Acrobatics or the Athletics check equal to the damage dealt by the basic attack.

Small Target (16th level): You gain a +4 bonus to AC against opportunity attacks from Large or larger enemies and a +2 bonus to AC against opportunity attacks from Medium and smaller enemies.

Giantslayer Exploits

Little Bait	Giantslayer Attack 11

Your vexing attack enrages your enemy, causing him to forget all targets other than you for a critical moment.

Encounter ✦ Martial, Weapon
Standard Action   **Melee** or **Ranged** weapon
Target: One creature
Attack: Strength vs. Reflex (melee) or Dexterity vs. Reflex (ranged)
Hit: 2[W] + Strength modifier damage (melee) or 2[W] + Dexterity modifier damage (ranged), and the target is dazed and takes a -5 penalty to attack rolls against your allies until the end of your next turn. If the target is Large or larger, it also takes a -2 penalty to AC until the end of your next turn.

Ride the Giant Down	Giantslayer Utility 12

You scramble onto the creature's back, distracting it and gaining a better position to bring it down.

Daily ✦ Martial
Move Action   **Melee** 1
Target: One Large or larger creature
Effect: You move into the target's space, provoking opportunity attacks as normal. Until you leave the target's space, the target grants combat advantage to you and your allies and takes a -2 penalty to attack rolls, and you grant combat advantage to other enemies. Any attack that damages you also deals half the attack's damage to the target. When the target moves, you move with it, staying in the same portion of the target's space.
   If the target hits you with a melee attack, it can slide you to a square adjacent to its space unless you succeed on a saving throw.
Special: If you're trained in Athletics, you don't grant combat advantage to other enemies because of being in the target's space, and you can make a saving throw to negate any pull, push, or slide that would move you out of the target's space.

Giantslayer's Strike	Giantslayer Attack 20

The precision and force of your attack shocks your gigantic foe.

Daily ✦ Martial, Reliable, Weapon
Standard Action   **Melee** or **Ranged** weapon
Target: One creature
Attack: Strength vs. AC (melee) or Dexterity vs. AC (ranged)
Hit: 4[W] + Strength modifier damage (melee) or 4[W] + Dexterity modifier damage (ranged), and the target is dazed (save ends). If the target is Large or larger, the attack deals 1[W] extra damage, and instead of being dazed, the target is stunned (save ends).

HELLBORN SHADOW

"My ancestors gave much to learn the secrets of the Nine Hells. Why shouldn't I benefit from their sacrifice?"

Prerequisites: Tiefling, ranger

Although you're a being of this world, you're cursed to carry the mark of an infernal pact made by your mortal ancestors. The weight of that heritage rests heavy on your soul. Yours has been the life of one apart—a life marred by the prejudice of others and of battle against foul creatures spawned from darkness.

You have long seen similar darkness within yourself, hiding it to avoid the hate of bigots or revealing it to evoke horror in your enemies. You have sought the ancient secrets of your people. You have overcome evil dreams and vile impulses to master your inner nature. Finally, you have tapped sinister knowledge of your immortal forebears to aid you in your quests.

It's irrelevant whether you obtained these secrets in catacombs once lost to the ravages of time, within your own being, or from tormenting visions. The point is that you've learned to unleash some of your hidden potential by speaking words of power that few mortals know. With the baleful utterances you have learned, you can unleash pain, fire, and shadow. You can transform yourself momentarily into a form like that of your greatest ancestors and take to the air.

The darkness you have allowed to creep into your being now colors your exploits. Your heroic acts and your reputation, as well as those of your comrades, are tainted by the devilish legacy you have willingly tapped. The finale of your story will ultimately determine if your end justified your means.

HELLBORN SHADOW PATH FEATURES

Hunter's Feast (11th level): Whenever you reduce your quarry to 0 hit points, you gain temporary hit points equal to 1 + your Constitution modifier.

Immolation Action (11th level): You can spend an action point to deal fire damage to your quarry equal to your Hunter's Quarry damage, instead of taking an extra action.

Hellfire Caress (16th level): Whenever you hit your quarry with a melee or a ranged attack, the target loses fire resistance and immunity until the end of your next turn.

HELLBORN SHADOW EXPLOITS

Shadowbite Strike — Hellborn Shadow Attack 11

Just before you loose your attack, you whisper a word of power to make your enemy more vulnerable to your attacks and to cover yourself in a thin veil of darkness.

Encounter ✦ Martial, Weapon
Standard Action — Melee weapon
Requirement: You must be wielding two melee weapons.
Targets: One or two creatures
Attack: Strength vs. AC (main weapon and off-hand weapon), two attacks
Hit: 1[W] + Strength modifier + Charisma modifier damage per attack, and the target gains vulnerable 5 to your attacks until the end of your next turn.
Effect: You gain concealment until the start of your next turn.

Wings of Devilry — Hellborn Shadow Utility 12

You surge aloft on tattered, leathery wings. When you land, they dissolve into foul-smelling smoke.

Encounter ✦ Martial
Move Action — Personal
Effect: You fly a number of squares equal to your speed and must land at the end of this movement. You then gain concealment until the end of your next turn.

Balefire Scourge — Hellborn Shadow Attack 20

With a word of power, infernal flames erupt all over your weapons, lending fire and speed to your attacks.

Daily ✦ Martial, Weapon
Standard Action — Close burst 1
Requirement: You must be wielding two melee weapons.
Target: Each enemy in burst you can see
Attack: Strength vs. AC
Hit: 2[W] + Strength modifier damage, and the target takes ongoing 10 fire damage and loses any fire resistance or immunity (save ends both).
Miss: Half damage.
Effect: You gain concealment until the end of your next turn.

HORIZON WALKER

"In time, these eyes will see all realms."

Prerequisite: Ranger

The world is vast, with few mapped places. It begs exploration, instilling wanderlust in brave hearts. Roving it is a test of skill and stamina, an ordeal that rewards the intrepid with amazing sights, exciting encounters, and more. Still, the world is only one place in the broader cosmos. Other planes also beckon to the curious wanderer. The trials and experiences they offer can defy the worldly imagination and force adaptation beyond mortal ken.

Horizon walker is the traditional name for a ceaseless roamer who seeks the unexplored regions of the universe. The appellation applies to members of a loose confederation of warriors who recognize one another as comrades on life's wondrous journey. Such travelers go from place to place, from plane to plane, developing their skills and a mystic connection with the environment. They return changed by their contact with other realms, and with knowledge to better protect the world most mortals know.

Like most horizon walkers, you have traveled the world. You learned about it and protect its inhabitants from otherworldly threats. Then you fearlessly set out into the wider universe, using your skills and the magical nature of your tie to the world to develop similar bonds with the far reaches of creation.

To this day, you're incapable of staying in one place long. Unseen locales summon you with their mystery. Your destiny whispers to you from an unknown vista. Each step you take moves you closer to it.

HORIZON WALKER PATH FEATURES

Wanderer's Action (11th Level): When you spend an action point to take a move action, you gain an action point after taking that action.

Shadowfell Sight (11th Level): You gain darkvision. If you are in the Shadowfell, you also gain a +5 bonus to Perception checks.

Astral Infusion (16th Level): You gain a bonus to death saving throws and to your healing surge value equal to your Wisdom modifier. If you are on the Astral Sea or in any divine dominion there, you can't die as a result of failing three death saving throws, although damage can still kill you.

HORIZON WALKER EXPLOITS

Worldly Strike	Horizon Walker Attack 11

You put the arcane energy of the earth into your strike, strengthening your blow against otherworldly creatures.

Encounter ✦ Arcane, Weapon
Standard Action — **Melee** or **Ranged** weapon
Attack: Strength vs. AC (melee) or Dexterity vs. AC (ranged)
Hit: 2[W] + Strength modifier damage (melee) or 2[W] + Dexterity modifier damage (ranged). If the target has an origin other than natural, the attack deals extra damage equal to your Wisdom modifier, and the target is dazed until the start of your next turn.

Fey Strider	Horizon Walker Utility 12

The piece of the Feywild you carry in your heart allows you to transcend space for a moment.

Encounter ✦ Arcane, Teleportation
Move Action — **Personal**
Effect: You can teleport a number of squares equal to 3 + your Wisdom modifier. If you're in the Feywild, you can teleport an additional 3 squares.
Special: If you have a beast companion and it is adjacent to you, it can teleport with you when you use this power.

Elemental Chaos Smite	Horizon Walker Attack 20

Elemental energy swirls within you, and you unleash it as you strike an enemy.

Daily ✦ Arcane, Weapon; Acid, Cold, Fire, Radiant, or Thunder
Standard Action — **Melee** or **Ranged** weapon
Target: One creature
Attack: Strength vs. AC (melee) or Dexterity vs. AC (ranged)
Hit: 3[W] + Strength modifier damage (melee) or 3[W] + Dexterity modifier damage (ranged). The damage type is your choice of acid, cold, fire, radiant, or thunder, and the target takes ongoing 10 damage of that damage type (save ends). If you're in the Elemental Chaos, the target instead takes ongoing 20 damage of that damage type (save ends).
Miss: Half damage, and no ongoing damage.

JIM PAVELEC

PACK RUNNER

"To run with the pack is to be one with the pack."

Prerequisites: Ranger, Beast Mastery class feature, beast companion (wolf)

Humanoids have taken clever beasts as companions since the beginning of time. The most prevalent among such animals are those from the canine family. Like humanoids, canines have a cooperative mentality and an established social order. It's not surprising that nearly every humanoid race that has the option to do so—from humans to goblins, eladrin to gnolls—keeps hounds or doglike beasts as pets.

Myth holds that, just as humanoids have adopted canines, so too have canines adopted humanoids. One such story is the tale of Kurngarl, or Kurn the Hunter. Soon enough after the fall of the tiefling empire that the hatred of that race was still widespread, unnamed human parents bore a tiefling child. The parents left the babe in an enchanted wood to die of exposure. By some twist of destiny—or, certain versions say, by Melora's fickle mercies—wolves found the infant instead. Yunulf, "the Lady of the Wolves," added the human child to her litter, naming him Horned Man.

Kurngarl developed uncanny skills with nature while living with his wolf family, learning from a variety of other animals as well. Eventually, a dwarf explorer named Fargrim found Kurngarl and took the tiefling child to the ancient dwarven hold of Durigirn. The young tiefling then became a citizen of the dwarven hold and roamed the wilderness surrounding it. Even so, he acknowledged no dwarven name in place of the one his wolf mother had given him. That he translated literally into Dwarven, accepting only the nickname Kurn as an alternative.

Kurngarl had many adventures, almost all with his wolf brother Grabor by his side. Kurn and Grabor were renowned as hunters and trackers among the dwarves of Durigirn. They are also mentioned in the legends of other races, enjoying a heroic reputation for battling monsters, especially gnolls and giants. Kurn the Hunter is reputed to have turned the animals of the wilderness against unjust people in civilized areas. As such, he is held as an example by Melora's followers.

Despite differences in your life's history, like Kurn, you have a preternatural connection with a canine beast. You and your companion function as a deadly unit among the larger pack made up of your other allies. For its part, your companion has taken cues from you, developing a level of competence and guile rivaling that of some humanoids. You have taken the wildness of the wolf into your spirit. Those who observe the two of you together find it hard to tell where the line between humanoid and beast is drawn.

PACK RUNNER PATH FEATURES

Runner's Action (11th Level): When you spend an action point to take an extra action, you can shift half your speed as a free action before or after taking the extra action.

Pack Chase (11th Level): If you and your beast companion move at least 2 squares during your turn, you both gain a +1 bonus to attack rolls until the start of your next turn.

Canine's Cunning (16th Level): If you are within 5 squares of your beast companion, you can command it to shift 1 square as a minor action. When you do this, you can also shift 1 square.

PACK RUNNER EXPLOITS

Pack Runner Assault   Pack Runner Attack 11

Working in unison, you and your wolf companion tear at an enemy from different angles, dividing the foe's attention.

Encounter ✦ Beast, Martial, Weapon
Standard Action   Melee weapon (beast 1)
Target: One creature
Effect: Before the primary attack, both you and your beast companion can shift 2 squares.
Primary Attack: Strength vs. AC
Hit: 2[W] + Strength modifier damage, and the target grants combat advantage to your beast companion for the secondary attack.
Effect: Your beast companion makes a secondary attack against the target.
Secondary Attack: Beast's attack bonus vs. Reflex
Hit: 1[B] + beast's Dexterity modifier damage, and the target is knocked prone.

Wolfskin   Pack Runner Utility 12

As you take on a canine aspect, your senses grow keener and your footsteps fleeter.

Daily ✦ Beast, Primal
Minor Action   Personal
Requirement: You must be within 5 squares of your beast companion.
Effect: You gain a +5 power bonus to Stealth and Perception checks and a +2 power bonus to speed. This effect lasts for 1 hour, until you take a minor action to end it, or until you are knocked unconscious.

Neck-Bite Pounce   Pack Runner Attack 20

Your wolf friend springs at your adversary, bowling the foe over and landing a vicious bite on a vital area.

Daily ✦ Beast, Martial
Standard Action   Melee beast 1
Target: One creature
Attack: Beast's attack bonus vs. AC
Hit: 3[B] + beast's Dexterity modifier damage, and the target is knocked prone and takes ongoing 10 damage (save ends).
Miss: No damage, and the target is slowed and takes ongoing 10 damage (save ends both).

Ruthless Punisher

"The most dangerous foes are those who know the difference between right and wrong yet choose to do evil. They also understand what dying really means."

Prerequisite: Ranger

For a mundane hunter or a common would-be hero, ordinary animals and beastlike monsters are worthy prey. Regardless of what such a creature is physically capable of, or the wrongs it's responsible for, it has only raw instinct or brutish cunning to use against its antagonist. Reaction is its only course. The beast lacks the abilities to reason and to plan, which are required for any but the most mindless of evil acts.

Humanoid creatures seldom suffer from this lack, this banality. Even a semblance of human intelligence, combined with the ability to use weapons and other skills, makes an adversary that much more dangerous. From common goblins to demon lords and deities, the most numerous wicked creatures in the cosmos live inside various humanoid frames. The form is similar enough in each instance that knowledge of one is a help against another, no matter how different the seeming. Malevolent or not, few creatures offer the challenge that a humanoid quarry does.

Long ago, whether for vengeance, righteousness, or pure gamesmanship, you chose to specialize in facing and taking out humanoid foes. You excel at tracking and opposing such canny foes, slaying the many who deserve death and retrieving a few for reward, profit, or justice. For you, the understanding of anatomy, the inflicting of pain, and the invoking of fear are weapons as effective as sword or bow.

You've been so successful that you have developed a merciless reputation. The mention of your name inspires terror among those who know they must face you. One day, you're sure, a humanoid adversary of mythic scope will tremble at your approach.

Ruthless Punisher Path Features

Ruthless Action (11th level): You can spend an action point to reroll any attack roll against a humanoid target designated as your quarry, instead of taking an extra action.

Most Dangerous Prey (11th level): Against any humanoid target designated as your quarry, you gain a bonus to damage rolls equal to your Wisdom modifier.

Ongoing Punishment (16th level): You gain a bonus to the ongoing damage you deal equal to your Wisdom modifier. You also gain combat advantage against humanoid enemies that are taking ongoing damage.

Ruthless Punisher Exploits

Crippling Shot — Ruthless Punisher Attack 11

A blow to the vitals causes your victim to stagger and whimper in pain.

Encounter ✦ Martial, Weapon
Standard Action   Melee **or** Ranged **weapon**
Target: One creature
Attack: Strength vs. Reflex (melee) or Dexterity vs. Reflex (ranged)

Hit: 1[W] + Strength modifier damage (melee) or 1[W] + Dexterity modifier damage (ranged), and the target is slowed until the end of your next turn. If the target is a humanoid, it is also weakened until the end of your next turn.

Named Dread — Ruthless Punisher Utility 12

Your name is terror among your humanoid foes.

Daily ✦ Fear, Martial
Minor Action   Close **burst 10**
Target: Each humanoid enemy in burst that can hear you
Effect: You speak your name, and the targets take a -2 penalty to attack rolls against you until the end of the encounter. If you're trained in Intimidate, you also gain combat advantage against the targets until the end of your next turn.

Bleed Away — Ruthless Punisher Attack 20

If your adversary fails to give ground under your assault, your wounding blows feed the earth with blood.

Daily ✦ Martial, Weapon
Standard Action   Melee **or** Ranged **weapon**
Target: One creature
Attack: Strength vs. Reflex (melee) or Dexterity vs. Reflex (ranged), three attacks

Hit: 1[W] + Strength modifier damage (melee) or 1[W] + Dexterity modifier damage (ranged) per attack. You slide the target 2 squares and can shift 2 squares after each hit.

Miss: No damage, and you slide the target 1 square and can shift 1 square after each miss.

Effect: The target can negate each slide as a free action, but it then takes ongoing 10 damage per square of forced movement negated.

SHARPSHOOTER

"The faster they come, the sooner I shoot 'em down."

Prerequisite: Ranger

Mastery of a chosen armament is a long-standing tradition among many peoples. Legends are full of examples: the fighter who is one with his sword or the assassin who can't miss with knives. Fables also tell of those who have consummate proficiency with the bow or the crossbow.

Some warriors acquire skill with the bow to avoid close combat. Others do so because ability and purpose lead them that way. Archers work for all sorts of causes, military to mercenary, noble to malevolent. One example is the battlefield archer (*Player's Handbook*), a tactical shooter that works well in the chaos of small-unit combat.

Unlike other archers, the sharpshooter's purpose is to become legendary for accuracy and skill, as well as for the number and sorts of foes defeated. Quick shooting, accuracy, and deadliness are the sharpshooter's trademarks, along with the ability to use a bow or a crossbow in ways that few others can. Some who would become the ultimate sharpshooter look for other archers to challenge in contests of skill or even in duels to the death.

You have honed your bow or crossbow skills with a desire to become the best of the best. You fire faster than most folk would think possible. When enemies try to move in close and shut you down, you shoot on without compromising defense. Those who watch you work could swear your arrows are alive. One day, you'll be targeting that one enemy whose defeat will make you a legend.

after Schoonover

2

SHARPSHOOTER PATH FEATURES

Rapid-Fire Action (11th level): When you spend an action point to take an extra action, you can make a ranged basic attack with a bow or a crossbow as a free action before or after taking the extra action.

Opportunity Fire (11th level): You can use a bow or a loaded crossbow to make opportunity attacks. These attacks don't provoke opportunity attacks.

Seeking Arrow (16th level): You don't take the normal penalty to attack rolls for concealment or cover when making a ranged attack against a creature designated as your quarry. You still take the penalty for total concealment or superior cover.

SHARPSHOOTER EXPLOITS

Stab and Shoot — Sharpshooter Attack 11

You drive your arrow into an adjacent enemy, pull it out, load it, and fire it at another foe.

Encounter ✦ Martial, Weapon
Standard Action   Melee 1
Requirement: You must be wielding a bow or a crossbow.
Primary Target: One creature
Primary Attack: Dexterity vs. AC
Hit: 1[W] + Dexterity modifier damage, and the target is dazed until the end of your turn. Make a secondary attack.
　Secondary Target: One creature other than the primary target in weapon range
　Secondary Attack: Dexterity vs. AC
　Hit: 2[W] + Dexterity modifier damage.

Perfect Aim — Sharpshooter Utility 12

You take the time to line up a deadly shot.

Encounter ✦ Martial, Weapon
Minor Action   Personal
Requirement: You must be wielding a ranged weapon.
Effect: Until the end of your next turn, your next ranged attack gains a power bonus to the attack and damage rolls equal to your Wisdom modifier. If you move or take damage before making a ranged attack, the bonus is lost.

Escalating Barrage — Sharpshooter Attack 20

With increasing accuracy and deadliness, you send your shots at multiple foes.

Daily ✦ Martial, Weapon
Standard Action   Ranged weapon
Primary Target: One creature
Primary Attack: Dexterity vs. AC
Hit: 2[W] + Dexterity modifier damage.
Effect: Make a secondary attack.
　Secondary Target: One creature other than the primary target
　Secondary Attack: Dexterity + 2 vs. AC
　Hit: 3[W] + Dexterity modifier damage.
Effect: Make a tertiary attack.
　Tertiary Target: One creature other than the primary and secondary targets
　Tertiary Attack: Dexterity + 4 vs. AC
　Hit: 4[W] + Dexterity modifier damage.

CHAPTER 2 | *Ranger*

SYLVAN ARCHER

"Drawing the bowstring is a spiritual oath. The flight of the arrow is its fulfillment."

Prerequisites: Elf, ranger

Like their eladrin cousins, elves have the time and the will to give everything they do a complex expression. To them, something worth doing at all is worth doing better than well—it's worth total dedication of body, mind, and soul. Any task merits mastering to the extent that the very process of doing it, even in training, is beautiful. Further, to the fey mind, combining seemingly disparate arts and joys into one form creates something more beautiful in the end. This is as true of archery as it is of any other activity.

Ages ago, after they entered the world and became separated from the eladrin, elves found it necessary to survive in the hostile wilds. Grace and awareness became their strengths. The bow became their chosen weapon for hunting and stealthy warfare.

The magic flowing in the fey soul has enabled more than one elf to forge a spiritual tie with the bow. Such archers are practiced at engaging targets in dense forests and areas fraught with cover. The sound of an enemy bowstring being drawn or the hint of movement in the undergrowth is enough to draw a reactive shot faster than any intended attack can come. A master of elven archery easily deals with multiple foes, and in time develops the uncanny ability to make arrows literally track their targets. Elven arrows can be said literally to have an enemy's name on them.

You carry on this glorious tradition. Stalking in untamed and dangerous places armed with only quiver and bow, you have become an exemplar of elven marksmanship. Your finely honed senses are second to none, and your aim is ever true. Among the most formidable of hunters, you have a shooting expertise that transcends the mundane skill of other archers. Your spirit reaches out to inform you of the unseen. If your skill and your amazing deeds carry you farther, elves who come to the way of the bow after you will hold you as the example that guides them.

SYLVAN ARCHER PATH FEATURES

Archer's Action (11th level): When you spend an action point to take an extra action, your ranged attack rolls take no penalties for cover, superior cover, concealment, or total concealment until the end of your next turn.

Sylvan Senses (11th level): You gain a +2 bonus to Perception checks.

Intuitive Hunter (16th level): When making ranged attacks, you add your Wisdom modifier to the extra damage dealt by your Hunter's Quarry class feature.

SYLVAN ARCHER EXPLOITS

Shaft Splitter	Sylvan Archer Attack 11

As your foe launches his attack, you loose a shot right down his sights.

Encounter ✦ Martial, Weapon
Immediate Interrupt   Ranged weapon
Trigger: An enemy hits you or an ally within 5 squares of you with a ranged attack
Target: The triggering enemy
Attack: Dexterity vs. Reflex
Hit: 2[W] + Dexterity modifier damage, and the target takes a –5 penalty to the triggering attack roll.

Elf-Eyed Archery	Sylvan Archer Utility 12

You can easily divide your attention between chosen targets.

Encounter ✦ Martial
Minor Action   Ranged sight
Target: One creature
Effect: You designate the target as your quarry, even if it isn't the closest enemy to you. The target doesn't count against your normal limit of one quarry at a time, although you can still deal your Hunter's Quarry damage only once per round.
Special: Using this power doesn't provoke opportunity attacks.

Named Arrow	Sylvan Archer Attack 20

Whispering your foe's name in Elven, you loose your arrow and watch it streak unerringly across the battlefield.

Daily ✦ Martial, Weapon
Standard Action   Ranged weapon
Target: One creature
Effect: If you speak the target's name when you use this power, you designate the target as your quarry and take no penalties to the attack roll for cover, superior cover, concealment, or total concealment.
Attack: Dexterity vs. Will
Hit: 4[W] + Dexterity modifier damage, and the target is dazed (save ends). If you spoke the target's name, instead of being dazed, the target is stunned (save ends).
Miss: Half damage, and the target is dazed until the end of its next turn. If you spoke the target's name, instead of being dazed, the target is stunned until the end of its next turn.

WILDCAT STALKER

"This cat is subtle and fierce, just like its master."

Prerequisites: Ranger, Beast Mastery class feature, beast companion (cat)

Independence, courage, and quickness of mind and body—the cat symbolizes all of these traits. It prefers to watch the world carefully from a good vantage before acting decisively. Normally calm and fastidiously clean, a feline loves to play but fights fearlessly when it must. It is a stealthy hunter that specializes in ambushes and deadly rushes, finishing its prey as quickly as possible. When surrounded by friends, the cat is industrious and protective, sharing what it has.

You see yourself in the cat, or a little of the cat in yourself. You too are a careful and swift hunter, with catlike grace and bravery. Surprise and swift attacks are your specialty, and few compare to you in your self-sufficiency.

Maybe that's why you chose a wild cat as a companion (or perhaps it was the cat that picked you). You have developed your feline qualities, growing in awareness, slyness, and sneakiness. Your beast companion has become a strong warrior at your side, using its predatory skills to bring down your common adversaries as if they were game.

As word of your deeds spreads, your cat's fame grows with yours. It has become an emblem that identifies you among those you meet, affect, and oppose. When your story is done, your cat will stand beside you in mythic chronicles, as if you and it were one.

WILDCAT STALKER PATH FEATURES

Neck Seeker (11th Level): You and your beast companion gain a +1 bonus to attack rolls and damage rolls against any bloodied enemy designated as your quarry.

Prowling Action (11th Level): When you spend an action point to take an extra action, you also gain concealment until the end of your next turn.

Cat's Quarry (16th Level): When you or your beast companion reduces an enemy to 0 hit points (whether or not that enemy is your quarry), you can designate a new quarry as a free action instead of as a minor action.

WILDCAT STALKER EXPLOITS

Cat-Eyed Strike   Wildcat Stalker Attack 11

Your sharp senses allow you to aim for a gap in your foe's defenses.

Encounter ✦ Beast, Martial, Weapon
Standard Action   **Melee** or **Ranged** weapon (beast 1)
Target: One creature
Attack: Strength vs. Reflex (melee) or Dexterity vs. Reflex (ranged)
Hit: 2[W] + Strength modifier damage (melee) or 2[W] + Dexterity modifier damage (ranged). If you have combat advantage against the target, the attack deals extra damage equal to your Wisdom modifier.

Lurk Unseen   Wildcat Stalker Utility 12

You and your cat move like mist in the grass.

Encounter ✦ Martial
Standard Action   **Close** burst 1
Requirement: You and your beast companion must have concealment.
Targets: You and your beast companion in burst
Effect: Each target has total concealment until the end of your next turn or until the target attacks.

Panther Pounce   Wildcat Stalker Attack 20

At your signal, your cat launches at your enemy, tearing with tooth and claw.

Daily ✦ Beast, Martial, Weapon
Standard Action   **Melee** beast 1
Target: One creature designated as your quarry
Attack: Beast's attack bonus vs. AC
Hit: 2[B] + beast's Dexterity modifier damage. If your beast companion was hidden from the target at the start of your turn, the attack deals 3[B] extra damage.
Miss: Half damage.
Effect: Before and after the attack, your beast companion can shift its speed, ignoring difficult terrain.

JIM PAVELEC

CHAPTER 3

ROGUE

"Many learn to break legs; a few learn to break wills. Some master deception, others agility. Me? I've got it all. Just tell me what you need done."

THE WORD "rogue" has many meanings, and those who fall into this class are as varied. Plenty of rogues grow up on the street, honing their talents to become hard-nosed toughs or sharp grifters. Others—foppish nobles or venturesome rakes with more cunning with a blade and the tongue than scruples—come from the opposite end of the social ladder. Many rogues grow up connected to the underworld and absorb those values. Some come from noncriminal backgrounds, developing skills that serve well in risky ventures. A few are or were spies or scouts for other powerful people or creatures.

You could be a rogue who relies on brute force or deception to get your way. Or you might possess great skill and fighting prowess. Perhaps you or your circumstances shaped you into someone who knows how to coerce others through threats, implied or direct.

This chapter supports the rogue builds presented in the *Player's Handbook*. It's also intended to support other sorts of rogue builds. It contains the following information.

✦ **New Rogue Builds:** The aerialist and the cutthroat offer two new ways to fulfill your function, which, of course, is to quickly finish off your enemies.

✦ **New Class Feature:** You now have three rogue tactics options to choose from, including the new Ruthless Ruffian.

✦ **New Rogue Powers:** Be cruel, be fast, or be both with a new array of exploits that reward one of numerous combat styles. Powers that have the rattling keyword leave your foes shaking in their boots.

✦ **New Paragon Paths:** Perfect your sort of skulduggery by choosing one of twelve new roguish paths. Be the lethal shot in the dark, teach your knives to take wing, swashbuckle, or deal death as an agent of the Raven Queen.

VINCENT PROCE

This book introduces two rogue builds: the aerialist and the cutthroat. The aerialist is a mobile striker who relies on the Acrobatics skill for an edge in attacks and maneuvers, whereas the cutthroat is a charming killer, using training in Intimidate to rattle foes.

AERIALIST ROGUE

All rogues are known for their agility and daring, but you take both to the next level. Ducking under a giant's club isn't enough; you leap over it and cartwheel to safety. You're a masterful mover and an expert top-story burglar, using your abilities to tumble into the fray, into high openings, and out of all sorts of tight spots. Dexterity is your primary ability score, because you rely on it for your attacks and acrobatic stunts. Charisma is secondary for you, useful in avoiding opportunity attacks if you employ the Artful Dodger tactic. Strength serves you well as a tertiary ability, helping your Athletics checks in particular.

Suggested Feat: Defensive Mobility (Human feat: Sure Climber)

Suggested Skills: Acrobatics, Athletics, Bluff, Perception, Stealth, Thievery

Suggested At-Will Powers: *deft strike, riposte strike*

Suggested Encounter Power: *fox's gambit**

Suggested Daily Power: *handspring assault**

*New option presented in this book

CUTTHROAT ROGUE

Leave smiles and misdirection to the tricksters. Instead, you use your animal magnetism in a more beastly way, oozing menace and implying a willingness to allow those who cross you to linger in pain. A friendly manner is for the weak; you achieve your way through tough words, hard looks, and the ability to back up either. Your attacks use Dexterity, so that should be your highest ability score. Charisma follows as a close second, essential for getting your way by using Intimidate. Strength comes in third; it's useful in delivering brutal attacks if you employ the Ruthless Ruffian tactic.

Suggested Feat: Press the Advantage (Human feat: Backstabber)

Suggested Skills: Bluff, Insight, Intimidate, Stealth, Streetwise, Thievery

Suggested At-Will Powers: *disheartening strike,* *sly flourish*

Suggested Encounter Power: *termination threat**

Suggested Daily Power: *checking jab**

*New option presented in this book

NEW CLASS FEATURE

Instead of selecting either Artful Dodger or Brutal Scoundrel as your rogue tactic, you can select Ruthless Ruffian.

Ruthless Ruffian: You are proficient with the club and the mace, and you can use those weapons with Sneak Attack or any rogue power that normally requires a light blade. If you use a club or a mace to deliver an attack that has the rattling keyword, add your Strength modifier to the damage roll.

NEW ROGUE POWERS

A rogue thrives on audacious exploits that keep the enemy guessing. An aerialist rogue, perhaps even more than other sorts of rogues, relies on powers that focus on skill and movement. If you're a cutthroat, you like exploits that focus your dark personality, especially those that have the rattling keyword. Nothing stops any rogue from dabbling in the new powers here. In fact, if you're a rogue worth your salt, one or more of these powers is bound to be just the trick you need to round out your repertoire.

NEW KEYWORD

Some powers in this chapter use the new rattling keyword.

Rattling: If you are trained in Intimidate and you deal damage with an attack that has this keyword, the target takes a -2 penalty to attack rolls until the end of your next turn. A creature immune to fear is not subject to this penalty.

LEVEL 1 AT-WILL EXPLOITS

Disheartening Strike	Rogue Attack 1

The bite of your weapon is deepened by the sting of your ire.

At-Will ✦ Martial, Rattling, Weapon
Standard Action   **Melee** or **Ranged** weapon
Requirement: You must be wielding a crossbow, a light blade, or a sling.
Target: One creature
Attack: Dexterity vs. AC
Hit: 1[W] + Dexterity modifier damage.
Increase damage to 2[W] + Dexterity modifier at 21st level.

SNEAK ATTACK

Is it just a matter of timing, attacking when your foe's back is turned or defenses down? Is it all about surprise, doing exactly what your enemy least expects? Or is it the surgical precision of your blade, striking right in the most vulnerable places? Sneak Attack damage isn't just extra dice you roll; it's what makes your attacks different from anyone else's. How can you make it feel unique?

LEVEL 1 ENCOUNTER EXPLOITS

Fox's Gambit	Rogue Attack 1

A distracting stab is all you need to foil your enemy's focus and step into a better position.

Encounter ✦ Martial, Weapon
Standard Action   **Melee** weapon
Prerequisite: You must be trained in Acrobatics.
Requirement: You must be wielding a light blade.
Target: One creature
Attack: Dexterity vs. Reflex
Hit: 1[W] + Dexterity modifier damage, and you negate any marks the target has applied. The target cannot mark any targets until the end of your next turn.
Effect: You can shift 1 square.
Artful Dodger: You can instead shift a number of squares equal to your Dexterity modifier.

Guarded Attack	Rogue Attack 1

Striking quickly, you remain ready to parry.

Encounter ✦ Martial, Weapon
Standard Action   **Melee** weapon
Requirement: You must be wielding a light blade.
Target: One creature
Primary Attack: Dexterity vs. AC
Hit: 2[W] + Dexterity modifier damage, and if the target makes a melee attack against you before the start of your next turn, you can make a secondary attack against it as an immediate interrupt.
Secondary Attack: Strength vs. AC
Hit: 1[W] + Strength modifier damage, and the target takes a -2 penalty to the triggering attack roll.

Impact Shot	Rogue Attack 1

Your shot slams your foe backward.

Encounter ✦ Martial, Weapon
Standard Action   **Ranged** weapon
Requirement: You must be wielding a crossbow, a light thrown weapon, or a sling.
Target: One creature
Attack: Dexterity vs. AC
Hit: 2[W] + Dexterity modifier damage, and you push the target 1 square.

Sly Lunge	Rogue Attack 1

You dart in to take advantage of lax defenses, and after striking, you're ready to capitalize on the same opening again.

Encounter ✦ Martial, Weapon
Standard Action   **Melee** weapon
Requirement: You must be wielding a light blade.
Target: One creature granting combat advantage to you
Attack: Dexterity vs. AC
Hit: 1[W] + Dexterity modifier damage, and you gain combat advantage against the target until the end of your next turn. If you don't apply your Sneak Attack damage to this attack, it deals 1d6 extra damage.
Brutal Scoundrel: The attack deals extra damage equal to your Strength modifier.

Termination Threat
Rogue Attack 1

Your attack unnerves your foe, possibly freezing it in its tracks.

Encounter ✦ Martial, Rattling, Weapon
Standard Action Melee weapon
Requirement: You must be wielding a light blade.
Target: One creature
Attack: Dexterity vs. AC
Hit: 1[W] + Dexterity modifier + Charisma modifier damage.
  Ruthless Ruffian: If the target is already taking the attack penalty from one of your rattling attacks, the target is also immobilized until the end of your next turn.

Unbalancing Shot
Rogue Attack 1

The impact of your shot leaves your enemy wobbly.

Encounter ✦ Martial, Weapon
Standard Action Ranged weapon
Requirement: You must be wielding a crossbow, a light thrown weapon, or a sling.
Target: One creature
Attack: Dexterity vs. AC
Hit: 2[W] + Dexterity modifier damage, and the target is slowed until the end of your next turn.

LEVEL 1 DAILY EXPLOITS

Checking Jab
Rogue Attack 1

You smile callously as your attack lands, cowing your enemy into an overcautious state.

Daily ✦ Martial, Rattling, Weapon
Standard Action Melee weapon
Requirement: You must be wielding a light blade.
Target: One creature
Attack: Dexterity vs. AC
Hit: 1[W] + Dexterity modifier damage, and the target is slowed (save ends). You have combat advantage against the target while it is slowed by this attack.
Miss: Half damage, and the target is not slowed.

Confounding Attack
Rogue Attack 1

Your attack causes your opponent to accidentally wallop his ally.

Daily ✦ Martial, Weapon
Standard Action Melee or Ranged weapon
Requirement: You must be wielding a crossbow, a light blade, or a sling.
Target: One creature
Attack: Dexterity vs. AC
Hit: 2[W] + Dexterity modifier damage.
Effect: As a free action, the target makes a melee basic attack against a creature of your choice adjacent to it. If you or the target has combat advantage against the creature and you haven't dealt your Sneak Attack damage during this round, you can deal your Sneak Attack damage against the creature.

Handspring Assault
Rogue Attack 1

Springing forward with feline agility, you lash out, cut deep, and roll away to safety.

Daily ✦ Martial, Reliable, Weapon
Standard Action Melee weapon
Prerequisite: You must be trained in Acrobatics.
Requirement: You must be wielding a light blade.
Target: One creature
Attack: Dexterity vs. AC
Hit: 3[W] + Dexterity modifier damage, and you can shift 2 squares.
Special: When charging, you can use this power in place of a melee basic attack.

Pommel Smash
Rogue Attack 1

You pound the pommel of your blade into your enemy's face.

Daily ✦ Martial, Weapon
Standard Action Melee weapon
Requirement: You must be wielding a light blade.
Target: One creature
Attack: Dexterity vs. AC
Hit: 3[W] + Dexterity modifier damage, and the target takes a -2 penalty to attack rolls (save ends).
Miss: Half damage, and the target takes a -2 penalty to attack rolls until the end of its next turn.

Precise Incision
Rogue Attack 1

You target an opening in your foe's armor and make a vicious cut.

Daily ✦ Martial, Reliable, Weapon
Standard Action Melee weapon
Requirement: You must be wielding a light blade.
Target: One creature
Attack: Dexterity vs. Reflex
Hit: 3[W] + Dexterity modifier damage.

Press the Advantage
Rogue Attack 1

Having just wounded your opponent, you follow up with a finishing move.

Daily ✦ Martial, Weapon
Free Action Melee weapon
Trigger: You bloody an enemy with a melee attack
Requirement: You must be wielding a light blade.
Target: The triggering enemy
Attack: Dexterity vs. AC
Hit: 2[W] + Dexterity modifier damage.
Miss: Half damage.

LEVEL 2 UTILITY EXPLOITS

Adaptable Flanker
Rogue Utility 2

The mere presence of an ally gives you all the advantage you need.

Encounter ✦ Martial
Minor Action Personal
Requirement: You and an ally must be adjacent to the same enemy.
Effect: You gain combat advantage against the enemy until the start of your next turn.

Double Take — Rogue Utility 2

Suspecting something is hidden, you concentrate your will on spotting it.

Encounter ✦ Martial
Minor Action   Personal
Prerequisite: You must be trained in Perception.
Effect: Make a Perception check with a bonus equal to your Charisma modifier.

Hop Up — Rogue Utility 2

Rolling with a blow that knocked you down, you hop up just a few steps away.

Encounter ✦ Martial
Immediate Reaction   Personal
Trigger: You are knocked prone
Prerequisite: You must be trained in Acrobatics.
Effect: You stand up and can shift 1 square.

Marked Escape — Rogue Utility 2

Through your subtlety, you end your enemy's mark.

Encounter ✦ Martial
Minor Action   Personal
Requirement: You must be marked.
Effect: The marked condition ends on you.

Reap the Rattled — Rogue Utility 2

Rattled foes are ripe fodder for your attacks.

Daily ✦ Martial
Minor Action   Personal
Prerequisite: You must be trained in Intimidate.
Effect: Select an enemy within line of sight that is taking the penalty from one of your rattling attacks. You gain combat advantage against that enemy until the end of your next turn.

Sneak in the Attack — Rogue Utility 2

You give your ally the advantage she needs to inflict a devastating attack.

Encounter ✦ Martial
Minor Action   Melee 1
Target: One creature
Effect: Until the start of your next turn, the next ally who hits the target and has combat advantage against it deals extra damage against it equal to your Sneak Attack damage.

LEVEL 3 ENCOUNTER EXPLOITS

Blade Vault — Rogue Attack 3

You bound into the air, driving your blade home as you land.

Encounter ✦ Martial, Weapon
Standard Action   Melee weapon
Requirement: You must be wielding a light blade.
Target: One creature
Effect: Before the attack, you can shift 2 squares. If you are trained in Athletics, ignore difficult terrain during the shift.
Attack: Dexterity vs. AC
Hit: 1[W] + Dexterity modifier damage. For every square you shifted as part of this power, the attack deals extra damage equal to your Strength modifier.

Defender's Cohort — Rogue Attack 3

Another warrior's vigilance is all you need to find the soft spot in your enemy's defenses.

Encounter ✦ Martial, Rattling, Weapon
Standard Action   Melee weapon
Requirement: You must be wielding a light blade.
Target: One creature
Attack: Dexterity vs. AC
Hit: 2[W] + Dexterity modifier damage. If the target is marked by an ally of yours, the attack deals extra damage equal to your Charisma modifier.

Enforced Threat — Rogue Attack 3

Your weapon backs up your threats, extracting its toll in blood.

Encounter ✦ Martial, Rattling, Weapon
Standard Action   Melee or Ranged weapon
Requirement: You must be wielding a crossbow, a light blade, or a sling.
Target: One creature
Attack: Dexterity vs. AC
  Ruthless Ruffian: If the target is taking the attack penalty from one of your rattling attacks, you gain combat advantage against the target for this attack.
Hit: 2[W] + Dexterity modifier damage.

Flamboyant Strike — Rogue Attack 3

By distracting your foe with a colorful flourish, you manage to attack from an unexpected angle.

Encounter ✦ Martial, Weapon
Standard Action   Melee weapon
Requirement: You must be wielding a light blade.
Target: One creature
Attack: Dexterity vs. AC
Hit: 2[W] + Dexterity modifier + Charisma modifier damage.
  Artful Dodger: You can shift 1 square.

Low Slash
Rogue Attack 3

Your blade bites your enemy's legs, momentarily hobbling him.

Encounter ✦ Martial, Weapon
Minor Action   **Melee** weapon
Requirement: You must be wielding a light blade.
Target: One creature
Attack: Dexterity vs. Reflex

Hit: 1[W] + Dexterity modifier damage, you slide the target 1 square, and the target is slowed until the end of your next turn. If you're flanking the target, the attack deals extra damage equal to your Strength modifier or Charisma modifier.

Nasty Backswing
Rogue Attack 3

You follow a missed attack with a surprising strike and a hasty sidestep.

Encounter ✦ Martial, Weapon
Free Action   **Melee** weapon
Trigger: You miss with a melee attack
Requirement: You must be wielding a light blade.
Target: One creature
Attack: Dexterity vs. AC. You have combat advantage for this attack.

Hit: 1[W] + Dexterity modifier damage, and you can shift 1 square.
  Brutal Scoundrel: The attack deals extra damage equal to your Strength modifier.

LEVEL 5 DAILY EXPLOITS

Compel the Craven
Rogue Attack 5

Your unnerving attack forces your foe to run away from you, heedless of its enemies.

Daily ✦ Fear, Martial, Rattling, Weapon
Standard Action   **Melee** or **Ranged** weapon
Requirement: You must be wielding a crossbow, a light blade, or a sling.
Target: One creature
Attack: Dexterity vs. Will

Hit: 2[W] + Dexterity modifier damage, and the target moves away from you a number of squares equal to your Charisma modifier, avoiding unsafe squares and difficult terrain if it can.
Miss: The target moves 1 square away from you, avoiding unsafe squares and difficult terrain if it can.

Downward Spiral
Rogue Attack 5

You spin about with your weapon, toppling your enemies.

Daily ✦ Martial, Rattling
Standard Action   **Close** burst 1
Requirement: You must be wielding a light blade.
Target: Each enemy in burst you can see
Attack: Dexterity vs. Reflex
Hit: 1[W] + Dexterity modifier damage.
Effect: You knock the target prone.

Driving Assault
Rogue Attack 5

The force of your rapid attacks throws your enemy from its feet.

Daily ✦ Martial, Weapon
Standard Action   **Melee** weapon
Requirement: You must be wielding a light blade.
Target: One creature
Attack: Dexterity vs. AC, two attacks

Hit: 1[W] + Dexterity modifier damage per attack, you push the target 1 square, and you can shift 1 square toward the target. If both attacks hit, you knock the target prone after the second push.
Miss: Half damage per attack.

Flashy Riposte
Rogue Attack 5

Under attack, you elegantly whirl and let your blade give a sharp reply, leaving your foe off balance.

Daily ✦ Martial, Rattling, Weapon
Immediate Reaction   **Melee** weapon
Trigger: An enemy makes a melee attack against you
Requirement: You must be wielding a light blade.
Target: The triggering enemy
Attack: Dexterity vs. AC
Hit: 2[W] + Dexterity modifier damage.
Effect: The target grants combat advantage to you and your allies until the end of your next turn.

Staggering Assault
Rogue Attack 5

You deal a savage strike that staggers your adversary.

Daily ✦ Martial, Weapon
Standard Action   **Melee** or **Ranged** weapon
Requirement: You must be wielding a crossbow, a light blade, or a sling.
Target: One creature
Attack: Dexterity vs. AC

Hit: 2[W] + Dexterity modifier damage, and the target is slowed (save ends). If the target is not bloodied when you make this attack, the attack deals 1[W] extra damage.
Effect: Until the end of the encounter, when you hit the target, it is slowed (save ends).

Surefooted Retort
Rogue Attack 5

Lessening the impact of an incoming attack, you swivel away from your foe and deliver a slash as you come about.

Daily ✦ Martial, Weapon
Immediate Interrupt   **Melee** weapon
Trigger: An enemy attacks you
Prerequisite: You must be trained in Acrobatics.
Requirement: You must be wielding a light blade.
Target: The triggering enemy
Attack: Dexterity vs. AC
Hit: 2[W] + Dexterity modifier damage.
Miss: Half damage.
Effect: If the triggering attack would knock you prone or slow you, negate the condition. Reduce any pull, push, or slide from the triggering attack by a number of squares equal to your Dexterity modifier.

LEVEL 6 UTILITY EXPLOITS

Ferret Out Frailty
Rogue Utility 6

You can always spot easy prey.

Encounter ✦ Martial
Minor Action   **Personal**
Prerequisite: You must be trained in Insight.
Effect: Until the beginning of your next turn, you gain combat advantage against one target within line of sight. If the target is taking the attack penalty from one of your rattling attacks, you instead gain combat advantage until the end of your next turn.

Fortuitous Dodge
Rogue Utility 6

You duck out of the way of an incoming attack, and it strikes another target.

Daily ✦ Martial
Immediate Reaction   **Melee** 1
Trigger: A melee or a ranged attack misses you
Target: One creature other than the attacker
Effect: The target is also targeted by the triggering attack. You can then shift 1 square.

Sidestep Stance
Rogue Utility 6

You go on the defensive against a particular opponent, watching carefully for its attacks.

Daily ✦ Martial, Stance
Minor Action   **Personal**
Prerequisite: You must be trained in Acrobatics.
Effect: Choose one enemy within 5 squares of you that you can see. Until the stance ends, you gain a +2 power bonus to AC against that enemy's melee attacks and ranged attacks if you can see the enemy. You can choose a new enemy as a minor action.

Threatening Glare
Rogue Utility 6

Your hostile visage warns enemies to beware your wrath.

Encounter ✦ Fear, Martial
Minor Action   **Personal**
Prerequisite: You must be trained in Intimidate.
Effect: Until the end of your turn, opportunity attacks against you deal half damage, and if an enemy makes an opportunity attack against you, you gain combat advantage against that enemy until the end of your next turn.

Vault Position
Rogue Attack 6

You assume a balanced pose, ready to leap away from danger at a moment's notice.

Daily ✦ Martial, Stance
Minor Action   **Personal**
Prerequisite: You must be trained in Acrobatics and Athletics.
Effect: Until the stance ends, you gain a +1 power bonus to Reflex. As a minor action, you can make an Athletics check to jump, but doing so ends the stance.

Vexing Flanker
Rogue Utility 6

Nimble feet and intense focus keep you on your foe.

Encounter ✦ Martial
Immediate Reaction   **Personal**
Trigger: An ally enters a square adjacent to an enemy adjacent to you
Effect: You can shift to any other square adjacent to the enemy.

LEVEL 7 ENCOUNTER EXPLOITS

Circling Predator — Rogue Attack 7

You wheel around your foe, attacking mercilessly.

Encounter ✦ Martial, Weapon
Standard Action   **Melee** weapon
Requirement: You must be wielding a light blade.
Target: One creature
Primary Attack: Dexterity vs. AC
Hit: 1[W] + Dexterity modifier damage.
Effect: You can shift 1 square and must end adjacent to the target. Then make a secondary attack against it.
    Secondary Attack: Dexterity vs. AC
    Hit: 1[W] + Dexterity modifier damage, and you gain combat advantage against the target until the end of your next turn.

Dismaying Slash — Rogue Attack 7

Your ripping strike saps your foe's determination.

Encounter ✦ Martial, Rattling, Weapon
Standard Action   **Melee** weapon
Requirement: You must be wielding a light blade.
Target: One creature
Attack: Dexterity vs. AC
Hit: 2[W] + Dexterity modifier damage, and the target takes a -2 penalty to saving throws until the end of your next turn.

From the Shadows — Rogue Attack 7

You spring from the shadows to strike, and then you fade away as if you were never there.

Encounter ✦ Martial, Weapon
Standard Action   **Melee** or **Ranged** weapon
Requirement: You must be wielding a crossbow, a light blade, or a sling.
Target: One creature
Effect: Before the attack, you can shift 2 squares. If the target could not see you before the shift, you gain combat advantage for this attack.
Attack: Dexterity vs. AC
Hit: 1[W] + Dexterity modifier damage, and you can shift 2 squares. If you have any cover or concealment after this shift, you can make a Stealth check as a free action.
    Artful Dodger: Before the attack and after the hit, you can instead shift a number of squares equal to 1 + your Charisma modifier.

Hectoring Strike — Rogue Attack 7

You deliver a strong attack, dampening your opponent's fighting spirit.

Encounter ✦ Martial, Rattling, Weapon
Standard Action   **Melee** or **Ranged** weapon
Requirement: You must be wielding a crossbow, a light blade, or a sling.
Target: One creature
Attack: Dexterity vs. AC
Hit: 1[W] + Dexterity modifier + Strength modifier damage.
    Brutal Scoundrel: You slide the target 1 square, and the target grants combat advantage to you until the end of your next turn.

Snap Shot — Rogue Attack 7

You strike as quickly as a coiled viper.

Encounter ✦ Martial, Weapon
Minor Action   **Ranged** weapon
Requirement: You must be wielding a crossbow, a light thrown weapon, or a sling.
Target: One creature
Attack: Dexterity vs. AC
Hit: 1[W] + Dexterity modifier damage.

Spring the Trap — Rogue Attack 7

You're surrounded—just as you planned.

Encounter ✦ Martial, Weapon
Standard Action   **Close** burst 1
Requirement: You must be wielding a light blade.
Target: Each enemy in burst you can see
Attack: Dexterity vs. AC
Hit: 1[W] + Dexterity modifier damage, and you can shift 1 square.
    Ruthless Ruffian: This power gains the rattling keyword.

LEVEL 9 DAILY EXPLOITS

Agonizing Shot — Rogue Attack 9

Your precise aim finds a weak spot.

Daily ✦ Martial, Weapon
Standard Action   **Ranged** weapon
Requirement: You must be wielding a crossbow, a light thrown weapon, or a sling.
Target: One creature
Attack: Dexterity vs. Reflex
Hit: 1[W] + Dexterity modifier damage, and the target is slowed and takes ongoing 10 damage (save ends both).
    Aftereffect: The target is slowed and takes ongoing 5 damage (save ends both).
Miss: Half damage, no ongoing damage, and the target is slowed (save ends).

Burst Fire — Rogue Attack 9

You loose missiles in an unpredictable pattern.

Daily ✦ Martial, Weapon
Standard Action   **Area** burst 1 within 10 squares
Requirement: You must be wielding a crossbow, a light thrown weapon, or a sling.
Target: Each enemy in burst you can see
Attack: Dexterity vs. Reflex
Hit: 2[W] + Dexterity modifier damage.
Miss: Half damage.

Into Harm's Way — Rogue Attack 9

You deliver a slashing feint, causing your enemy to stumble into more danger.

Daily ✦ Martial, Weapon
Standard Action   **Melee** weapon
Requirement: You must be wielding a light blade.
Target: One creature
Attack: Dexterity vs. Will
Hit: 2[W] + Dexterity modifier damage, and you slide the target 2 squares. Then an ally of yours can make a melee basic attack against the target as a free action.
Miss: Half damage.

Not It — Rogue Attack 9

Your sly attack directs your foe's attention to your ally.

Daily ✦ Martial, Weapon
Standard Action　　　**Melee** or **Ranged** weapon
Requirement: You must be wielding a crossbow, a light blade, or a sling.
Target: One creature
Attack: Dexterity vs. AC
Hit: 3[W] + Dexterity modifier damage, and an ally adjacent to you or the target marks the target until the start of your next turn.
Miss: Half damage, and no mark.

Not Worth My Time — Rogue Attack 9

With a vicious blow and a callous shove, you judge your foe unworthy of further attention.

Daily ✦ Martial, Rattling, Weapon
Standard Action　　　**Melee** weapon
Requirement: You must be wielding a light blade.
Target: One creature
Attack: Dexterity vs. AC
Hit: 2[W] + Dexterity modifier damage, and you push the target 1 square. The target is then immobilized (save ends).
Miss: Half damage, no push, and the target is immobilized until the end of its next turn.

Rogue's Recovery — Rogue Attack 9

With a cunning attack, you create a new opportunity for yourself.

Daily ✦ Martial, Weapon
Standard Action　　　**Melee** or **Ranged** weapon
Requirement: You must be wielding a crossbow, a light blade, or a sling.
Target: One creature
Attack: Dexterity vs. AC
Hit: 2[W] + Dexterity modifier damage.
Effect: If you have used all your encounter attack powers, you regain the use of a rogue encounter attack power you have used during this encounter. Or if you have combat advantage against the target, you can instead deal 2[W] extra damage with the attack.

Swift Strike — Rogue Attack 9

Your brutal efficiency makes your enemy pay for its lack of initiative.

Daily ✦ Martial, Weapon
Standard Action　　　**Melee** or **Ranged** weapon
Requirement: You must be wielding a crossbow, a light blade, or a sling.
Target: One creature
Attack: Dexterity vs. AC
Hit: 3[W] + Dexterity modifier damage. If the target has not taken an action during this encounter, the attack deals 1[W] extra damage.
Miss: Half damage.

Vexing Escape — Rogue Attack 9

Your timely attack allows you to break away from combat, and you remain one step ahead of your foe thereafter.

Daily ✦ Martial, Weapon
Standard Action　　　**Melee** weapon
Requirement: You must be wielding a light blade.
Target: One creature
Attack: Dexterity vs. AC
Hit: 3[W] + Dexterity modifier damage, and you can shift a number of squares equal to your Charisma modifier.
Miss: Half damage, and you can shift 1 square.
Effect: Until the end of the encounter, each time the target enters a square adjacent to you, you can shift 1 square as an immediate reaction.

Vexing Sting — Rogue Attack 9

Despite your foe's armor, you drive your point home, disheartening him.

Daily ✦ Martial, Reliable, Weapon
Standard Action　　　**Melee** or **Ranged** weapon
Requirement: You must be wielding a crossbow, a light blade, or a sling.
Target: One creature
Attack: Dexterity vs. Reflex
Hit: 3[W] + Dexterity modifier damage, and the target takes a -2 penalty to attack rolls (save ends).

LEVEL 10 UTILITY EXPLOITS

Brisk Stride — Rogue Utility 10

Leaping across minor obstacles, you dart across the battlefield.

Encounter ✦ Martial
Move Action　　　**Personal**
Prerequisite: You must be trained in Athletics.
Effect: You can move your speed + 4. During this movement and until the end of your next turn, you can move across difficult terrain at your normal speed.

Combat Tumbleset — Rogue Utility 10

You deftly somersault into position.

Encounter ✦ Martial
Move Action　　　**Personal**
Prerequisite: You must be trained in Acrobatics.
Effect: You can shift your speed and can shift through squares occupied by enemies during this movement.

Executioner's Mien — Rogue Utility 10

Every one of your attacks exudes a murderous intent that unnerves your adversaries.

Daily ✦ Martial, Stance
Minor Action　　　**Personal**
Prerequisite: You must be trained in Intimidate.
Effect: Until the stance ends, all your attacks gain the rattling keyword.

Gap in the Armor
Rogue Utility 10

You take a moment to find a weak point in your opponent's defenses.

Daily ✦ Martial
Minor Action   **Personal**
Prerequisite: You must be trained in Perception.
Effect: Choose an enemy within 5 squares of you. You gain a +2 power bonus to attack rolls against that enemy until the end of the encounter.

Peripheral Concealment
Rogue Utility 10

You slip away, and others briefly lose track of where you are.

Daily ✦ Martial
Standard Action   **Personal**
Prerequisite: You must be trained in Stealth.
Requirement: No creature is within 3 squares of you.
Effect: You become hidden until you attack or until the end of your next turn.

LEVEL 13 ENCOUNTER EXPLOITS

Bounding Escape
Rogue Attack 13

You attack and then jump away from your foe without leaving yourself open to counterattack.

Encounter ✦ Martial, Weapon
Standard Action   **Melee** or **Ranged** weapon
Prerequisite: You must be trained in Athletics.
Requirement: You must be wielding a crossbow, a light blade, or a sling.
Target: One creature
Attack: Dexterity vs. AC
Hit: 2[W] + Dexterity modifier damage.
Effect: You can jump horizontally a number of squares equal to your Strength modifier or jump vertically half that number of squares. This movement does not provoke opportunity attacks from the target.
     Artful Dodger: This movement does not provoke opportunity attacks from any enemy.

Cunning Cyclone
Rogue Attack 13

A series of lightning-fast attacks does devastating work to your opponents.

Encounter ✦ Martial, Rattling, Weapon
Standard Action   **Close** burst 1
Requirement: You must be wielding a light blade.
Target: Each enemy in burst you can see
Attack: Dexterity vs. AC
Hit: 1[W] + Dexterity modifier damage.
Special: If you have combat advantage against more than one target, you can deal one die of Sneak Attack damage to each target that you have combat advantage against, rather than dealing all your Sneak Attack damage to one target. This counts as one use of Sneak Attack, regardless of the number of targets.

Daunting Attack
Rogue Attack 13

Your attack resonates with your cold-blooded intent, overwhelming your enemy's resolve.

Encounter ✦ Martial, Rattling, Weapon
Standard Action   **Melee** weapon
Requirement: You must be wielding a light blade.
Targets: One creature
Attack: Dexterity vs. AC
Hit: 1[W] + Dexterity modifier damage, and the target is dazed until the end of your next turn.
     Ruthless Ruffian: If the target is already taking the penalty to attack rolls from one of your rattling attacks, instead of being dazed, the target is stunned until the end of your next turn.

Powerful Shot
Rogue Attack 13

The sharp force of your shot causes your foe to stumble.

Encounter ✦ Martial, Weapon
Standard Action   **Ranged** weapon
Requirement: You must be wielding a crossbow, a light thrown weapon, or a sling.
Target: One creature
Attack: Dexterity vs. AC
Hit: 3[W] + Dexterity modifier damage, you push the target 1 square, and the target is slowed until the end of your next turn.

Skip Shot
Rogue Attack 13

Your missile careens off your foe and grazes another enemy.

Encounter ✦ Martial, Weapon
Standard Action   **Ranged** weapon
Requirement: You must be wielding a crossbow, a light thrown weapon, or a sling.
Target: One creature
Attack: Dexterity vs. Reflex
Hit: 2[W] + Dexterity modifier damage, and an enemy within 3 squares of the target takes damage equal to your Dexterity modifier.

Toppling Slash — Rogue Attack 13

Your decisive cut forces your opponent to stumble and fall.

Encounter ✦ Martial, Rattling, Weapon
Standard Action   **Melee** weapon
Requirement: You must be wielding a light blade.
Target: One creature
Attack: Dexterity vs. AC
Hit: 2[W] + Dexterity modifier damage, and you push the target 1 square and knock it prone.
  Brutal Scoundrel: The attack deals extra damage equal to your Strength modifier, and you push the target 1 extra square.

LEVEL 15 DAILY EXPLOITS

Bold Feint — Rogue Attack 15

With a rakish flourish of your weapon, you misdirect your foe's thrust into his ally.

Daily ✦ Martial, Reliable, Weapon
Immediate Interrupt   **Melee** weapon
Trigger: An enemy hits you with a melee attack and another enemy is within its reach
Prerequisite: You must be trained in Bluff.
Target: The attacking enemy
Attack: Charisma vs. Will
Hit: Choose an enemy within the target's reach. That enemy is instead the target of the triggering attack.

Finish It — Rogue Attack 15

A lethal stab hastens your foe's demise.

Daily ✦ Martial, Weapon
Standard Action   **Melee** weapon
Requirement: You must be wielding a light blade.
Target: One bloodied creature
Attack: Dexterity vs. AC
Hit: 3[W] + Dexterity modifier damage, and ongoing 5 damage. The ongoing damage lasts until the creature is no longer bloodied.
Miss: Half damage, and no ongoing damage.

Mind-Boggling Onslaught — Rogue Attack 15

Your fearsome attack shakes your enemy to the core—a situation you can later take advantage of.

Daily ✦ Martial, Rattling, Weapon
Standard Action   **Melee** or **Ranged** weapon
Requirement: You must be wielding a crossbow, a light blade, or a sling.
Target: One creature
Attack: Dexterity vs. AC
Hit: 2[W] + Dexterity modifier damage.
Effect: Whether or not this rattling attack deals damage, the target takes the –2 penalty to attack rolls until the end of your next turn.
Sustain Minor: The penalty to attack rolls lasts until the end of your next turn, or you can end the penalty and daze the target until the end of your next turn.

Ripple Effect — Rogue Attack 15

Your tumbling swipe sends your foe headlong into another enemy, which sends it stumbling.

Daily ✦ Martial, Weapon
Standard Action   **Melee** weapon
Prerequisite: You must be trained in Acrobatics.
Requirement: You must be wielding a light blade.
Primary Target: One creature
Primary Attack: Dexterity vs. Reflex
Hit: 3[W] + Dexterity modifier damage, and you slide the primary target 4 squares.
Miss: Half damage, and you slide the primary target 1 square.
Effect: Make a secondary attack after the slide.
  Secondary Target: One enemy adjacent to the primary target
  Secondary Attack: Dexterity vs. Reflex
  Hit: 1d6 + Dexterity modifier damage, and you slide the secondary target 1 square.

Vicious Cooperation — Rogue Attack 15

Your attack gives your comrade the perfect opening to thump your opponent.

Daily ✦ Martial, Weapon
Standard Action   **Melee** weapon
Requirement: You must be wielding a light blade.
Target: One creature you're flanking
Attack: Dexterity vs. AC
Hit: 4[W] + Dexterity modifier damage.
Effect: An ally flanking the target with you can make a melee basic attack against it as a free action. You can deal Sneak Attack damage to the target if either you or the ally hit it.

Wounding Strike — Rogue Attack 15

You strike, intending to inflict grave injury.

Daily ✦ Martial, Weapon
Standard Action   **Melee** or **Ranged** weapon
Requirement: You must be wielding a crossbow, a light blade, or a sling.
Target: One creature
Attack: Dexterity vs. AC
Hit: 3[W] + Dexterity modifier damage. If the target is not bloodied before you make this attack, the attack also deals ongoing 10 damage (save ends).
Miss: Half damage.

LEVEL 16 UTILITY EXPLOITS

Anticipate Attack — Rogue Utility 16

You sense the attack before it comes.

Encounter ✦ Martial
Immediate Interrupt   **Personal**
Trigger: You are hit by an attack
Requirement: You must be trained in Insight.
Effect: You gain a +4 bonus to all defenses until the end of your next turn.

Defensive Roll
Rogue Utility 16

As you evade an attack, you tumble into a better spot.

Encounter ✦ Martial
Immediate Reaction   **Personal**
Trigger: You are missed by an attack
Prerequisite: You must be trained in Acrobatics
Effect: You can shift your speed.

Denying Stance
Rogue Utility 16

The attacks of your enemies allow you to better size them up and avoid future blows.

Daily ✦ Martial, Stance
Minor Action   **Personal**
Effect: Until the stance ends, each time an enemy misses you with a melee or a ranged attack, that enemy takes a −2 penalty to its next attack roll against you.

Grasshopper Leap
Rogue Utility 16

You jump, covering a jaw-dropping distance.

Encounter ✦ Martial
Free Action   **Personal**
Trigger: You make an Athletics check to jump
Prerequisite: You must be trained in Athletics.
Effect: Treat the Athletics check as if you had rolled a 20.

Magpie Filch
Rogue Utility 16

You covertly snatch something from a foe distracted by your successful attack.

Daily ✦ Martial
Free Action   **Melee 1**
Trigger: You hit a creature with a melee attack
Prerequisite: You must be trained in Thievery.
Requirement: You must have a hand free.
Target: The triggering creature
Effect: You take a small object from the target as if you had made a successful Thievery check to pick pocket.

Opportunistic Relocation
Rogue Utility 16

You capitalize on the distraction caused by downing a foe, slyly repositioning for your next maneuver.

Encounter ✦ Martial
Move Action   **Personal**
Requirement: You must have reduced an enemy to 0 hit points during this turn.
Effect: You can shift your speed.

Vigilant Footwork
Rogue Utility 16

You parry and dodge close-quarters attacks with amazing focus, never hampering your offense.

Daily ✦ Martial, Stance, Weapon
Minor Action   **Personal**
Requirement: You must be wielding a light blade.
Effect: Until the stance ends, you gain a +1 power bonus to AC and Reflex against melee attacks.

LEVEL 17 ENCOUNTER EXPLOITS

Audacious Strike
Rogue Attack 17

You lunge forward recklessly, then roll defensively to the side.

Encounter ✦ Martial, Weapon
Standard Action   **Melee weapon**
Requirement: You must be wielding a light blade.
Target: One creature
Effect: Before the attack, you can move 4 squares.
Attack: Dexterity vs. AC
Hit: 3[W] + Dexterity modifier damage.
Effect: You can shift 2 squares.

Blistering Outburst
Rogue Attack 17

In a flurry of lunges and strikes, you leave nearby foes unable to give decisive counterattacks.

Encounter ✦ Martial, Weapon
Standard Action   **Close burst 1**
Requirement: You must be wielding a light blade.
Target: Each creature in burst you can see
Attack: Dexterity vs. Fortitude
Hit: 1[W] + Dexterity modifier damage, and the target takes a −2 penalty to attack rolls until the end of your next turn.

Escape Artist's Gambit
Rogue Attack 17

You take a parting shot as you wriggle free and scramble away.

Encounter ✦ Martial, Weapon
Standard Action   **Melee weapon**
Prerequisite: You must be trained in Acrobatics.
Attack: Dexterity vs. AC
Hit: 2[W] + Dexterity modifier damage, and you can shift 1 square. If you are immobilized, slowed, or both, those conditions end before you shift, and you automatically escape if you are grabbed.
   Artful Dodger: You can instead shift a number of squares equal to 1 + your Dexterity modifier.

Guerrilla Blitz
Rogue Attack 17

The speed and accuracy displayed during your daring assault causes your enemies to momentarily overcompensate when attacking you.

Encounter ✦ Martial, Weapon
Standard Action   **Melee or Ranged weapon**
Requirement: You must be wielding a crossbow, a light blade, or a sling.
Target: One creature
Effect: Before the attack, you can move your speed.
Attack: Dexterity vs. AC
Hit: 2[W] + Dexterity modifier damage.
   Brutal Scoundrel: The attack deals extra damage equal to your Strength modifier.
Effect: Until the start of your next turn, you gain a +1 power bonus to AC and Reflex for every 2 squares you moved as part of this power.

No Escape — Rogue Attack 17

Your enemy tries to escape, but you leave it lying in its tracks.

Encounter ✦ Martial, Weapon
Immediate Interrupt   **Ranged** weapon
Trigger: An enemy leaves a square adjacent to you or enters a square where it has cover or concealment against you
Requirement: You must be wielding a crossbow, a light thrown weapon, or a sling.
Target: The triggering enemy
Attack: Dexterity vs. AC
Hit: 2[W] + Dexterity modifier damage, and you knock the target prone.

Stinging Squall — Rogue Attack 17

Spooked by your flurry of jabs, nearby adversaries are unable to make anything but feeble retaliatory strikes against you.

Encounter ✦ Martial, Rattling, Weapon
Standard Action   **Close** burst 1
Requirement: You must be wielding a light blade.
Target: Each enemy in burst you can see
Attack: Dexterity vs. AC
Hit: 1[W] + Dexterity modifier damage, and the target is weakened when making attacks against you until the end of your next turn.
    Ruthless Ruffian: The attack deals extra damage equal to your Charisma modifier, and the target is weakened when making any attack (not just against you).

LEVEL 19 DAILY EXPLOITS

Bloodbath Attack — Rogue Attack 19

Your vicious attack leaves the enemy lying in a pool of his own blood.

Daily ✦ Martial, Weapon
Standard Action   **Melee** weapon
Requirement: You must be wielding a light blade.
Target: One creature
Attack: Dexterity vs. AC
Hit: 3[W] + Dexterity modifier damage, you knock the target prone, and it takes ongoing damage equal to your Strength modifier (save ends).
Effect: Until the end of the encounter, whenever you hit the target, the target takes ongoing damage equal to your Strength modifier (save ends).

Blood Squall — Rogue Attack 19

Your blade flashes like lightning, and fountains of blood erupt from the foes around you.

Daily ✦ Martial, Weapon
Standard Action   **Close** burst 1
Requirement: You must be wielding a light blade.
Target: Each enemy in burst you can see
Attack: Dexterity vs. AC
Hit: 2[W] + Dexterity modifier damage, and ongoing 10 damage (save ends).
Miss: Half damage, and no ongoing damage.

Daunting Barrage — Rogue Attack 19

A blistering volley of projectiles knocks your enemies for a loop.

Daily ✦ Martial, Rattling, Weapon
Standard Action   **Close** blast 5
Requirement: You must be wielding a crossbow, a light thrown weapon, or a sling.
Target: Each enemy in blast you can see
Attack: Dexterity vs. AC
Hit: 3[W] + Dexterity modifier damage, and the target is dazed (save ends).
Miss: Half damage, and the target is not dazed.

Marked Beating — Rogue Attack 19

Using the distraction caused by an ally, you brutalize your foe, leaving it off kilter.

Daily ✦ Martial, Weapon
Standard Action   **Melee** or **Ranged** weapon
Requirement: You must be wielding a crossbow, a light blade, or a sling.
Target: One creature marked by an ally
Attack: Dexterity vs. Reflex
Hit: 5[W] + Dexterity modifier damage, and the target is dazed and takes a -2 penalty to all defenses (save ends both).
Miss: Half damage, the target is dazed until the end of your next turn, and no penalty to defenses.

Stolen Vitality — Rogue Attack 19

Your vicious assault leaves your enemy unable to move quickly, and you gain a burst of confidence from the deed.

Daily ✦ Martial, Weapon
Standard Action   **Melee** weapon
Requirement: You must be wielding a light blade.
Target: One creature
Attack: Dexterity vs. AC
Hit: 4[W] + Dexterity modifier damage, and the target is slowed (save ends). You gain temporary hit points equal to 10 + your Charisma modifier.
Miss: Half damage, the target is slowed until the end of your next turn, and no temporary hit points.

Strong-Arm Loyalty — Rogue Attack 19

You browbeat your wounded foe with a cruel attack, forcing compliance for a short time.

Daily ✦ Martial, Weapon
Standard Action   **Melee** weapon
Prerequisite: You must be trained in Intimidate.
Requirement: You must be wielding a light blade.
Target: One bloodied creature
Attack: Dexterity vs. Will
Hit: 2[W] + Dexterity modifier damage, and the target is dominated until the start of your next turn or until it is attacked.
Miss: Half damage, and the target is immobilized until the start of your next turn or until it is attacked.

Uncanny Ricochet
Rogue Attack 19

Your attack has such force that if it fails to hit one opponent, it might career into another.

Daily ✦ Martial, Weapon
Standard Action   **Ranged** weapon
Requirement: You must be wielding a crossbow, a light thrown weapon, or a sling.
Primary Target: One creature
Primary Attack: Dexterity vs. Reflex
Hit: 4[W] + Dexterity modifier damage.
Miss: Make a secondary attack with combat advantage.
   Secondary Target: One creature within 3 squares of the primary target
   Secondary Attack: Dexterity vs. Reflex
   Hit: 4[W] + Dexterity modifier damage.
   Miss: Half damage.

LEVEL 22 UTILITY EXPLOITS

Mountebank's Flight
Rogue Utility 22

You steal a bit of magic to stow away on another creature's teleportation.

Encounter ✦ Martial, Teleportation
Immediate Reaction   **Personal**
Trigger: A creature within 5 squares of you teleports
Effect: You teleport to any square adjacent to the triggering creature.

Scoundrel's Epiphany
Rogue Utility 22

The answer is on the tip of your tongue.

Daily ✦ Martial
Free Action   **Personal**
Trigger: You make a Dungeoneering or a Streetwise check to remember or discover a useful bit of information
Prerequisite: You must be trained in Dungeoneering or Streetwise.
Effect: If you are trained in the skill, don't roll for the check; you are considered to have rolled a 25 and then add your skill check bonus. If you are not trained in the skill, you gain a +5 bonus to the check.

Seize the Moment
Rogue Utility 22

It's time to make your move.

Daily ✦ Martial
No Action   **Personal**
Trigger: You make an initiative check at the beginning of an encounter
Effect: You gain a +20 bonus to your initiative check. Until the end of your first turn in the encounter, you gain a +2 power bonus to attack rolls and a +4 power bonus to speed.

Thief of Fortune
Rogue Utility 22

You make your own luck by stealing it from others.

Daily ✦ Martial
No Action   **Personal**
Trigger: Your attack misses or you fail a saving throw
Requirement: You must be able to see another creature.
Effect: Reroll the triggering attack roll or saving throw and use the new result. One creature you can see takes a -2 penalty to attack rolls and saving throws until the end of your next turn.

Unnerving Footwork
Rogue Utility 22

Your amazing footwork shows you to be a superior combatant, disheartening enemies that draw near.

Daily ✦ Martial, Stance
Minor Action   **Personal**
Prerequisite: You must be trained in Intimidate.
Effect: Until the stance ends, any creature that ends its turn adjacent to you takes a -2 penalty to attack rolls against you until the end of its next turn.

Wall Crawl
Rogue Utility 22

You scramble upward with preternatural speed.

At-Will ✦ Martial
Move Action   **Personal**
Prerequisite: You must be trained in Acrobatics and Athletics.
Effect: You climb a number of squares equal to your speed minus your armor's check penalty.

LEVEL 23 ENCOUNTER EXPLOITS

Blindside
Rogue Attack 23

Your attack comes from such an unexpected angle that your adversary is taken aback.

Encounter ✦ Martial, Weapon
Standard Action   **Melee** or **Ranged** weapon
Requirement: You must be wielding a crossbow, a light blade, or a sling.
Target: One creature
Attack: Dexterity vs. AC
Hit: 4[W] + Dexterity modifier damage, and if you have combat advantage against the target, it is dazed until the start of your next turn.

Crack Shot
Rogue Attack 23

Your lightning-fast shots send your opponents sprawling.

Encounter ✦ Martial, Weapon
Standard Action   **Area** burst 1 within 10 squares
Requirement: You must be wielding a crossbow, a light thrown weapon, or a sling.
Target: Each enemy in burst you can see
Attack: Dexterity vs. AC
Hit: 3[W] + Dexterity modifier damage, and you knock the target prone.

Collapsing Riposte
Rogue Attack 23

When your enemy overreaches to attack you, you cut his legs out from under him.

Encounter ✦ Martial, Weapon
Immediate Reaction   **Melee** weapon
Trigger: An enemy misses you with a melee attack
Requirement: You must be wielding a light blade.
Target: The triggering enemy
Attack: Dexterity vs. AC
Hit: 3[W] + Dexterity modifier damage, and you knock the target prone.
   Artful Dodger: The target is also dazed until the end of your next turn.

Death Dance
Rogue Attack 23

Masterfully lunging and weaving, you deliver a series of powerful attacks and then slip to a new location.

Encounter ✦ Martial, Weapon
Standard Action   Close burst 1
Requirement: You must be wielding a light blade.
Target: Each enemy in burst you can see
Attack: Dexterity vs. AC
Hit: 2[W] + Dexterity modifier damage.
   Brutal Scoundrel: The attack deals extra damage equal to your Strength modifier.
Effect: You can shift 2 squares.

Felling Gash
Rogue Attack 23

You cut the legs out from under your foe so brutally that its head hits the ground before its feet do.

Encounter ✦ Martial, Rattling, Weapon
Standard Action   Melee weapon
Requirement: You must be wielding a light blade.
Target: One creature
Attack: Dexterity vs. Reflex
Hit: 4[W] + Dexterity modifier damage, and you knock the target prone.
   Ruthless Ruffian: The target is also dazed until the end of your next turn.

Fettering Shot
Rogue Attack 23

With a clever shot, you pin your target to the spot.

Encounter ✦ Martial, Weapon
Standard Action   Ranged weapon
Requirement: You must be wielding a crossbow, a light thrown weapon, or a sling.
Target: One creature
Attack: Dexterity vs. AC
Hit: 4[W] + Dexterity modifier damage, and the target is immobilized until the end of your next turn.

LEVEL 25 DAILY EXPLOITS

Acrobatic Assault
Rogue Attack 25

With tumbling lunges, you deliver a sharp blow to each nearby enemy and return to your starting position.

Daily ✦ Martial, Weapon
Standard Action   Melee weapon
Prerequisite: You must be trained in Acrobatics.
Requirement: You must be wielding a light blade.
Target: One creature
Attack: Dexterity vs. AC
Hit: 3[W] + Dexterity modifier damage.
Miss: Half damage.
Effect: You can shift 4 squares and repeat the attack against a second target. You can then shift 4 squares and repeat the attack against a third target.

SEHANINE'S BLESSING

Fickle Sehanine is the trickster of the gods, relying on misdirection and deceit to pursue her goals. Rogues who work in the shadows often ask her blessing while gazing at the moon, and then act quickly before her attention wanders.

Cruel Pursuit
Rogue Attack 25

Your initial probing attack makes your enemy lurch to one side, allowing you to move up and finish with a wounding strike.

Daily ✦ Martial, Weapon
Standard Action   Melee weapon
Requirement: You must be wielding a light blade.
Target: One creature
Primary Attack: Dexterity vs. Reflex
Hit: 3[W] + Dexterity modifier damage, and you slide the target a number of squares equal to 1 + your Charisma modifier. You can then shift a number of squares equal to 3 + your Charisma modifier to a square adjacent to the target.
Miss: Half damage, you slide the target 2 squares, and you can then shift 3 squares to a square adjacent to the target.
Effect: Make a secondary attack against the target.
   Secondary Attack: Dexterity vs. Reflex
   Hit: 3[W] + Dexterity modifier damage.
   Miss: Half damage.

Gory Slash
Rogue Attack 25

Your bladed savagery opens a gushing wound that cripples your foe with pain.

Daily ✦ Martial, Weapon
Standard Action   Melee weapon
Requirement: You must be wielding a light blade.
Target: One creature
Attack: Dexterity vs. AC
Hit: 4[W] + Dexterity modifier damage, and the target takes ongoing 10 damage and is immobilized (save ends both).
Miss: Half damage, and ongoing 5 damage (save ends). The target is immobilized until the start of your next turn.

Magnetic Shot
Rogue Attack 25

You distract your adversary just long enough to deliver a shot that bypasses armor.

Daily ✦ Martial, Weapon
Standard Action   Melee or Ranged weapon
Requirement: You must be wielding a crossbow, a light blade, or a sling.
Target: One creature
Attack: Dexterity vs. Reflex
Hit: 6[W] + Dexterity modifier + Strength modifier + Charisma modifier damage.
Miss: Half damage.

Rogue's Resurgence
Rogue Attack 25

You strike with murderous exactness and then pull a deadly exploit back out of your bag of tricks.

Daily ✦ Martial, Weapon
Standard Action   Melee or Ranged weapon
Requirement: You must be wielding a crossbow, a light blade, or a sling.
Target: One creature
Attack: Dexterity vs. AC
Hit: 4[W] + Dexterity modifier damage.
Effect: If you have used all your encounter attack powers, you regain the use of a rogue encounter attack power you have used during this encounter. Or if you have combat advantage against the target, you can instead deal 4[W] extra damage with the attack.

Shocking Execution — Rogue Attack 25

You viciously lunge for a wounded enemy's throat and shock its allies.

Daily ✦ Martial, Rattling, Weapon
Standard Action   **Melee** weapon
Prerequisite: You must be trained in Intimidate.
Requirement: You must be wielding a light blade.
Target: One bloodied creature
Attack: Dexterity vs. Fortitude
Hit: 4[W] + Dexterity modifier damage, and each enemy within 3 squares of you takes a –2 penalty to attack rolls (save ends).
Miss: Half damage, and each enemy within 3 squares of you takes a –2 penalty to attack rolls until the start of your next turn.

Visceral Strike — Rogue Attack 25

You cut open your foe across the middle, drastically hampering her actions.

Daily ✦ Martial, Weapon
Standard Action   **Melee** weapon
Requirement: You must be wielding a light blade.
Target: One creature
Attack: Dexterity vs. AC
Hit: 4[W] + Dexterity modifier damage, and the target is stunned (save ends).
Aftereffect: The target is weakened and slowed (save ends both).
Miss: Half damage, and the target is weakened and slowed until the end of your next turn.

LEVEL 27 ENCOUNTER EXPLOITS

Hurling Pounce — Rogue Attack 27

As you send one foe staggering away from you, you spring on another.

Encounter ✦ Martial, Weapon
Standard Action   **Melee** weapon
Requirement: You must be wielding a light blade.
Primary Target: One creature
Primary Attack: Dexterity vs. AC
Hit: 3[W] + Dexterity modifier damage, and you push the primary target 2 squares. You can then shift 2 squares and make a secondary attack.
Brutal Scoundrel: You can instead push the primary target a number of squares equal to 1 + your Strength modifier.
Secondary Target: One creature other than the primary target
Secondary Attack: Dexterity vs. AC
Hit: 2[W] + Dexterity modifier damage.

Safe Bet — Rogue Attack 27

With an initial strike, you set yourself up to spring at your enemy if she dares to attack again.

Encounter ✦ Martial, Weapon
Standard Action   **Melee** or **Ranged** weapon
Requirement: You must be wielding a crossbow, a light blade, or a sling.
Target: One creature
Attack: Dexterity vs. AC
Hit: 4[W] + Dexterity modifier damage. If the target makes an attack before the start of your next turn, you can shift a number of squares equal to your Dexterity modifier and make a basic attack against the target as an immediate interrupt.

3

Skirmishing Strike — Rogue Attack 27

You move hastily to take your shot and then depart.

Encounter ✦ Martial, Weapon
Minor Action   **Melee** weapon
Requirement: You must be wielding a light blade.
Target: One creature
Attack: Dexterity - 2 vs. AC
Hit: 3[W] + Dexterity modifier damage, and you can shift 1 square.
  Artful Dodger: You can instead shift a number of squares equal to your Charisma modifier.

Stunning Assist — Rogue Attack 27

The fighter distracts him, and you shut him down.

Encounter ✦ Martial, Weapon
Standard Action   **Melee or Ranged** weapon
Requirement: You must be wielding a crossbow, a light blade, or a sling
Targets: One creature
Attack: Dexterity vs. AC
Hit: 3[W] + Dexterity modifier damage, and the target is dazed until the end of your next turn. If the target is marked by any of your allies, it is stunned instead of dazed.

Stupefying Violence — Rogue Attack 27

Your enemy reels from your shocking belligerence.

Encounter ✦ Martial, Rattling, Weapon
Standard Action   **Melee or Ranged** weapon
Requirement: You must be wielding a crossbow, a light blade, or a sling.
Targets: One creature
Attack: Dexterity vs. AC
Hit: 4[W] + Dexterity modifier damage, and you slide the target 2 squares.
  Ruthless Ruffian: You instead slide the target a number of squares equal to 2 + your Charisma modifier.

LEVEL 29 DAILY EXPLOITS

Cagey Killer — Rogue Attack 29

You smile and flick your weapon; your enemy stares unmoving at the deep wound.

Daily ✦ Martial, Weapon
Standard Action   **Melee or Ranged** weapon
Requirement: You must be wielding a crossbow, a light blade, or a sling
Target: One creature
Attack: Dexterity vs. AC
Hit: 3[W] + Dexterity modifier damage, and the target is stunned (save ends).
  Aftereffect: The target is dazed (save ends).
Miss: Half damage, and the target is dazed (save ends).

THE SWASHBUCKLER

The rogue is an ideal class for the swashbuckler famed in fiction. You could opt for cloth armor instead of leather, using a parrying dagger (see *Adventurer's Vault*) to help your AC. Pick a mix of acrobatic and trickster powers, relying on Dexterity and Charisma. It's worth a feat to get proficiency with the rapier, which is the best light blade.

Deathweaving Strike — Rogue Attack 29

Your attack sends the enemy lurching past your comrades, who take advantage by making attacks of their own.

Daily ✦ Martial, Reliable, Weapon
Standard Action   **Melee** weapon
Requirement: You must be wielding a light blade.
Target: One creature
Attack: Dexterity vs. Reflex
Hit: 3[W] + Dexterity modifier damage, and you slide the target a number of squares equal to 1 + your Charisma modifier. Each of your allies adjacent to the target at any point during this forced movement can make a basic attack against the target as an opportunity action. Each ally's attack has combat advantage and deals extra damage equal to your Charisma modifier on a hit.

A Murder of One — Rogue Attack 29

You flip and flit, stab and slash, as if flying among your foes.

Daily ✦ Martial, Weapon
Standard Action   **Melee** weapon
Prerequisite: You must be trained in Acrobatics.
Requirement: You must be wielding a light blade.
Primary Target: One creature
Primary Attack: Dexterity vs. AC
Hit: 4[W] + Dexterity modifier damage.
Effect: You can shift 3 squares and can shift through squares occupied by enemies during this movement. Make a secondary attack.
  Secondary Target: One creature other than the primary target
  Secondary Attack: Dexterity vs. AC
  Hit: 3[W] + Dexterity modifier damage. If the primary attack hit, this attack deals 1[W] extra damage.
Effect: You can shift 3 squares and can shift through squares occupied by enemies during this movement. Make a tertiary attack.
  Tertiary Target: One creature other than the primary and secondary targets
  Tertiary Attack: Dexterity vs. AC
  Hit: 2[W] + Dexterity modifier damage. If the primary or the secondary attack hit, this attack deals 1[W] extra damage.

Sight-Stealing Shot — Rogue Attack 29

You attack your foe in the eyes, leaving him dumbfounded and temporarily unable to see.

Daily ✦ Martial, Weapon
Standard Action   **Ranged** weapon
Requirement: You must be wielding a crossbow, a light thrown weapon, or a sling.
Target: One creature
Attack: Dexterity vs. Reflex
Hit: 4[W] + Dexterity modifier damage, and the target is blinded and dazed (save ends both).
Miss: Half damage, and the target is dazed until the end of its next turn.

AVANDRA'S LUCK

The swashbuckler's creed—"Luck favors the bold"—is part of Avandra's teachings. Daring rogues are more likely to thank her for good luck received than ask for it in advance. Through decisive action, they claim her luck as their own.

CLOAKED SNIPER

"You tell me—is it better to win with a shot from the dark or to lose up close?"

Prerequisites: Rogue, trained in Stealth

The advantage of getting the drop on an enemy is acknowledged far and wide. Equally prized is the benefit of taking out important targets with little risk. No one is better at accomplishing either task than a trained sharpshooter, and the sharpshooter's weapon of choice is the crossbow.

Nations and mercenary groups train specialized soldiers to use crossbows in this fashion. Underworld organizations do the same. Any such soldier is essentially an assassin who knows how to use a crossbow to slay from a distance without attracting notice. Dwarves in particular prize this exception to their normally straightforward battle tactics. That race produces fine snipers.

Such shooters don't shy away from a normal fight. They understand that reconnaissance and a plan, along with the ability to strike unseen from a great distance, are great advantages in a combat situation. A good ambush leaves the enemy weakened and confused, giving any follow-up assault a better chance of working.

You have chosen to hone your skills along these lines. You prefer to strike from hiding with a well-placed shot and to remain unobserved during a confrontation, aiding your allies by picking off foes without ever drawing notice. The hand crossbow is your preferred weapon.

Sniping is the ultimate tactic for you. The sound of a bolt finding its target is the sweet toll of victory. A bolt you fire might take out a sentry in a single hit, as well as sending your enemies scurrying for cover. If you miss, no matter. You can slink back into the shadows until you have a chance to shoot again.

CLOAKED SNIPER PATH FEATURES

Crossbow Savant (11th level): You add 5 squares to the normal range of any crossbow you wield and 10 squares to the long range. Treat a hand crossbow as an off-hand weapon, and treat any crossbow that has the load minor property as having the load free property instead.

Sniper Action (11th level): When you spend an action point to make a ranged basic attack and you have combat advantage against the target of the attack, you can add your Sneak Attack damage even if you have already dealt Sneak Attack damage during this round. If the attack hits, you can shift 1 square.

Versatile Combatant (16th level): When you are armed with a melee weapon in your main hand and a hand crossbow in your off hand, you do not provoke opportunity attacks when attacking with your hand crossbow.

CLOAKED SNIPER EXPLOITS

Sudden Bolt	Cloaked Sniper Attack 11

From the edge of sight, your well-placed bolt knocks your enemy silly.

Encounter ✦ Martial, Weapon
Minor Action   **Ranged** weapon
Requirement: You must be wielding a crossbow.
Target: One creature
Attack: Dexterity vs. Reflex
Hit: 2[W] + Dexterity modifier damage. If you are hidden from the target when you make this attack, the target is dazed until the end of your turn.

Unseen Shot	Cloaked Sniper Utility 12

They saw your attack but have no idea where it came from.

At-Will ✦ Martial
Free Action   **Personal**
Trigger: You miss with a ranged attack while hidden
Effect: You remain hidden if you have any cover or concealment. You can also shift 1 square.

Bolt from Nowhere	Cloaked Sniper Attack 20

Your bolt sails across the battlefield and sends your enemies into a panic.

Daily ✦ Martial, Weapon
Standard Action   **Ranged** weapon
Requirement: You must be wielding a crossbow.
Primary Target: One creature
Primary Attack: Dexterity vs. AC
Hit: 4[W] + Dexterity modifier damage.
Miss: Half damage.
Effect: Make a secondary attack, which has the fear keyword.
  Secondary Target: The primary target and each enemy you can see within 3 squares of it
  Secondary Attack: Dexterity vs. Will
  Hit: Until the end of your next turn, the secondary target takes a -2 penalty to attack rolls and grants combat advantage to you and your allies.

DARING ACROBAT

"Agile movement is as much offensive as it is defensive."

Prerequisites: Rogue, trained in Acrobatics

Acrobatics is a widespread and popular talent. All people, from nobles to peasants, enjoy acrobatics shows, whether amid the finery of court or the debris of the street. A few venturesome religious rites, especially those that pay homage to Avandra or Kord, require the skill. Mastery of the body is part of numerous education philosophies, and acrobatics is unmatched in cultivating fitness and balance. Thieves and burglars use the skill to ply their trade. Training is easy to find and widely accepted. Some youngsters attain a level of mastery well before they reach adolescence.

Not to be underestimated is the value of such proficiency on the battlefield. A combatant who is adept at acrobatics can maneuver like no other. The adroit use of the skill opens up advantages that other warriors can't attain and allows the acrobat to avoid being pinned down. Movement becomes quicker and smoother as the acrobat uses the whole body as a tool, rather than just relying on the feet and the legs. It's obvious why some martial training includes instruction in acrobatics.

It's also clear that the adventurer has even more use for acrobatics than a warrior or a soldier does. Explorers routinely face perils that are best overcome with agility, poise, and a sense of one's body. More than one fortune seeker owes life and limb to his dedicated schooling in acrobatics.

To say that of you is a gross understatement, however. It doesn't matter if you came by your skill in a formal academy, from family tradition, or through the school of hard knocks. You have made acrobatics not only an art form, but also a martial style all your own.

You flabbergast friend and foe alike with your talent. Using it, you routinely accomplish tricks that seem beyond mortal capacity. With your flamboyant derring-do, you deliver terrible attacks and deftly capitalize on the smallest openings.

DARING ACROBAT PATH FEATURES

Acrobatic Action (11th level): When you spend an action point to take an extra action, you can take a move action in addition to taking an extra action.

Tumbling Positions (11th level): You do not grant combat advantage to enemies when you are balancing, climbing, or prone.

Agile Charge (16th level): When you begin a charge, you gain a +1 bonus to AC and Reflex until the start of your next turn. Also, after completing a charge, you can take further actions (if you have any left).

DARING ACROBAT EXPLOITS

Wild Tumble Cut — Daring Acrobat Attack 11

With acrobatic flair, you rush in to deliver a vicious cut but are left momentarily off balance.

Encounter ✦ Martial, Weapon
Standard Action　　　　**Melee** weapon
Requirement: You must be wielding a light blade, and you must charge and use this power in place of a melee basic attack.
Target: One creature
Attack: Dexterity vs. AC
Hit: 4[W] + Dexterity modifier damage, and the target gains combat advantage against you until the start of your next turn.

Flawless Stunt — Daring Acrobat Utility 12

Your concentration and long hours of practice make all the difference in pulling off a trick.

Encounter ✦ Martial
Minor Action　　　　**Personal**
Effect: You gain a +5 bonus to Acrobatics and Athletics checks until the end of your turn.

Dramatic Finish — Daring Acrobat Attack 20

You drive your blade deep into your wounded foe, knowing you have something in reserve as a follow-up.

Daily ✦ Healing, Martial, Weapon
Standard Action　　　　**Melee** weapon
Requirement: You must be wielding a light blade.
Target: One creature
Attack: Dexterity vs. AC
Hit: 4[W] + Dexterity modifier damage, or 6[W] + Dexterity modifier damage if either you or the target is bloodied.
Effect: If this attack fails to reduce the target to 0 hit points, you can either make a melee basic attack against the target with a +5 bonus to the attack roll or spend a healing surge.
Special: When charging, you can use this power in place of a melee basic attack.

DEATH DEALER

"Killing's my game."

Prerequisite: Rogue

Some people are born killers. That penchant can be channeled in as many ways as there are reasons for slaughter. Some slay for religion or creed, others for power or influence, and still others for money, vengeance, glory, or just plain relief. Many who have a knack for murder take up violent professions, from soldier or town guard to gladiator or assassin. A few, whatever their reasons, make a career out of slaying monsters.

Killing is grim business, no matter who or what ends up dead. Nobody takes going to the grave lightly. Hands-off methods, such as poison, can sometimes work, as can stealthy techniques. Otherwise, direct and bloody conflict is the only way to go about butchery.

Strangely, a lot of would-be killers think that combat has rules. You know differently: In battle, fair play, honor, and mercy are for chumps. Fighting is all about dancing with death and being one of those still standing when the music ends. Maybe you came by your "philosophy" while being schooled as an assassin or hired sword. Of course, an adventurer's life has plenty of object lessons along the same lines: Kill or be killed.

When you start a fight, you take a little time to size up the competition. After that, it's all bloody business.

If someone has the nerve to attack you, you make that fool pay in such a way that anyone watching will think twice about facing you. Nobody escapes you unless they have the ability to take you out of the fight, or you want the story of your prowess to get around.

However you gained your skills, they are honed in accordance with your brutal creed. Those who go up against you risk everything. As proven by the boost you sometimes get from brutalizing our adversaries, you take at least a little pleasure in your work.

DEATH DEALER PATH FEATURES

No Respite (11th level): Enemies adjacent to you take a -2 penalty to saving throws.

Slaying Action (11th level): When you spend an action point to take an extra action, you gain a +2 bonus to each damage die until the start of your next turn.

Unfair Advantage (16th level): When you hit a bloodied foe with a melee attack, you gain temporary hit points equal to your Strength modifier or Charisma modifier (your choice).

DEATH DEALER EXPLOITS

Sizing Strike	Death Dealer Attack 11

Your attack is only probing, but what you see gives you confidence and your enemy pause.

Encounter ✦ Martial, Rattling, Weapon
Standard Action   **Melee** weapon
Requirement: You must be wielding a light blade.
Target: One creature
Attack: Dexterity vs. AC
Hit: 1[W] + Dexterity modifier damage, and you gain 10 temporary hit points. If you have combat advantage against the target, add your Strength modifier or Charisma modifier (your choice) to the damage roll and to the temporary hit points gained.

Gruesome Kill	Death Dealer Utility 12

You finish off your adversary with efficient butchery, and no other foe wants any part of you.

At-Will ✦ Martial
Free Action   **Personal**
Trigger: You reduce an enemy to 0 hit points
Effect: Each enemy that can see you takes a -2 penalty to attack rolls against you until the start of your next turn.

Death Dealer Assault	Death Dealer Attack 20

The wound you open tags your foe as yours.

Daily ✦ Martial, Weapon
Standard Action   **Melee** weapon
Requirement: You must be wielding a light blade.
Target: One creature
Attack: Dexterity vs. AC
Hit: 3[W] + Dexterity modifier damage.
Effect: The target takes ongoing 10 damage (save ends). Until the target saves against this damage, you can shift 1 square toward it as a minor action.

RON LEMEN

DREAD FANG

"You're caught in my web of shadows, poor little insect. Now it's time to die."

Prerequisites: Drow, rogue

Deceive your prey into a weak tactical position. Strike without being seen. Kill without allowing a counterattack. Don't sever a limb when you can cut off the head. Reward your enemies with death so horrifying that all others fear to oppose you. Live to fight again. All of these are drow rules of warfare, which young drow learn well just to get by in their treacherous society.

The drow are famous for slaughter, murdering all who get in their way. Countless folk have suffered the cruel kiss of a drow priestess's whip or the vile magic of a drow warlock. Innumerable slaves have lived and died as the wicked and capricious whims of their drow masters demanded. From this world you have come, and like others before you, you have found sanctuary in the arts of death. You learned the rudiments of drow warfare among your school-age peers. You mastered the blade-and-crossbow fighting style of the drow warrior to improve your station among your people. Better to be a valued killer than a slave or a sacrifice.

Maybe you smelled the deceptions and half-truths in your society, put up with the lies of the Spider Queen, until you could take no more. Perhaps the internecine warfare between drow houses left you without allies in the vast Underdark. You abandoned your past. Estranged from your homeland, you joined with other wanderers and continued your training. You have sought to become death incarnate and have succeeded well beyond the normal warriors of your people.

DREAD FANG PATH FEATURES

Spider Assassin (11th level): You deal one extra die of Sneak Attack damage against a target that could not see you at the start of your turn.

Dread Sneak Action (11th level): When you spend an action point to make an attack against a target granting combat advantage to you, you can deal Sneak Attack damage even if you have already dealt Sneak Attack damage during this round.

Sinister Presence (16th level): When you reduce an enemy to 0 hit points, pick a second enemy within 5 squares of you. You gain combat advantage against the second enemy until the end of your next turn.

DREAD FANG EXPLOITS

Fang and Web Strike	Dread Fang Attack 11

With expert precision, you drive your blade through your opponent and loose a bolt at the same time.

Encounter ✦ Martial, Weapon
Standard Action　　　　**Melee** or **Ranged** weapon
Requirement: You must be wielding a crossbow and a light blade.
Targets: One or two creatures
Attack: Dexterity vs. AC (melee or ranged), two attacks
Hit: 2[W] + Dexterity modifier damage per attack.
Special: Using this power doesn't provoke opportunity attacks.

Spider Feint	Dread Fang Utility 12

You feint, causing your opponent to flinch as you slip past.

Encounter ✦ Martial, Weapon
Minor Action　　　　**Close** burst 5
Target: One creature in burst you can see
Effect: You gain a +5 bonus to AC against the target's opportunity attacks until the end of your next turn.

Venomous Sting	Dread Fang Attack 20

Using your dark fey power, you deliver a deep and toxic wound.

Daily ✦ Martial, Poison, Reliable, Weapon
Standard Action　　　　**Melee** or **Ranged** weapon
Requirement: You must be wielding a crossbow or a light blade.
Target: One creature
Primary Attack: Dexterity vs. AC
Hit: 2[W] + Dexterity modifier damage. Make a secondary attack against the target.
Secondary Attack: Dexterity vs. Fortitude
Hit: The target is weakened and takes ongoing 5 poison damage (save ends both).

BETH TROTT

Flying-Blade Adept

"Any monkey can stab someone. Now, throwing to kill—that's got style."

Prerequisites: Rogue, Quick Draw feat

Among common folk, knife and shuriken throwing are forms of entertainment and sport. Competitors throw under calm conditions at stationary targets. At the extreme, carnival throwers toss blades at a moving mark, or sport throwers have to put up with rowdy onlookers and too much drink.

It takes a special breed of warrior to specialize in throwing blades in actual combat. The clash of steel, the rush of magical forces, and the screams of the wounded and dying are far more than taproom distractions. Moreover, the idea of tossing away a weapon seems tantamount to suicide. Still, anyone who has mastered the technique of hurling blades in battle knows that doing so helps to keep one out of harm's way.

Being such an expert takes guts, discernment, smarts, and quickness. The hurler must be brave enough to throw away a weapon, and to stand fast when the enemy recognizes the danger that he or she presents. The thrower's senses must be accurate enough to discern when to move and where. Furthermore, perception is nothing without the good judgment to exploit opportunities and to carry the right array of blades. And all this means little if the wielder lacks the agility or speed to take advantage of whatever battle situation arises.

You are such an expert with light thrown blades. Swift enough to draw weapons in rapid succession and to knock an arrow out of the air, you have little to fear when you throw a blade. Your talent allows you to hit with terrifying accuracy, to bounce your blades off one target and into another, and even to punch holes in enemy armor. You have even been known to throw so quickly that you can hit every target in your field of vision.

Flying-Blade Adept Path Features

Deadeye Blade (11th level): When you throw a light blade, it has the high crit property.

Flying-Blade Action (11th level): When you spend an action point to take an extra action, you can also make a ranged basic attack with a light blade as a free action.

Armor-Piercing Blade (16th level): The first time you score a critical hit against a target with a ranged attack using a light blade, that target takes a -2 penalty to AC until the end of the encounter.

Flying-Blade Adept Exploits

Ricochet Blade — Flying-Blade Adept Attack 11

Your blade wounds, then careens off your target and into a nearby foe.

Encounter ✦ Martial, Weapon
Standard Action — Ranged weapon
Requirement: You must be wielding a light blade with the light thrown property.
Target: One creature
Attack: Dexterity vs. AC
Hit: 3[W] + Dexterity modifier damage, and an enemy within 3 squares of the target takes damage equal to your Dexterity modifier.

Nimble Deflection — Flying-Blade Adept Utility 12

With a practiced eye, you follow a projectile's path and knock it out of the air.

Encounter ✦ Martial, Weapon
Immediate Interrupt — Ranged weapon
Trigger: A creature hits you with a ranged attack
Requirement: You must be wielding a light blade with the light thrown property.
Effect: You make a ranged basic attack, treating the attacking creature's attack roll as the target AC. If your attack hits, the triggering attack misses.

Bladed Fusillade — Flying-Blade Adept Attack 20

You unleash a volley of thrown blades.

Encounter ✦ Martial, Rattling, Weapon
Standard Action — Close blast 5
Requirement: You must be wielding a light blade with the light thrown property.
Target: Each enemy in blast you can see
Attack: Dexterity vs. AC
Hit: 3[W] + Dexterity modifier damage.
Miss: Half damage.

GUILDMASTER THIEF

"Me and my crew, we'll get the job done. Top-story jobs to shakedowns—we're all in."

Prerequisites: Rogue, trained in Thievery

Whoever says crime doesn't pay just isn't good enough to pull it off. For the organized and resourceful, there's always an angle.

Thieves' guilds are criminal gangs that crop up mostly in urban areas. A single guild might manage or influence illegal activities such as assassination, blackmail, burglary, espionage, fencing stolen goods, grifting, smuggling, loan sharking, pickpocketing, piracy, racketeering, robbery, thuggery, and so on. A guild might also direct legal enterprises as legitimate business ventures, as cover, or as a way to control the flow of information. For instance, many thieves' guilds have their fingers in begging, bounty hunting, mercenary work, gambling, prostitution, shipping, and even street cleaning and lamp lighting.

Because a guild's business can be so varied, and because it often has trouble with legal authorities and rival gangs, it must divide its profitable interests between various centers of control. Those centers have bosses, who report to those higher in the chain of command. Thus, guilds have complicated hierarchies, clear divisions of authority, and codes of behavior that can border on downright law-abiding in some respects. A guildmaster typically leads a portion of a guild, and some guilds have a grand master who oversees a guild's entire operation.

You might be an actual guildmaster, or maybe you grew up in the criminal world and know what's what on the street and in a brawl. Your experience has left you able to run a criminal crew on jobs and in fights. You're a great skirmisher who knows how to get a job done right while helping out your pals with some "world-wise management."

GUILDMASTER THIEF PATH FEATURES

Guildmaster's Action (11th level): When you spend an action point to take an extra action, instead of deducting the action point from your total you can deduct it from the total of any willing ally you can see. Similarly, as long as you are willing and conscious, any ally who can see you can deduct an action point from your total instead of from his or her total when spending an action point to take an extra action. The normal limit of action points spent during an encounter still applies.

Whenever you spend an ally's action point to take an extra action, you gain a +2 bonus to attack rolls until the start of your next turn.

Thieving Crew (11th level): Allies within 5 squares of you gain a +2 bonus to Stealth checks and Thievery checks.

Thick as Thieves (16th level): Any ally flanking with you gains a bonus to melee damage rolls equal to your Charisma modifier.

GUILDMASTER THIEF EXPLOITS

Guild Beatdown	Guildmaster Thief Attack 11

You strike your foe, cuing your friend to take a cheap shot.

Encounter ✦ Martial, Weapon
Standard Action — **Melee** or **Ranged** weapon
Requirement: You must be wielding a crossbow, a light blade, or a sling.
Target: One creature
Attack: Dexterity vs. AC
Hit: 2[W] + Dexterity modifier damage, and one ally adjacent to the target can make a melee basic attack against it as a free action. If the ally hits and has combat advantage, that attack deals 1d6 extra damage.

Shifty Direction	Guildmaster Thief Utility 12

With cutthroat timing, you help your ally carefully maneuver.

Encounter ✦ Martial
Immediate Reaction — **Close** burst 5
Trigger: An ally within 5 squares of you is missed by an attack
Target: The triggering ally in burst
Effect: The target can shift a number of squares equal to your Charisma modifier.

Biting Repositioning	Guildmaster Thief Attack 20

Your attack creates just the right opportunity for you and your crew to back off—or to change the flow of the battle.

Daily ✦ Martial, Weapon
Standard Action — **Melee** or **Ranged** weapon
Requirement: You must be wielding a crossbow, a light blade, or a sling.
Target: One creature
Attack: Dexterity vs. AC
Hit: 4[W] + Dexterity modifier damage, and you and each ally within 5 squares of you can shift a number of squares equal to 1 + your Charisma modifier.
Miss: Half damage, and you or one ally within 5 squares of you can shift a number of squares equal to 1 + your Charisma modifier.

Halfling Quickblade

"I told you once, mate. I'm the fastest blade there is. Ain't braggin' if it's true."

Prerequisites: Halfling, rogue

Halflings have a long tradition of using light blades with great skill. Whether a tool of survival or an implement of battle, the simple dagger has much to recommend it. Even one as small as a halfling can hide a dagger on the body for use in a tight spot. A small body coupled with a small weapon means greater mobility and deadliness enhanced by a better chance for stealthy attacks.

Halflings also have a history of using light blades in their art and performances. Carving, acrobatic blade tricks, knife juggling, dagger throwing, and even dances that incorporate blades are common among halflings. For them, such activities are a natural meeting of physical traits and handy tools.

As with almost every other aspect of their life, halflings have a variety of stories that explain their propensity for using blades. Such yarns include the daring tales of Barras Quickblade, whose surname is probably one of convenient fiction.

Barras's legend begins when he was a lad who provided for his clan by stalking game with nothing but a

knife and his wits. The legend grows into a spirited saga of an adventurous halfling who, along with a band of other intrepid characters, confronts ogres, yuan-ti, and worse with a tongue as pointed as his blade.

In the end, most stories have it that Barras sacrificed himself to save his comrades by leading a group of fomorians on a reckless chase through the Feywild. Darker versions say that Barras's spirit is still trapped, kept prisoner by the twisted fey. Halflings prefer to think that he passed from the world and that he stands at Avandra's side as her immortal companion.

You have the flair and the growing reputation to be a quickblade. Your fighting style is like that of your celebrated forebear. Perhaps, given time, your legend will be even greater.

Halfling Quickblade Path Features

First Cut (11th level): When you have combat advantage due to your First Strike class feature, add 1 to each die of Sneak Attack damage dealt by the attack.

Chancy Action (11th level): You can spend an action point to regain the use of the *second chance* racial power, instead of taking an extra action.

Ultimate Quickblade (16th level): You gain a bonus to initiative checks equal to your Charisma modifier.

Halfling Quickblade Exploits

Slash and Dash — Halfling Quickblade Attack 11

After delivering two sharp cuts, you scamper to a safe position.

Encounter ✦ Martial, Weapon
Standard Action   **Melee** weapon
Requirement: You must be wielding a light blade.
Targets: One or two creatures
Attack: Dexterity vs. AC, two attacks
Hit: 2[W] + Dexterity modifier damage per attack.
Effect: If you have combat advantage against every target of the attack, you can shift your speed and must end in a space that is not adjacent to a target of the attack.

Quickblade Scarper — Halfling Quickblade Utility 12

Your surprising quickness makes it impossible to hit you solidly.

Daily ✦ Martial
Move Action   **Personal**
Effect: You can shift your speed, and you take half damage from all attacks until the start of your next turn.

Quickblade Form — Halfling Quickblade Attack 20

You move quickly, with your dagger poised to retaliate.

Daily ✦ Martial, Stance, Weapon
Minor Action   **Personal**
Effect: When an adjacent enemy makes an opportunity attack against you, you can make a melee basic attack with a light blade against that enemy as a free action. Until the stance ends, you can make this attack only once per round.

MASTER SPY

"I've seen the things you never intended me to see, heard whispers meant only for your conspirators. I know you well enough to take you down."

Prerequisite: Rogue

In halls of power, on the field of battle, and even among those who seek what is long lost, reliable information is king. Those in the know have an advantage over their allies and enemies and readily know the difference between the two. Thus have persons skilled in acquiring secrets always had ample work and reasons to hone their skills. Such agents learn how to conceal their true motives and cover their tracks while focusing on attaining their goals. Any lapse in precision can mean death.

Long ago, you learned how to sneak into places where you're not welcome. No secret is safe from your expertise and trickery. Subterfuge is your stock-in-trade. You know how best to peer into the intentions of your enemies, and you work undercover with the greatest of ease. Most of your enemies never know that you are in their midst, and you always manage to turn their ignorance against them.

MASTER SPY PATH FEATURES

Cover Action (11th level): Whenever you spend an action point to take an extra action, you gain concealment at the end of that action. Until the end of your next turn, you have concealment and take no

penalty to Stealth checks for moving more than 2 squares or for running.

Deadly Bluff (11th level): You can make a Bluff check to gain combat advantage against an adjacent enemy as a minor action instead of as a standard action (*Player's Handbook*, page 183). If your check beats the enemy's Insight check, the enemy grants combat advantage to you and your allies until the end of your next turn.

Double Agent (16th level): Once per encounter, when an enemy you can see targets one of its allies with a power or an ability, you can choose to gain the benefit of that power or ability as if you were one of its targets as well.

MASTER SPY EXPLOITS

Lingering Revelation — Master Spy Attack 11

Your surprising attack slashes open your foe, causing the enemy to leave a trail you easily follow.

Encounter ✦ Martial, Weapon
Standard Action   **Melee** or **Ranged** weapon
Requirement: You must be wielding a crossbow, a light blade, or a sling.
Target: One creature
Attack: Dexterity vs. Will
Hit: 3[W] + Dexterity modifier damage, and the target cannot turn invisible or make Stealth checks until the end of your next turn.
Effect: You gain a +5 bonus to Insight checks and Perception checks opposed by the target until the end of the encounter.

Quick Change — Master Spy Utility 12

Your cunning actions plant a seed of doubt. Are you friend or foe?

Encounter ✦ Martial
Minor Action   **Ranged** 5
Target: One creature
Effect: Make a Bluff check opposed by the target's Insight check. If you succeed, the target considers you an ally for the purpose of auras, opportunity attacks, and powers until the end of your next turn or until you attack the target or its allies.

Spymaster's Edge — Master Spy Attack 20

You slip your weapon past your enemy's defenses, using your knowledge of its tactics to stay one step ahead.

Daily ✦ Martial, Weapon
Standard Action   **Melee** or **Ranged** weapon
Requirement: You must be wielding a crossbow, a light blade, or a sling.
Target: One creature
Attack: Dexterity vs. Will
Hit: 3[W] + Dexterity modifier damage, and the target takes a -5 penalty to attack rolls against you (save ends).
Miss: Half damage, and the target takes a -2 penalty to attack rolls against you (save ends).
Effect: Until the end of the encounter, whenever the target moves, you can move your speed or shift 1 square as an immediate reaction.

RAKISH SWASHBUCKLER

"With a face like that, it's no wonder your mother loves me best!"

Prerequisite: Rogue

Life is too short to take seriously. Danger lurks in every shadow, and an enemy waits behind every door. Those who spend every waking moment thinking about all the bad things that could happen never leave the house.

Instead of wringing your hands, you throw away all your worries and take a devil-may-care attitude. Sure, some say you will end up raking the coals of the Nine Hells because of your decadent living. In the end, though, who's the happier: you and your adventurous, libertine ways or the hidebound drudge shuddering under his covers?

On one hand, you're a charmer. Others find your infectious wit and bravado winsome. But you're also irreverent, irresponsible, and reckless. What's worst is that sometimes you have the hardest time keeping your mouth shut. Whether cracking a joke in the middle of a solemn funeral or shouting a barrage of insults at a demon, you can't help but stir up trouble. Deep down, you know life might be easier if you straightened up, but where's the fun in that?

When you face a serious challenge, your skill with weapons comes to the fore. Your tongue and your body language become secondary instruments of derision. You seed your exploits with cutting insults and disdain, goading your enemies into overextending or making other mistakes. When an enemy gives you an opening, you press the advantage. In the end, you stand triumphantly over a fallen foe, showing once again who's the greater fool is.

RAKISH SWASHBUCKLER PATH FEATURES

Incorrigible Action (11th level): Whenever you spend an action point to take an extra action, enemies take a -2 penalty to attack rolls against you until the start of your next turn.

Vexing Foe (11th level): Enemies marked by anyone other than you take a -2 penalty to attack rolls against you (this is in addition to the penalty from being marked). Enemies marked by you grant combat advantage to your allies.

Dastardly Opportunist (16th level): Whenever an ally scores a critical hit against an enemy adjacent to you, you can make a melee basic attack against that enemy as an immediate reaction.

RAKISH SWASHBUCKLER EXPLOITS

Abashing Stab — Rakish Swashbuckler Attack 11

With words or body language, you mock your foe as you deliver a cutting attack.

Encounter ✦ Martial, Weapon
Standard Action   Melee weapon
Requirement: You must be wielding a light blade.
Target: One creature
Attack: Dexterity vs. AC
Hit: 3[W] + Strength modifier damage, and the target is marked until the start of your next turn. Until the start of your next turn, the target takes a -2 penalty to attack rolls against you but gains a +5 bonus to damage rolls against you.

Mocking Footwork — Rakish Swashbuckler Utility 12

A derisive combat style keeps foes off balance.

Daily ✦ Martial, Stance
Minor Action   Personal
Effect: Until the stance ends, each time you hit an enemy that you have combat advantage against, you can either shift 1 square or slide the enemy 1 square.

Cutting Assault — Rakish Swashbuckler Attack 20

Your scornful manner puts your foe on the defensive, allowing you to make a sharp follow-up.

Daily ✦ Martial, Weapon
Standard Action   Melee 1
Requirement: You must be wielding a light blade.
Target: One creature
Primary Attack: Charisma vs. Will
Hit: The target is weakened and slowed (save ends both).
Miss: The target is slowed until the end of its next turn.
Effect: Make a secondary attack against the target. The target is then marked until the end of the encounter, until you are knocked unconscious, or until another mark supersedes this one.
Secondary Attack: Dexterity vs. Reflex. If the primary attack hit, you have combat advantage against the target.
Hit: 2[W] + Dexterity modifier damage.

Raven Herald

"All beings come to an end. Seeing to that is my task."

Prerequisites: Rogue, must worship the Raven Queen

The transition to death is a holy road on which all living things are pilgrims. Every creature steps onto that road at birth. When fate's appointed hour comes, every creature steps off into whatever waits beyond the finite and visible path. So it has been, and so it should be. These are the truths of the Raven Queen.

Yet some do not hold to the proper path. Brazen mortals defy the natural order by avoiding that righteous hour of ending. A few do so by magic or other means, the most common of which is to become undead.

Undead aren't, in and of themselves, offensive to the Raven Queen. Still, shambling dead brought back to a mockery of life through foul magic deserve to be destroyed. So do those undead that defy true death by serving other entities, such as Orcus or Vecna. A few bold souls manage to elude death without otherwise blaspheming the Raven Queen's edicts. Still, demise must come for them in time as well.

It is the duty of any who serve the Raven Queen to bring down the proud, showing them the equality that only death provides. Within temples where the Raven Queen is esteemed above all others, the clergy offers support and training for those who would be her instruments of death. Cults form around the ideal of righteous killing, of becoming heralds of death. Common folk know of the Raven Queen's heralds and

RON LEMEN

whisper of their mission when sudden loss of life visits the prideful, the wicked, or those cursed by undeath.

You have consciously devoted yourself to becoming a tool in the Raven Queen's wintry hands. Perhaps you came to this commitment on your own, or maybe you have an affiliation with the Raven Queen's hierarchy in the world. The origin of your connection to the mistress of winter makes little difference. As a harbinger of destiny, you know that every foe who falls before you has met its appropriate end.

Raven Herald Path Features

Death Rites (11th level): You gain the Ritual Caster feat and training in Religion. You also gain a +4 bonus to death saving throws.

Slaying Action (11th level): When you spend an action point to make a melee basic attack against an adjacent enemy that is bloodied or has the undead keyword, you gain a +2 bonus to the attack roll.

Radiant Striker (16th level): Each time you deal Sneak Attack damage, you can choose for that damage to be radiant damage.

Raven Herald Exploits

Unraveling Blow	Raven Herald Attack 11

You see the threads of fate tying your foe to existence, and you cut them.

Encounter ✦ Martial, Weapon
Standard Action — Melee weapon
Target: One creature
Attack: Dexterity vs. AC
Hit: 2[W] + Dexterity modifier damage. If the target is bloodied when you make the attack or has the undead keyword, the attack deals 1[W] extra damage and you add one die to Sneak Attack damage dealt through this attack.

Death's Veil	Raven Herald Utility 12

With the Raven Queen's blessing and your nearness to death, you become spiritlike.

Daily ✦ Divine
Immediate Reaction — Personal
Trigger: An enemy bloodies you
Effect: You become invisible and insubstantial until the end of your next turn.

Herald the End	Raven Herald Attack 20

Your merciless strike shakes your foe to the core of its being. It then sees an end to its existence.

Daily ✦ Martial, Weapon
Standard Action — Melee weapon
Target: One creature
Attack: Dexterity vs. AC
Hit: 4[W] + Dexterity modifier damage, and the target is dazed (save ends). If the target is bloodied or has the undead keyword, it is instead stunned (save ends).
Miss: Half damage, and if the target is bloodied or has the undead keyword, it is dazed until the end of its next turn.

STRONG-ARM ENFORCER

"This is going to hurt you a lot more than it hurts me."

Prerequisites: Rogue, trained in Intimidate

The world has no shortage of bullies. In every town and every neighborhood roams a lout with more muscle than sense, and more bravado than backbone. Every gang has an enforcer or a leg breaker. Yet it takes more than a mean streak and a hard head to rise above mere thuggery.

Unlike such roughnecks, who are so often craven at heart, you have cold iron beneath your hardened visage. You have the skill and the mettle to make good on threats you offer. Intimidation, to you, is just fair warning, an omen foretelling the cost of crossing you.

Like most of your kind, you might have started with a criminal outfit or learned how to get along in the harsh training ground of the streets. Such unsavory surroundings taught you to survive. A reputation for handing out grim rewards to your enemies slowly enabled you to avoid fights through the use of your bladed stare. For a few of you, formal training as an interrogator or operative taught you to use fear and pain as a principal means of getting the job done. In any case, fear is as useful in battle as it is outside it.

You have set your mind to this harsh fact and have realized that most interactions are all about getting in and getting out on top. If the other guy believes you can and will hurt him if you need to, dealings are much more likely to go in your favor.

Although stealth and subterfuge have uses, combat isn't a subtle solution. You favor techniques that keep your enemies shaken. A traumatized, fearful, or angry foe is more likely to make a mistake. Encouraging such missteps—gleefully at times—you make yourself a target through your brutality. Then you and your allies capitalize on those slip-ups to win the day.

STRONG-ARM ENFORCER PATH FEATURES

Promise of Pain (11th level): When you spend an action point to take an extra action, attacks you make until the start of your next turn gain the rattling keyword.

Vicious Courage (11th level): When you hit with a rattling attack and have combat advantage against the target, you gain temporary hit points equal to your Charisma modifier.

Strong-Arm Mark (16th level): When you hit with a rattling attack and have combat advantage against the target, you can choose to mark the target until the end of your next turn. Until the end of your next turn, you also gain a bonus to damage rolls against the target equal to your Charisma modifier.

STRONG-ARM ENFORCER EXPLOITS

Painful Reminder	Strong-Arm Enforcer Attack 11

You thump your adversary one more time, in case he forgot you're top dog.

Encounter ✦ Martial, Rattling, Weapon
Standard Action   **Melee** weapon
Requirement: You must be wielding a light blade.
Target: One creature you hit on your previous turn
Attack: Dexterity vs. Will
Hit: 2[W] + Dexterity modifier damage, and the target is marked until the end of your next turn.
 Ruthless Ruffian: You slide the target 1 square.

Implied Threat	Strong-Arm Enforcer Utility 12

Even when you manage to be polite, you have a threatening air.

Encounter ✦ Martial
Minor Action   **Personal**
Effect: Until the end of the encounter, you gain a power bonus to Intimidate checks equal to your Strength modifier.

Callous Strike	Strong-Arm Enforcer Attack 20

The cruelty of your attack causes other foes to withdraw from you.

Daily ✦ Martial, Rattling, Weapon
Standard Action   **Melee** weapon
Requirement: You must be wielding a light blade.
Primary Target: One creature
Primary Attack: Dexterity vs. AC
Hit: 3[W] + Dexterity modifier damage. Make a secondary attack, which has the fear keyword.
Secondary Target: Each enemy within 1 square of you
Secondary Attack: Charisma vs. Will
 Hit: The secondary target moves 1 square away from you.
Miss: Half damage, and no secondary attack.

TIEFLING HELLSTALKER

"Manifestations of the darkest flames of Hell cover me. You'll see the genuine article soon enough."

Prerequisites: Tiefling, rogue

Supernatural might comes naturally to a tiefling. Blood tied to the dark history of devils makes the reason for this obvious. In a vestigial form, this power lends vehemence to a tiefling's retaliation against attackers. History has shown that a tiefling who wishes to do so can reach inward for even more power, manifesting it in a variety of ways.

Those ways are mirrored in devils and their home. When mortals speak of the Nine Hells, they refer to fire, smoke, and the burning wrath of fiends. But the truth is more complex. The hells have ice, storms, and shadow. They even have combinations of these, the elements mixing in strange and unnatural ways to produce oddities such as lightless fire.

Some tieflings prefer to live up to expectations, displaying talent with anger and flame. They evoke terror by playing the devil's part. But they lack subtlety, which is a devil's best tool. They fail to acknowledge that mortals most fear what they can't see.

Drawing on the darkness within, a darkness that extends from the hells, a tiefling can gain uncanny advantages against enemies. Eyes can be dimmed, darkness and invisibility can be pierced, and flesh can be burned without light.

You know this, because you have learned to summon the darkness enshrouding your soul. By coupling it with your deadly martial skills, you become a terror in lightless halls under the earth, as well as on shadowed streets and in moonless wilds. Where light does find you, you snuff it in the sight of your foes. Eventually, the shadows you call up will be able to, at times, burn your enemies like extraplanar blackfire.

TIEFLING HELLSTALKER PATH FEATURES

Hell's Shadows (11th level): When you have concealment or total concealment, you gain a +1 bonus to all defenses.

Hellstalker Action (11th level): You can spend an action point to gain concealment until the end of your next turn, instead of taking an extra action.

Gloom Wrath (16th level): Your *infernal wrath* racial power also grants combat advantage to you for your next attack roll against an enemy that hit you since your last turn.

TIEFLING HELLSTALKER EXPLOITS

RON LEMEN

Dimming Blow	Tiefling Hellstalker Attack 11

To the senses of the one you strike, gloom covers you.

Encounter ✦ Martial, Weapon
Standard Action Melee or Ranged weapon
Requirement: You must be wielding a crossbow, a light blade, or a sling.
Target: One creature
Attack: Dexterity vs. Reflex
Hit: 2[W] + Dexterity modifier damage, and you become invisible to the target until the end of your next turn.

Devil's Sight	Tiefling Hellstalker Utility 12

You tap your heritage and gain a piercing vision.

Daily ✦ Martial
Minor Action Personal
Effect: Until the end of the encounter, you gain darkvision and the ability to perceive invisible creatures and objects as if they were visible.

Blackfire Wind	Tiefling Hellstalker Attack 20

Shadowy blazes engulf your foes and dim your image as you strike true.

Daily ✦ Fire, Martial, Weapon
Standard Action Close burst 1
Target: Each enemy in burst you can see
Attack: Dexterity vs. Reflex
Hit: 2[W] + Dexterity modifier damage, and ongoing 10 fire damage (save ends).
Effect: You are invisible to the targets until the end of your next turn.

CHAPTER 4

WARLORD

"Recklessness is still a tactical choice, and adaptability is an asset to any leader. If putting your own skin on the line saves your friends some pain, I say recklessness is more fun."

WHETHER CALLED to lead by talent or fate, or trained to lead as a soldier or a noble, a warlord must always acknowledge the importance of the team. A warlord forms the core of a squad, using martial know-how to manipulate any battle toward a favorable outcome. The notion of martial leadership includes countless techniques of command. Raw charisma can push allies to new heights, and strategic genius can create triumph where none seems possible. However, those are only two possibilities among many.

You could be the kind of leader who likes hard-hitting tactics and living on the edge. Maybe you just prefer to risk yourself rather than your friends, knowing that you have the guile and strength to pull off your style of daring leadership. Instead, you might prefer to play it fast and loose, observing the tactical situation and solving the problem with astounding ingenuity.

Rouse your allies to wrath and determination, come up with incisive tactics on the fly, create openings with your headlong rushes, or mix and match your strategies. No matter how you prefer to lead your allies to victory, this chapter is for you. In it, you'll find the following information.

✦ **New Warlord Builds:** Charge into battle as an aggressive bravura warlord, or test your creativity and battle acumen as a resourceful warlord.

✦ **New Class Features:** Two alternative choices give you the opportunity to focus your warlord even more sharply on one of the new builds.

✦ **New Warlord Powers:** Trick your enemies into overextending, and then make them pay. If you prefer more subtle methods, the exploits in this section also have you and your allies covered.

✦ **New Paragon Paths:** Channel your knack for leading into one of twelve new paths. Lead by following the example of a deity, march to traditional methods set by legendary generals, or let the law of the frontier be your guide.

MARK TEDIN

As alternatives to the warlord builds described in the *Player's Handbook*, this chapter presents two types of warlords and two groups of warlord powers that explore new leadership approaches. The bravura warlord centers on one set of these powers and the resourceful warlord on the other. These new powers can be useful to any warlord, however.

BRAVURA WARLORD

You lead through a combination of daring attacks and aggressive tactics. Using your powers is risky, but the rewards for success are great. You help your allies find the nerve to profit from bold maneuvers and punch into enemies head-on. Compared to other warlords, you're oriented more toward handling heavy fighting yourself, and your attack powers rely mainly on Strength. Charisma is your second priority, for it lets you get away with your audacious stunts yet maintain the respect of your comrades. Mental acuity and quick reflexes in battle are valuable to any warlord, so Intelligence is also important to you. The Bravura Presence class feature is designed to complement this build.

Suggested Feat: Improved Bravura* (Human feat: Action Surge)

Suggested Skills: Endurance, Heal, History, Intimidate

Suggested At-Will Powers: *brash assault,* *furious smash*

Suggested Encounter Power: *luring focus**

Suggested Daily Power: *fearless rescue**

*New option presented in this book

RESOURCEFUL WARLORD

You don't limit yourself to a particular set of tactics, instead adapting to the mistakes and openings your enemies provide and endeavoring to create opportunities. You lead through a diverse selection of shouted commands, ongoing stratagems, martial stances, and flexible plans. Allies can expect help in a wide variety of circumstances. As is typical for a warlord, Strength is your primary ability, but your powers make use of Intelligence and Charisma, encouraging you to pick and choose among the powers that other traditions have to offer. The Resourceful Presence class feature is designed to complement this build.

Suggested Feat: Improved Resources* (Human feat: Durable)

Suggested Skills: Athletics, Diplomacy, Endurance, Heal

Suggested At-Will Powers: *commander's strike,* *opening shove**

Suggested Encounter Power: *hammer formation**

Suggested Daily Power: *calculated assault**

*New option presented in this book

NEW CLASS FEATURES

These two variants of the Commanding Presence class feature are available to any warlord. You can pick one of them instead of another version, such as Inspiring Presence or Tactical Presence.

Bravura Presence: When an ally who can see you spends an action point to take an extra action and uses the action to make an attack, the ally can choose to take advantage of this feature before the attack roll. If the ally chooses to do so and the attack hits, the ally can either make a basic attack or take a move action after the attack as a free action. If the attack misses, the ally grants combat advantage to all enemies until the end of his or her next turn.

Resourceful Presence: When an ally who can see you spends an action point to take an extra action and uses the action to make an attack, that attack gains a bonus to damage equal to one-half your level + your Intelligence modifier. If the attack hits no target, the ally gains temporary hit points equal to one-half your level + your Charisma modifier.

NEW WARLORD POWERS

A warlord commands the field with a variety of powers that bolster allies and define the warlord as a warrior and leader. The bravura style of leadership is the ultimate lead-from-the-front method, complete with brash stunts that bait your enemies to give your comrades the upper hand. A resourceful warlord is the best at adaptability and can mold exploits designed for this leadership technique. This section also expands the abilities of all warlords, with some powers focused on other warlord builds and general exploits usable by any worthy commander.

LEVEL 1 AT-WILL EXPLOITS

Brash Assault	Warlord Attack 1

Your bold lunge leaves you open to an enemy's counterattack, but that's just what you want.

At-Will ✦ Martial, Weapon
Standard Action   **Melee** weapon
Target: One creature
Attack: Strength vs. AC
Hit: 1[W] + Strength modifier damage.
Increase damage to 2[W] + Strength modifier at 21st level.
Effect: The target can make a melee basic attack against you as a free action and has combat advantage for the attack. If the target makes this attack, an ally of your choice within 5 squares of the target can make a basic attack against the target as a free action and has combat advantage for the attack.

Opening Shove	Warlord Attack 1

You knock your foe off-balance while shouting a quick command to an ally.

At-Will ✦ Martial, Weapon
Standard Action   **Melee** weapon
Target: One creature
Attack: Strength vs. Reflex
Hit: You push the target 1 square. Then choose one ally you can see. That ally either shifts a number of squares equal to your Intelligence modifier or makes a melee basic attack against the target.

LEVEL 1 ENCOUNTER EXPLOITS

Hammer Formation	Warlord Attack 1

You signal your allies to attack with abandon, dishing out as much damage as possible.

Encounter ✦ Martial, Weapon
Standard Action   **Ranged** weapon
Requirement: You must be wielding a heavy thrown weapon.
Target: One creature
Attack: Strength vs. AC
Hit: 1[W] + Strength modifier damage, and each ally adjacent to you deals 1[W] extra damage on a hit with the next attack he or she makes before the start of your next turn.
Resourceful Presence: Each ally within a number of squares equal to your Charisma modifier can deal the extra damage.

Luring Focus	Warlord Attack 1

Your attack wounds your adversary, and another enemy moves closer, hoping to take advantage of your concentration.

Encounter ✦ Martial, Weapon
Standard Action   **Melee** weapon
Target: One creature
Attack: Strength vs. Fortitude
Hit: 1[W] + Strength modifier damage. Choose another enemy within 5 squares of you and pull it 1 square.
Bravura Presence: Pull the enemy a number of squares equal to your Charisma modifier.
Special: When charging, you can use this power in place of a melee basic attack.

Myrmidon Formation	Warlord Attack 1

Knowing that regrouping increases morale, you attack while calling for your allies to fall into line.

Encounter ✦ Martial, Weapon
Standard Action   **Melee** weapon
Requirement: You must be using a shield.
Target: One creature
Attack: Strength vs. AC
Hit: 2[W] + Strength modifier damage.
Effect: At the start of your next turn, each ally adjacent to you gains 5 temporary hit points.

Concentrated Attack · Warlord Attack 1

You and your companion combine your attacks to deliver a nasty blow.

Daily ✦ Martial, Weapon
Standard Action · Melee weapon
Target: One creature
Attack: Strength vs. AC
Hit: 2[W] + Strength modifier damage.
Effect: One ally within 10 squares of you can make a basic attack against the target as a free action. The ally gains a bonus to the attack roll and the damage roll equal to your Intelligence modifier.

Fearless Rescue · Warlord Attack 1

One of your allies falls, and without regard for your own well-being, you rush to make the attacker pay. Your bravery inspires your ally to fight on.

Daily ✦ Healing, Martial, Weapon
Immediate Reaction · Melee weapon
Trigger: An enemy within 5 squares of you reduces an ally to 0 hit points or fewer
Target: The triggering enemy
Effect: Before the attack, you can move to the nearest square from which you can attack the target.
Attack: Strength + 1 vs. AC
Hit: 2[W] + Strength modifier damage.
Effect: The ally can spend a healing surge and regains an additional 1d6 hit points for every opportunity attack you provoke while moving to the target.

Nimble Footwork · Warlord Attack 1

You attack and step to one side, allowing an ally to slip closer.

Encounter ✦ Martial, Weapon
Standard Action · Melee weapon
Target: One creature
Hit: 2[W] + Strength modifier damage, and you can shift 1 square. After you shift, one ally within 2 squares of you can shift 1 square as a free action.

LEVEL 1 DAILY EXPLOITS

Calculated Assault · Warlord Attack 1

Your attack proves your superior command of the situation.

Daily ✦ Martial, Reliable, Weapon
Standard Action · Melee weapon
Target: One creature
Attack: Strength vs. AC
Hit: 1[W] + Strength modifier damage, and one of your allies within 5 squares of you gains a power bonus to damage rolls against the target equal to 1 + your Intelligence modifier until the end of the encounter. You can transfer the bonus to another ally within 5 squares of you as a minor action.

Lead by Example · Warlord Attack 1

You step forward to attack, showing your allies how it's done—and whom to hit next.

Daily ✦ Martial, Weapon
Standard Action · Melee weapon
Target: One creature
Effect: Before the attack, you can shift 1 square.
Attack: Strength vs. AC
Hit: 2[W] + Strength modifier damage, and your allies gain combat advantage against the target until the start of your next turn.
Miss: Two allies within 5 squares of you can each shift 1 square and make a basic attack as a free action.

LEVEL 2 UTILITY EXPLOITS

Adaptive Stratagem · Warlord Utility 2

Your companion has the ability and the will. You provide the plan and the motivation.

Encounter ✦ Martial
Minor Action · Close burst 10
Target: One ally in burst
Effect: Until the end of your next turn, the ally gains his or her choice of a power bonus to damage rolls equal to your Intelligence modifier or a power bonus to saving throws equal to your Charisma modifier.
Resourceful Presence: The ally gains both bonuses.

Covering Maneuver
Warlord Utility 2

Responding to your expertise, one ally steps in to cover another's recovery.

Encounter ✦ Martial
Free Action   **Close** burst 5
Trigger: You or an ally within 5 squares of you uses second wind
Target: One ally in burst other than the triggering character
Effect: The target can shift 1 square as a free action. In addition, an enemy in the burst is marked by the target until the end of the enemy's next turn.

Heroic Effort
Warlord Utility 2

On the brink of exhaustion, you still manage to rally your allies.

Daily ✦ Martial
Minor Action   **Close** burst 10
Requirement: You must be bloodied.
Target: Each ally in burst
Effect: The target can add your Charisma modifier to damage rolls until you are no longer bloodied. Also, you gain temporary hit points equal to your level + your Charisma modifier.

Inspired Belligerence
Warlord Utility 2

You lead your allies to use your enemies' defensive openings to deliver more punishment.

Encounter ✦ Martial
Minor Action   **Close** burst 5
Target: One enemy in burst granting combat advantage to you or an ally
Effect: Until the start of your next turn, all your allies gain combat advantage against the target.
    Inspiring Presence: Until the start of your next turn, your allies add your Charisma modifier to damage rolls against the target.

Motivated Recovery
Warlord Utility 2

At your encouragement, an injured ally exploits an opportunity to shine.

Daily ✦ Martial
Minor Action   **Close** burst 5
Target: One bloodied ally in burst
Effect: The target regains the use of second wind and gains a power bonus to his or her next attack roll equal to your Charisma modifier.

Reckless Opportunity
Warlord Utility 2

You hurl an impulsive command at an ally, hoping that he understands it properly.

Encounter ✦ Martial
Minor Action   **Close** burst 5
Targets: One enemy in burst and you or one ally in burst
Effect: The targets make opposed initiative checks. The winner gains combat advantage against the loser until the end of the winner's next turn.
    Bravura Presence: You or your ally gains a power bonus to the initiative check equal to your Charisma modifier.

Repositioning Command
Warlord Utility 2

With a single word from you, your allies shift to more advantageous positions.

Daily ✦ Martial
Move Action   **Close** burst 5
Targets: You and each ally in burst
Effect: Each target can shift 1 square.
    Tactical Presence: Increase the burst to 10.

Rub Some Dirt on It
Warlord Utility 2

With a wisecrack, you give your comrade a little courage despite his wounds.

Encounter ✦ Martial
Minor Action   **Melee** touch
Target: You if you're bloodied or one bloodied ally
Effect: The target gains temporary hit points equal to 5 + your Charisma modifier.

LEVEL 3 ENCOUNTER EXPLOITS

Bloody Ending
Warlord Attack 3

You cunningly aim to finish off a wounded foe.

Encounter ✦ Martial, Weapon
Standard Action   **Melee** weapon
Target: One bloodied creature
Attack: Strength vs. AC
Hit: 2[W] + Strength modifier + Intelligence modifier damage.
    Resourceful Presence: Your allies gain a +2 power bonus to attack rolls against the enemy until the end of your next turn.

Dicey Predicament
Warlord Attack 3

Surrounded by enemies, you fake weakness and make them careless. Then you suddenly strike.

Encounter ✦ Martial, Weapon
Standard Action   **Melee** weapon
Requirement: You must be flanked.
Target: One creature
Attack: Strength vs. AC
Hit: 2[W] + Strength modifier damage, and all enemies adjacent to you grant combat advantage to all your allies within 5 squares of you until the end of your next turn.
    Bravura Presence: The attack deals extra damage equal to your Charisma modifier.

Flattening Charge
Warlord Attack 3

The force of your hurtling attack knocks your enemy flat or leaves your defenses down.

Encounter ✦ Martial, Weapon
Standard Action   **Melee** weapon
Requirement: You must charge and use this power in place of a melee basic attack.
Target: One creature
Attack: Strength vs. Fortitude
Hit: 1[W] + Strength modifier damage, and you knock the target prone.
    Bravura Presence: If the attack hits, this power is not expended.
Miss: The target gains combat advantage against you until the start of your next turn.

Follow Me In
Warlord Attack 3

You rush into battle with a decisive attack, rallying a friend behind you.

Encounter ✦ Martial, Weapon
Standard Action   **Melee** weapon
Target: One creature
Attack: Strength vs. AC
Hit: 2[W] + Strength modifier damage, and one ally within 10 squares of you gains a +2 power bonus to speed until the end of your next turn.
  Tactical Presence: If the ally charges while the bonus to speed is in effect, the ally's movement during the charge does not provoke opportunity attacks.
Special: When charging, you can use this power in place of a melee basic attack.

Shielding Retaliation
Warlord Attack 3

You step in front of an attack meant for your ally and give the attacker a staggering blow. Your friend can then move to a better position.

Encounter ✦ Martial, Weapon
Immediate Interrupt   **Melee** 1
Trigger: An adjacent enemy hits an ally with an opportunity attack
Effect: The opportunity attack hits you instead.
Target: The triggering enemy
Attack: Strength vs. AC
Hit: 2[W] + Strength modifier damage, and the ally can shift 2 squares.

LEVEL 5 DAILY EXPLOITS

Pike Hedge
Warlord Attack 5

Setting yourself to foil enemy movement, you're ready to strike anyone who comes near.

Daily ✦ Martial, Weapon
Immediate Reaction   **Melee** weapon
Trigger: An enemy enters a square within your reach
Requirement: You must be wielding a reach weapon.
Target: The triggering enemy
Attack: Strength vs. AC
Hit: 1[W] + Strength modifier damage.
Effect: Whenever an enemy enters a square adjacent to you or to an ally adjacent to you, you deal damage to that enemy equal to your Strength modifier as an opportunity action. This effect lasts until the end of the encounter.

A Rock and a Hard Place
Warlord Attack 5

You focus to work in concert with your companion, harrying your opponent with relentless blows.

Daily ✦ Martial, Stance, Weapon
Minor Action   **Personal**
Effect: Until the stance ends, whenever an enemy adjacent to you attacks an ally of yours and misses, you deal damage to the enemy equal to your Intelligence modifier as a free action.
  Tactical Presence: If the enemy is marked by an ally, deal 1[W] + Intelligence modifier damage instead.

Scent of Victory
Warlord Attack 5

As your enemies stagger from their wounds, you can smell victory. Your allies respond with a furious assault.

Daily ✦ Martial
Standard Action   **Close** burst 5
Target: Each ally in burst
Effect: Each target can make a melee basic attack as a free action against a bloodied enemy adjacent to him or her.

Situational Advantage
Warlord Attack 5

Your attack against an unprepared enemy gives you and your allies a decided advantage.

Daily ✦ Martial, Weapon
Standard Action   **Ranged** weapon
Requirement: You must be wielding a heavy thrown weapon.
Target: One creature
Attack: Strength vs. AC
Hit: 3[W] + Strength modifier damage.
Miss: Half damage.
Effect: Until the end of your next turn, you and each ally within 10 squares of you deal extra damage equal to your Intelligence modifier when hitting with combat advantage.
  Resourceful Presence: Your extra damage is 1[W] + Intelligence modifier instead.

Staggering Spin
Warlord Attack 5

With a wild, wheeling attack, you send your foes careening into your allies' waiting weapons.

Daily ✦ Martial, Weapon
Standard Action   **Close** burst 1
Target: Each enemy in burst
Attack: Strength vs. Fortitude
Hit: 1[W] + Strength modifier damage, and you push the target 1 square. If the target is then adjacent to any of your allies, those allies can make a melee basic attack against the target as an opportunity action.
Miss: Half damage, and no push.

LEVEL 6 UTILITY EXPLOITS

Encouraging Stance
Warlord Utility 6

With a daunting bearing, you unleash a litany of oaths as you attack, pushing your allies onward.

Daily ✦ Martial, Stance
Minor Action   **Personal**
Effect: Until the stance ends, when you hit with a melee attack, choose a bloodied ally within 5 squares of you. That ally gains temporary hit points equal to 5 + your Charisma modifier.
  Bravura Presence: You can choose to grant the temporary hit points when you miss with a melee attack, but that grants the target of the attack combat advantage against you until the end of your next turn.

Forward Observer
Warlord Utility 6

Discerning the proper angle of fire, you point out concealed enemies to your allies.

At-Will ✦ Martial
Minor Action   **Personal**
Effect: Choose one enemy you can see. Until the end of your next turn, any ally who can see or hear you doesn't take the normal penalty to attack rolls for cover or concealment when attacking that enemy (the penalties for superior cover and total concealment still apply).

Guileful Switch
Warlord Utility 6

You spring a trap on your opponents, surprising them with your clever stratagem.

Encounter ✦ Martial
Minor Action   **Personal**
Effect: You and one ally you can see switch places in the initiative order. Your turn ends when you use this power, and the ally takes his or her next turn immediately, even if he or she has already acted during this round. You then act when your ally would have acted.

Phalanx Formation
Warlord Utility 6

You and your allies link shields for better defense.

Daily ✦ Martial, Stance
Minor Action   **Personal**
Requirement: You must be using a shield.
Effect: Until the stance ends, whenever you are adjacent to any ally who is using a shield, you and the ally gain a +1 power bonus to AC and Reflex.

Rousing Words
Warlord Utility 6

As your ally's spirit wanes, you manage to pick just the right words to inspire him.

Encounter ✦ Healing, Martial
Minor Action   **Close** burst 5
Target: You or one ally in burst
Effect: The target can spend two healing surges.
   Inspiring Presence: The target regains additional hit points equal to 5 + your Charisma modifier.

Tactical Supervision
Warlord Utility 6

You lend your expertise to your ally to help her strike a foe.

Encounter ✦ Martial
Immediate Interrupt   **Close** burst 10
Trigger: An ally makes a basic attack, a bull rush, or a charge within 10 squares of you
Target: The triggering ally in burst
Effect: The target gains a power bonus to the attack roll equal to your Intelligence modifier.

Tempting Target
Warlord Utility 6

You invite attack and distract your foes in the process.

Daily ✦ Healing, Martial, Stance
Minor Action   **Personal**
Effect: Until the stance ends, you grant combat advantage to all enemies, but any enemies adjacent to you grant combat advantage to your allies.
   Bravura Presence: When an enemy adjacent to you becomes bloodied or is reduced to 0 hit points, you regain hit points equal to your Charisma modifier.

LEVEL 7 ENCOUNTER EXPLOITS

Deadly Returns
Warlord Attack 7

You create an opening that allows an ally to capitalize on your foe's aggression.

Encounter ✦ Martial, Weapon
Standard Action
Target: One creature
Attack: Strength vs. AC
Hit: 2[W] + Strength modifier damage, and you choose one ally within 5 squares of you. Until the end of your next turn, if the target makes a melee attack against you or the ally, the ally can make an opportunity attack against the target.

Phalanx Assault
Warlord Attack 7

From behind your ready shield, you pound your foe and bark an order, calling for defensive tactics.

Encounter ✦ Martial, Weapon
Standard Action   **Melee** weapon
Requirement: You must be using a shield.
Target: One creature
Attack: Strength vs. AC
Hit: 2[W] + Strength modifier damage, and allies adjacent to you gain a +2 power bonus to AC and Reflex until the end of your next turn.
   Resourceful Presence: Adjacent allies gain the +2 power bonus to AC and Reflex even if you miss.

Provoke Overextension
Warlord Attack 7

You goad the enemy into pressing too far, setting up your ally's counterstrike.

Encounter ✦ Martial, Weapon
Standard Action   **Melee** weapon
Target: One creature
Attack: Strength vs. AC
Hit: 2[W] + Strength modifier damage, and the target must make a basic attack against you as a free action. If the basic attack misses, an ally of yours can make a basic attack against the target as a free action.
   Bravura Presence: You gain a bonus to your AC against the target's basic attack equal to your Charisma modifier and your ally gains the same bonus to his or her basic attack's damage roll.

Sacrificial Lure
Warlord Attack 7

Your wild strike lands solidly and inspires a comrade, but it leaves you vulnerable.

Encounter ✦ Martial, Weapon
Standard Action   **Melee** weapon
Target: One creature
Attack: Strength vs. AC
Hit: 2[W] + Strength modifier + Charisma modifier damage. Until the start of your next turn, one ally within 5 squares of you gains a power bonus to his or her next attack roll equal to your Charisma modifier.
Effect: You take a -2 penalty to AC until the start of your next turn.

LEVEL 9 DAILY EXPLOITS

Blood Designation — Warlord Attack 9

The blood you've drawn acts as a target for your comrades.

Daily ✦ Martial, Weapon
Standard Action   **Melee** weapon
Target: One creature
Attack: Strength vs. AC
Hit: 2[W] + Strength modifier damage.
Effect: The target takes ongoing 5 damage (save ends). As long as the ongoing damage persists, your allies gain combat advantage against the target.
     Inspiring Presence: Add your Charisma modifier to the ongoing damage.

Denying Mark — Warlord Attack 9

Your smite incites your enemy to focus on you, but only with weaker attacks.

Daily ✦ Martial, Weapon
Standard Action   **Melee** weapon
Target: One creature
Attack: Strength vs. AC
Hit: 3[W] + Strength modifier damage, and the target is marked (save ends).
Miss: Half damage, and the target is marked until the end of its next turn.
Effect: The target cannot recharge its powers as long as it is marked by this power.
     Bravura Presence: The target also cannot spend action points as long as it is marked by this power.

Stirring Force — Warlord Attack 7

With a mighty strike, you spur your friends to shake off their hindrances.

Encounter ✦ Martial, Weapon
Standard Action   **Melee** weapon
Target: One creature
Attack: Strength vs. AC
Hit: 2[W] + Strength modifier damage, and any ally within 2 squares of you can make a saving throw.
     Resourceful Presence: Your allies gain a power bonus to the saving throws equal to your Intelligence modifier.

Disheartening Flurry — Warlord Attack 9

The skill you show with your series of attacks dismays your enemies.

Daily ✦ Martial, Weapon
Standard Action   **Close** burst 1
Target: Each enemy in burst you can see
Attack: Strength vs. AC
Hit: 2[W] + Strength modifier damage.
Miss: Half damage.
Effect: The target takes a -2 penalty to saving throws until the end of the encounter.

War of Attrition — Warlord Attack 7

Little by little, your allies turn the tide against the enemy.

Encounter ✦ Martial, Weapon
Standard Action   **Melee** weapon
Target: One creature
Attack: Strength vs. AC
Hit: 2[W] + Strength modifier damage. Until the start of your next turn, any ally who can see you gains a +1 power bonus to attack rolls and damage rolls with basic attacks and at-will powers.
     Inspiring Presence: The bonus equals your Charisma modifier.

Stay on Target — Warlord Attack 9

You and your comrades train your fire on an enemy drawing near.

Daily ✦ Martial, Weapon
Immediate Reaction   **Ranged** 3
Trigger: An enemy enters a square within 3 squares of you
Requirement: You must be wielding a heavy thrown weapon.
Target: The triggering enemy
Attack: Strength vs. AC
Hit: 1[W] + Strength modifier + Intelligence modifier damage.
Miss: Half damage.
Effect: Each ally within 2 squares of you can make a ranged basic attack against the target as an immediate reaction, with a bonus to the damage roll equal to your Intelligence modifier.

Warlord's Recovery Warlord Attack 9

You point out an opportunity perfect for an ally's attacks, re-newing your own determination to end this fight.

Daily ✦ Martial
Standard Action   **Close** burst 5
Target: One ally in burst
Effect: As a free action, the target can make an attack us-ing an encounter attack power that he or she has already used during this encounter. Also, if you have used all your encounter attack powers, you regain the use of a war-lord encounter attack power you have used during this encounter.

LEVEL 10 UTILITY EXPLOITS

Bolstering Shout Warlord Utility 10

Your war cry quickly rallies your allies.

Encounter ✦ Healing, Martial
Minor Action   **Close** burst 10
Target: Each ally in burst
Effect: Until the end of your next turn, each target regains additional hit points equal to your Charisma modifier when he or she uses second wind. Each target can also choose to use second wind as a minor action but gain no bonus to defenses from it.

Instant Planning Warlord Utility 10

Your instinctive reactions to the situation turn the tide in your favor.

Daily ✦ Martial
Minor Action   **Close** burst 5
Targets: You and each ally in burst
Effect: Until the end of your next turn, every target gains your choice of a power bonus to attack rolls equal to your Charisma modifier, a power bonus to speed equal to your Charisma modifier, or a power bonus to all defenses equal to your Intelligence modifier.
    Resourceful Presence: You can grant a different bonus to each target.

Marked Revelation Warlord Utility 10

With a fake command and your ally's practiced response, you identify that ally as a danger that your enemies should heed.

Encounter ✦ Martial
Standard Action   **Close** burst 3
Target: Each unmarked enemy in burst
Effect: The targets are marked by an ally of your choice until the end of your next turn.
    Tactical Presence: Increase the burst to 5.

Rallying Deflection Warlord Utility 10

You catch the arrow on your shield and send your ally forward to meet the shooter.

Encounter ✦ Martial
Immediate Interrupt   **Personal**
Trigger: An enemy hits you with a ranged attack
Requirement: You must be using a shield.
Effect: Reduce the attack's damage by one-half your level. One ally within 5 squares of the attacker can charge the attacker as a free action.

Strider Stance Warlord Utility 10

You stand ready to change position quickly or to point out op-portunities for your allies to do so.

Daily ✦ Martial, Stance
Minor Action   **Personal**
Effect: Until the stance ends, once on each of your turns you can use a move action to shift 1 square and gain a +2 power bonus to damage rolls until the start of your next turn, or you can use a move action to allow an ally within 5 squares of you to do the same as a free action.

Unintended Feint Warlord Utility 10

As your ally misses, you spot an opening that the attack cre-ated. You point it out so that your friend can immediately take advantage of it.

Daily ✦ Martial
Immediate Reaction   **Close** burst 5
Trigger: An ally within 5 squares of you misses with an attack
Target: The triggering ally in burst
Effect: The target can reroll the attack and has combat advantage for it.

WARLORD GODS

As mentioned in the *Player's Handbook*, warlords favor martial gods such as Bahamut and Kord, and warlords with strong strategic leanings often follow Erathis or Ioun. Three paragon paths in this book reflect those preferences for warlord gods: the battlelord of Kord (page 118), the dujun of Erathis (page 122), and the platinum warlord (page 127), devoted to Bahamut.

LEVEL 13 ENCOUNTER EXPLOITS

Befuddling Cry | Warlord Attack 13

Your warning shout allows your ally to turn an opening into an advantage.

Encounter ✦ Martial
Immediate Interrupt   **Close** burst 5
Trigger: An enemy within 5 squares of you hits an ally with an opportunity attack
Target: The triggering ally in burst
Effect: The target makes a melee basic attack against the attacking enemy as a free action. If this attack hits, the attacking enemy rerolls the opportunity attack against a different creature of your choice within its reach.
    Resourceful Presence: The enemy gains a bonus to the new attack and damage rolls equal to your Charisma modifier.

Grim Mark | Warlord Attack 13

Your sidling approach belies your excruciating follow-up, which opens your opponent to attacks from your allies.

Encounter ✦ Martial, Weapon
Standard Action   **Melee** weapon
Target: One creature
Effect: Before the attack, you can shift 2 squares.
Attack: Strength vs. AC
Hit: 2[W] + Strength modifier damage, and the target is dazed and marked until the end of your next turn.
    Resourceful Presence: While the target is marked by this power, your allies gain a power bonus to damage rolls against the target equal to your Charisma modifier.

Headstrong Bravery | Warlord Attack 13

You smite your enemy without regard for your safety, inciting the enemy against you and your allies against it.

Encounter ✦ Martial, Weapon
Standard Action   **Melee** weapon
Target: One creature
Attack: Strength vs. Fortitude
Hit: 3[W] + Strength modifier damage, and you mark the target until the end of your next turn. Until the start of your next turn, you grant combat advantage to all enemies, and your allies gain a +2 power bonus to damage rolls against the target.
    Bravura Presence: Your allies instead gain a power bonus to damage rolls against the target equal to 2 + your Charisma modifier.
Special: When charging, you can use this power in place of a melee basic attack.

Pincer Maneuver | Warlord Attack 13

At your command, two of your allies move to flank a foe.

Encounter ✦ Martial
Standard Action   **Close** burst 5
Targets: One or two allies in burst
Effect: Each target can shift 3 squares and make a melee basic attack against an adjacent enemy as a free action. If the target is flanking the enemy, he or she gains a bonus to the damage roll equal to your Charisma modifier.
    Bravura Presence: The target gains a power bonus to the attack roll equal to your Charisma modifier.

Unified in Blood | Warlord Attack 13

Rushing to defend a friend in trouble, you make a bold attack. Your friend then defends himself by your example.

Encounter ✦ Martial, Weapon
Immediate Interrupt   **Melee** weapon
Trigger: An enemy within 5 squares of you bloodies an ally
Target: The triggering enemy
Effect: Before the attack, you can move your speed.
Attack: Strength vs. AC
Hit: 2[W] + Strength modifier damage, and the bloodied ally can make a basic attack against the target as a free action.

Ventured Gains | Warlord Attack 13

Rushing to take your adversary down a notch, you ignore your defenses but allow your allies to take advantageous shots.

Encounter ✦ Martial, Weapon
Standard Action   **Melee** weapon
Target: One creature
Attack: Strength vs. Fortitude
Hit: 2[W] + Strength modifier damage. If this attack bloodies the target, two of your adjacent allies can each make a basic attack against the target as a free action.
    Bravura Presence: Each ally gains a power bonus to the basic attack roll equal to your Charisma modifier.
Effect: You grant combat advantage to all enemies until the start of your next turn.

Withdrawal Gambit | Warlord Attack 13

With an interposing attack, you give your companions the determination and the space to improve the tactical situation.

Encounter ✦ Martial, Weapon
Standard Action   **Melee** weapon
Target: One creature
Attack: Strength vs. AC
Hit: 3[W] + Strength modifier damage, and each of your allies adjacent to the target can make a saving throw and then shift 1 square as a free action.
    Tactical Presence: Each ally gains a power bonus to the saving throw equal to your Charisma modifier, and each can instead shift a number of squares equal to 1 + your Intelligence modifier.

LEVEL 15 DAILY EXPLOITS

Anticipate Attack | Warlord Attack 15

Maneuvering to make your enemy open itself up to attack, you deliver a passing blow. Your comrades follow up with strikes of their own.

Daily ✦ Martial, Weapon
Immediate Interrupt   **Melee** 1
Trigger: An adjacent enemy hits you with a melee attack
Target: The triggering enemy
Attack: Strength vs. Reflex
Hit: 2[W] + Strength modifier damage, and you can shift 1 square.
Effect: Each ally adjacent to the target can make an opportunity attack against it and has combat advantage for the attack.
    Tactical Presence: Each ally gains a bonus to the damage roll equal to your Intelligence modifier.

Arkhosia's Fury — Warlord Attack 15

In a traditional dragonborn maneuver, you storm in, smite an enemy, spin away, and punish yet another foe.

Daily ✦ Martial, Weapon
Standard Action   **Melee** weapon
Target: One creature
Attack: Strength vs. AC

Hit: 3[W] + Strength modifier damage, and you can shift 2 squares.
Miss: Half damage, and you can shift 1 square.
Effect: After you shift, you can make a basic attack against a different target.
Special: When charging, you can use this power in place of a melee basic attack.

Formidable Smash — Warlord Attack 15

Your strike leaves your foe hesitant to attack you or anyone near you.

Daily ✦ Martial, Weapon
Standard Action   **Melee** weapon
Target: One creature
Attack: Strength vs. AC

Hit: 3[W] + Strength modifier damage. Until the end of the encounter, the target takes a -2 penalty to attack rolls against you or any ally who is adjacent to you when it attacks (the target takes no penalty if it is immune to fear).
Miss: Half damage, and no penalty.

Grim Instruction — Warlord Attack 15

With a remarkable show of skill, you school your foe, revealing the flaws in its fighting style.

Daily ✦ Martial, Reliable, Weapon
Standard Action   **Melee** weapon
Target: One creature
Attack: Strength vs. Fortitude

Hit: 3[W] + Strength modifier damage, and the target takes a -2 penalty to attack rolls and grants combat advantage to you and your allies (save ends both).

Infectious Determination — Warlord Attack 15

With each strike you deliver, your allies gain more resolve to grab victory from the jaws of defeat.

Daily ✦ Healing, Martial, Weapon
Standard Action   **Melee** weapon
Target: One creature
Primary Attack: Strength vs. AC
Hit: 2[W] + Strength modifier damage.
Miss: Half damage.
Effect: As a free action, each ally within 5 squares of you can make a saving throw. Make a secondary attack against the target.
  Resourceful Presence: Each ally gains a power bonus to the saving throw equal to your Intelligence modifier.
  Secondary Attack: Strength vs. Fortitude
  Hit: 1[W] + Strength modifier damage, and you knock the target prone. Each ally within 5 squares of you can spend a healing surge as a free action.
  Resourceful Presence: Each ally adds your Charisma modifier to the hit points regained.

War Master's Assault — Warlord Attack 15

You orchestrate a devastating coordinated attack.

Daily ✦ Martial
Standard Action   **Close** burst 3
Targets: You and each ally in burst
Effect: Each target can charge or make a basic attack as a free action, with a power bonus to the attack roll and the damage roll equal to your Charisma modifier.

LEVEL 16 UTILITY EXPLOITS

Decisive Timing — Warlord Utility 16

Practice has honed your party's maneuvering to near perfection.

Encounter ✦ Martial
No Action   **Close** burst 5
Trigger: You and your allies make initiative checks at the beginning of an encounter
Targets: You and two allies in burst or three allies in burst
Effect: You swap the initiative check results of the targets.
  Tactical Presence: Until the end of his or her first turn in the encounter, the target with the lowest initiative result gains a power bonus to damage rolls equal to your Intelligence modifier.

Encouraging Remark — Warlord Utility 16

You whisper a few words of support to a comrade heading back into the fray.

Encounter ✦ Martial
Standard Action   **Melee** 1
Target: One ally
Effect: The target gains temporary hit points equal to 10 + your Charisma modifier. Until the end of your next turn, the target also gains a power bonus to damage rolls, one defense, or saving throws equal to your Charisma modifier.

Flanking Stance — Warlord Utility 16

You take up a vulnerable position that forces your enemies into disadvantageous positions as well.

Daily ✦ Martial, Stance
Minor Action   **Personal**
Effect: Until the stance ends, any enemy adjacent to you gains combat advantage against you but grants combat advantage to your allies.
  Bravura Presence: Allies gain a bonus to melee damage rolls against enemies adjacent to you equal to your Charisma modifier.

Side by Side — Warlord Utility 16

You and an ally form a deadly team, fighting in tandem.

Daily ✦ Martial, Stance
Minor Action   **Melee** 1
Target: One ally
Effect: Until the stance ends, you and the target both gain a +2 power bonus to attack rolls, AC, and Reflex when you're adjacent to each other.

Warning Shout — Warlord Utility 16

Hearing your call of alarm, your friend leaps for cover.

Daily ✦ Martial
Immediate Interrupt   **Close** burst 5
Trigger: An ally within 5 squares of you is hit by a ranged or an area attack
Target: The triggering ally in burst
Effect: The target can shift a number of squares equal to 1 + your Intelligence modifier.

LEVEL 17 ENCOUNTER EXPLOITS

Bloody Termination — Warlord Attack 17

Your adversary reels from wounds, and you mean to bring that torment to an end.

Encounter ✦ Martial, Weapon
Standard Action   **Melee** weapon
Target: One bloodied creature
Attack: Strength vs. AC
Hit: 3[W] + Strength modifier + Charisma modifier damage.
     Resourceful Presence: If the attack's damage doesn't reduce the target to 0 hit points, make a melee basic attack against the target, with a bonus to the attack roll and the damage roll equal to your Charisma modifier.

Deadly Inspiration — Warlord Attack 17

Your bold strike inspires your allies to show off their fighting prowess.

Encounter ✦ Martial, Weapon
Standard Action   **Melee** weapon
Target: One creature
Attack: Strength vs. Reflex
Hit: 2[W] + Strength modifier damage, and allies within 5 squares of you deal 1[W] extra damage with their at-will weapon attacks that hit until the start of your next turn.

Girding Strike — Warlord Attack 17

You smite your enemy as you shout encouragement to your allies, imparting the vigor they need to push on.

Encounter ✦ Healing, Martial, Weapon
Standard Action   **Melee** weapon
Target: One creature
Attack: Strength vs. AC
Hit: 3[W] + Strength modifier damage, and each ally within 10 squares of you regains the use of second wind.
     Resourceful Presence: Any ally who uses second wind before the end of your next turn regains additional hit points equal to your Charisma modifier.

MARTIAL HEALING

What explains your warlord's ability to heal your allies' wounds? It might seem almost magical—and certainly at the highest levels it is superhuman. But your *inspiring word* is fundamentally a reflection of your ability to get your allies to do their best. Under your leadership, they can draw on reserves they didn't know they had, perform heroic deeds they never thought they could, and keep fighting when the pain and terror would otherwise bring them down.

WAYNE ENGLAND

Into the Breach! — Warlord Attack 17

You leap forward boldly, shouting a battle cry that fills your allies with the same courage.

Encounter ✦ Martial, Weapon
Standard Action   Melee weapon
Target: One creature
Attack: Strength vs. AC
Hit: 2[W] + Strength modifier damage, and one ally within 5 squares of you can charge the target as a free action.
   Inspiring Presence: The charging ally gains a power bonus to the attack roll and the damage roll equal to your Charisma modifier.
Special: When charging, you can use this power in place of a melee basic attack.

LEVEL 19 DAILY EXPLOITS

Exhorted Counterattack — Warlord Attack 19

You shout a warning to a comrade under fire, who avoids the brunt of the attack and responds with a vicious counterattack.

Daily ✦ Healing, Martial
Immediate Reaction   Close burst 20
Trigger: An ally within 20 squares of you is hit by an enemy
Target: The triggering ally in burst
Effect: The target regains hit points as if he or she had spent a healing surge and then makes two basic attacks against the attacking enemy as an opportunity action. If either basic attack hits, the enemy is dazed (save ends).
   Inspiring Presence: The ally regains additional hit points equal to your Charisma modifier and gains a bonus to the damage rolls equal to your Charisma modifier.

Inspiring Charge — Warlord Attack 19

Giving your companions a quick signal, you charge forward to glory, inspiring them.

Daily ✦ Healing, Martial, Weapon
Standard Action   Melee weapon
Target: One creature
Attack: Strength vs. AC
Hit: 4[W] + Strength modifier damage.
Effect: As a free action, each ally within 10 squares of you can shift a number of squares equal to your Charisma modifier and then spend a healing surge.
Special: When charging, you can use this power in place of a melee basic attack.

Storm of Carnage — Warlord Attack 19

For you and your comrades, every miss is just a new opportunity.

Daily ✦ Martial, Weapon
Standard Action   Melee weapon
Target: One creature
Attack: Strength vs. AC
Hit: 4[W] + Strength modifier damage.
Miss: Make a melee basic attack against the target.
Effect: Until the end of the encounter, each time you or an adjacent ally misses with an encounter or a daily melee attack power, that character can make a melee basic attack against the same target as a free action.

Unleash Hell — Warlord Attack 19

On your command, you and your allies unleash a ranged barrage upon your enemies.

Daily ✦ Martial, Weapon
Standard Action   Ranged weapon
Requirement: You must be wielding a heavy thrown weapon.
Target: One creature
Attack: Strength vs. AC. The attack can score a critical hit on a roll of 18–20.
Hit: 4[W] + Strength modifier damage.
Effect: Each ally within 5 squares of you can make a ranged basic attack against an enemy as a free action, with a power bonus to the attack roll and the damage roll equal to your Charisma modifier. Until the end of your next turn, any ranged attack made by you or your allies can score a critical hit on a natural roll of 18–20.

LEVEL 22 UTILITY EXPLOITS

Avenge Me — Warlord Utility 22

As you succumb to your injuries, you shout out a call for retribution.

Daily ✦ Healing, Martial
Immediate Interrupt   Close burst 10
Trigger: You are reduced to 0 hit points or fewer by an enemy
Target: Each ally in burst
Effect: Each target can spend a healing surge and regain additional hit points equal to your Charisma modifier. Until the end of the encounter, the targets gain a +2 power bonus to attack rolls and damage rolls.

Bloodthirsty Offensive — Warlord Utility 22

You have your foes against the wall, and you focus your attention on finishing the job.

Daily ✦ Martial, Stance
Minor Action   Personal
Effect: Until the stance ends, you grant combat advantage to all enemies. In addition, you and each ally within 10 squares of you gain a +2 power bonus to attack rolls against bloodied enemies. Also, each time you or an ally within 10 squares of you spends an action point to take an extra action, that character can make a basic attack as a free action before taking the extra action.
   Bravura Presence: You and each ally within 10 squares of you gain a bonus to damage rolls against bloodied enemies equal to your Charisma modifier.

Quickening Order — Warlord Utility 22

You aim to win the fight before your foes can respond.

Daily ✦ Martial
No Action   Close burst 10
Trigger: You and your allies make initiative checks at the beginning of an encounter
Targets: You and each ally in burst
Effect: Each target gains a bonus to the initiative check equal to your Intelligence modifier, and during each target's first turn, he or she gains a bonus to attack rolls and damage rolls equal to your Intelligence modifier.

Rush of Battle
Warlord Utility 22

You raise your voice above the din, encouraging your allies to make a rapid series of attacks.

Daily ✦ Martial
Minor Action   **Close** burst 5
Target: Each ally in burst
Effect: Until the start of your next turn, each target can make basic attacks as minor actions.
     Resourceful Presence: Each target gains a bonus to the basic attack rolls equal to your Intelligence or Charisma modifier.

Stirring Declaration
Warlord Attack 22

As you attack, you cheer your friends on toward victory.

Daily ✦ Martial, Stance
Minor Action   **Personal**
Requirement: You must be trained in Diplomacy.
Effect: Until the stance ends, each time you hit an enemy with an attack, allies within 10 squares of you gain temporary hit points equal to 5 + your Charisma modifier. You and your allies gain a bonus to saving throws against fear effects equal to your Charisma modifier.
     Inspiring Presence: Each time you hit an enemy with an attack, one ally within 10 squares of you can make a saving throw.

LEVEL 23 ENCOUNTER EXPLOITS

Blood Begets Blood
Warlord Attack 23

With a brutal strike and a marshalling cry, you open your enemy's defenses. Your allies respond with a coordinated assault.

Encounter ✦ Martial, Weapon
Standard Action   **Melee** weapon
Target: One creature
Attack: Strength vs. AC
Hit: 3[W] + Strength modifier damage. If the target is bloodied or reduced to 0 hit points by this attack, two allies within 5 squares of you can each make a basic attack as a free action.
     Resourceful Presence: If the target is bloodied or reduced to 0 hit points by this attack, three allies within 5 squares of you can each make a basic attack as a free action.

Daring Display
Warlord Attack 23

You fling yourself against your enemy brutally, unleashing a fury that draws the eye of nearby enemies.

Encounter ✦ Martial, Weapon
Standard Action   **Melee** weapon
Target: One creature
Attack: Strength vs. Fortitude
Hit: 4[W] + Strength modifier damage, and you mark and grant combat advantage to every enemy within 2 squares of you until the end of your next turn. Each of the enemies that attacks you grants combat advantage to your allies until the end of its next turn.
     Bravura Presence: The attack deals extra damage equal to your Charisma modifier, and you can shift 1 square, whether or not you hit.

Quickening Force — Warlord Attack 23

The punishing blow you land on your enemy causes your allies to take heart and defy ill fortune.

Encounter ✦ Martial, Weapon
Standard Action   Melee weapon
Target: One creature
Attack: Strength vs. AC
Hit: 4[W] + Strength modifier damage, and each ally within 5 squares of you can make a saving throw.
   Resourceful Presence: Your allies gain a power bonus to the saving throw equal to your Charisma modifier.

Ringing Clarity — Warlord attack 23

The clang of your steel on your enemy's armor clears the cobwebs from your allies' heads.

Encounter ✦ Martial, Weapon
Standard Action   Melee weapon
Target: One creature
Attack: Strength vs. AC
Hit: 4[W] + Strength modifier damage, and the marked condition ends on any ally within 10 squares of you. Also, each ally within 10 squares of you automatically saves against a charm or a fear effect that a save can end.

Shutdown Smite — Warlord Attack 23

A well-placed attack throws your foe out of prime fighting form for a moment.

Encounter ✦ Martial, Weapon
Standard Action   Melee weapon
Target: One creature
Attack: Strength vs. Will
Hit: 3[W] + Strength modifier damage, and the target cannot recharge any of its powers or use action points until the end of your next turn.
   Tactical Presence: The target also takes a penalty to saving throws equal to your Intelligence modifier until the end of your next turn.

Wounding Focus — Warlord Attack 23

You open a small wound on your foe as a pinpoint target for your allies.

Encounter ✦ Martial, Weapon
Standard Action   Melee weapon
Target: One creature
Attack: Strength vs. Reflex
Hit: 2[W] + Strength modifier damage. Until the start of your next turn, your allies gain combat advantage against the target and a power bonus to damage rolls against it equal to your Intelligence modifier.

WARLORD PERSONALITIES

Different warlord builds suggest different personalities. An inspiring or bravura warlord might exhort allies to mighty deeds through poetic speech or inspire allies through brave, perhaps even foolhardy, action. A tactical warlord might be more of a thinker, calculating odds, planning three rounds ahead in every fight, and mapping out each ally's best position. A resourceful warlord combines a thinking approach with keen instincts to find the best plan in each moment, changing strategies as circumstances shift.

LEVEL 25 DAILY EXPLOITS

Precision Stance — Warlord Attack 25

You take on a watchful bearing, lending your allies your battle acumen, allowing their wilder strikes to hit home more often.

Daily ✦ Martial, Stance
Minor Action   Personal
Effect: Until the stance ends, when an ally within 5 squares of you misses with an attack, you can take an immediate interrupt to allow the ally to reroll the attack roll with a bonus equal to your Intelligence modifier.

Primordial Onslaught — Warlord Attack 25

You attack like a force of nature, driving your opponents before you.

Daily ✦ Martial, Weapon
Standard Action   Close burst 1
Target: Each enemy in burst
Attack: Strength vs. Will
Hit: 4[W] + Strength modifier damage.
Effect: Until the end of the encounter, each time you or an ally attacks any target of this power, you can slide the target 1 square after resolving the attack.

Sleeping Dragon Lure · Warlord Attack 25

You land a light blow to make yourself look weak, and when a foe gives in to temptation and attacks you, you explode in a burst of violence.

Daily ✦ Martial, Weapon
Standard Action   **Melee** weapon
Primary Target: One creature
Primary Attack: Strength vs. AC
Hit: 2[W] + Strength modifier damage.
Effect: You grant combat advantage to enemies that make melee attacks against you until the start of your next turn. If an enemy hits you with a melee attack while this effect lasts, you can make a secondary attack against the attacker as an immediate interrupt. You can shift 1 square closer to the secondary target before making the secondary attack. If no enemy attacks you in melee before the start of your next turn, you regain the use of this power.
  Secondary Target: The attacking creature
  Secondary Attack: Strength vs. AC
  Hit: 4[W] + Strength modifier damage.
  Bravura Presence: You gain a bonus to the secondary attack's attack roll and damage roll equal to your Charisma modifier.

Victorious Destiny · Warlord Attack 25

Your decisive strike turns the tide of battle as your allies find renewed ferocity.

Daily ✦ Martial, Reliable, Weapon
Standard Action   **Melee** weapon
Requirement: You must be bloodied.
Target: One creature
Attack: Strength vs. AC
Hit: 6[W] + Strength modifier damage, and allies gain a +2 bonus to attack rolls until the end of the encounter.

Warlord's Resurgence · Warlord Attack 25

With deific speed and precision, you call out an opening for an ally's attack. You also spot an opportunity that you can later exploit.

Daily ✦ Martial
Standard Action   **Close** burst 10
Target: One ally in burst
Effect: As a free action, the target can make an attack using an encounter attack power that he or she has already used during this encounter, and the target gains a +2 bonus to the attack roll. Also, if you have used all your encounter attack powers, you regain the use of a warlord encounter attack power you have used during this encounter.

Wave of Defeat · Warlord Attack 25

You and your comrades hurl your foes backward in a furious simultaneous assault.

Daily ✦ Martial, Weapon
Standard Action   **Melee** weapon
Target: One creature
Attack: Strength vs. Fortitude
Hit: 4[W] + Strength modifier damage, and you push the target 2 squares.
Miss: Half damage, and no push.
Effect: Each ally within 5 squares of you can make a melee basic attack as a free action. On a hit, the ally can push his or her target 1 square.

LEVEL 27 ENCOUNTER EXPLOITS

Abrupt Skirmish · Warlord Attack 27

Using feigned weakness or harsh words, you goad your enemies to attack you. Your allies instantly fall upon your foes in turn.

Encounter ✦ Martial, Weapon
Standard Action   **Close** burst 2
Target: Each enemy in burst you can see
Effect: You pull each target 1 square to a space adjacent to you. You can't pull a target that can't end adjacent to you. You then attack one of the targets.
Attack: Strength vs. AC
Hit: 4[W] + Strength modifier damage. Each enemy adjacent to you can make a melee basic attack against you as a free action, but each of your allies can make a basic attack against the enemy as an opportunity action triggered by the enemy's attack.
  Bravura Presence: Each ally gains a power bonus to the attack roll and the damage roll equal to your Charisma modifier.

Brutal Setup · Warlord Attack 27

After a cautious approach, you deliver a wicked smite and your enemy staggers, becoming an obvious target for your friends.

Encounter ✦ Martial, Weapon
Standard Action   **Melee** weapon
Targets: One or two creatures
Effect: Before the attack, you can shift 3 squares.
Attack: Strength vs. AC, one attack per target
Hit: 2[W] + Strength modifier damage, and the target is dazed until the end of your next turn.
  Tactical Presence: Until the end of the encounter, your allies gain a power bonus to attack rolls against dazed enemies equal to your Intelligence modifier.

Eye of the Storm · Warlord Attack 27

With a gale of fierce swings, you give your enemies cause to consider you dangerous and your allies cause for hope.

Encounter ✦ Healing, Martial, Weapon
Standard Action   **Close** burst 1
Target: Each enemy in burst you can see
Attack: Strength vs. AC
Hit: 2[W] + Strength modifier damage, and you mark the target until the end of your next turn.
Effect: Until the end of your next turn, any of your allies who hit enemies marked by this power can use a free action either to make a saving throw or to spend a healing surge.
  Resourceful Presence: If an ally makes the saving throw, he or she gains a power bonus to the roll equal to your Intelligence modifier. If an ally spends the healing surge, he or she regains additional hit points equal to your Charisma modifier.

WARLORDS AND POLEARMS

A polearm is a great weapon for a warlord. Many warlord powers rely on specific positioning, granting benefits to allies adjacent to you or the target you're attacking. The reach of a polearm can help you get into the right position to make the best use of those powers.

Uplifting Assault — Warlord Attack 27

Your successful strike fills you with renewed hope that you can use to inspire your comrades.

Encounter ✦ Martial, Weapon
Standard Action   **Melee** weapon
Target: One creature
Attack: Strength vs. AC

Hit: 4[W] + Strength modifier damage, and you gain an additional use of *inspiring word* for this encounter.

 Inspiring Presence: Until the start of your next turn, you can use *inspiring word* as an immediate reaction triggered by an ally taking damage.

Warlord's Indignation — Warlord Attack 27

An enemy dares to strike you, and you hurl him to the ground in retaliation. Your allies then make him pay for his insolence.

Encounter ✦ Martial, Weapon
Immediate Reaction   **Melee** weapon
Trigger: An enemy hits you with a melee attack
Target: The triggering enemy
Attack: Strength vs. Fortitude

Hit: 2[W] + Strength modifier damage, and you knock the target prone. Each of your allies can then make a basic attack against the target as an opportunity action.

LEVEL 29 DAILY EXPLOITS

Deific Rallying — Warlord Attack 29

You loose a tremendous shout, giving your allies confidence and instant attacks.

Daily ✦ Martial, Weapon
Standard Action   **Close** burst 20
Target: Each ally in burst

Effect: Each target gains 20 temporary hit points and can make a basic attack as a free action.

 Inspiring Presence: Each target gains additional temporary hit points and a bonus to the basic attack's damage roll equal to your Charisma modifier.

Flawless Snare — Warlord Attack 29

With a practiced swing, you throw yourself off balance, making yourself into bait and your allies the waiting trap.

Daily ✦ Martial, Weapon
Standard Action   **Melee** weapon
Target: One creature
Attack: Strength vs. AC

Hit: 6[W] + Strength modifier damage.

Effect: You mark the target and grant combat advantage to it until the end of your next turn. Whenever the target attacks you before the end of your next turn, each ally within 10 squares of you can make a basic attack against it as an opportunity action triggered by its attack.

 Bravura Presence: Each ally gains a bonus to the basic attack's attack roll and damage roll equal to your Charisma modifier.

Special: When charging, you can use this power in place of a melee basic attack.

Inexorable Surge — Warlord Attack 29

You deliver a spectacular attack, filling your allies with lethal resolve against your adversaries.

Daily ✦ Martial, Reliable, Weapon
Standard Action   **Melee** weapon
Target: One creature
Attack: Strength + 2 vs. AC

Hit: 6[W] + Strength modifier damage. Until the end of the encounter, your allies gain a bonus to damage rolls against the target equal to your Charisma modifier. When the target is reduced to 0 hit points, choose another enemy within 5 squares of it, and your allies gain the bonus to damage rolls against that enemy. Each time the chosen enemy is reduced to 0 hit points, choose a different enemy within 5 squares of it.

Perfect Front — Warlord Attack 29

With practiced form, you and your allies create a battle line that allows you to attack with godlike precision.

Daily ✦ Martial, Stance
Minor Action   **Personal**

Effect: Until the stance ends, as long as you are adjacent to an ally, roll twice each time you make an attack roll and use the higher result. Any ally adjacent to you gains the same benefit.

 Tactical Presence: You gain the benefit when within 2 squares of an ally, and an ally within 2 squares of you gains the benefit as well.

Wake of Devastation — Warlord Attack 29

Your furious weapon thrusts leave many trails of blood.

Daily ✦ Martial, Weapon
Standard Action   **Close** burst 1
Target: Each enemy in burst you can see
Attack: Strength vs. AC

Hit: 3[W] + Strength modifier damage.

Effect: Each target takes ongoing 15 damage (save ends). Each target taking ongoing damage grants combat advantage to you and your allies.

 Resourceful Presence: You can reduce the damage to 1[W] to add 15 to the ongoing damage, or you can increase the damage to 5[W] by forgoing the ongoing damage.

RALLYING CRY

"Steady," Anastrianna said. Cawing wildly, the shadowravens swarmed closer, and her allies shifted uneasily beside her. "Steady," she said again.

Suddenly, the ravens shot forward like swift arrows shot from a hellish bow. Behind them, their master, a tall sorrowsworn draped in black shrouds, strode forward, its baleful eyes fixed on Anastrianna. She cast her eyes around the barren field. Her friends clutched their weapons, waiting for her word.

"Now!" she cried. "In Corellon's name!"

She felt her own heart surge with elation as her friends leaped forward. She saw their faces refreshed, their courage strong, as each one cut into their enemies. The Raven Queen's minions would die this day, and Anastrianna herself would tell the tale as long as she lived.

BATTLELORD OF KORD

"Fame find me or death take me, I'll storm any field in Kord's name."

Prerequisite: Warlord

Both Kord and Bane exult in battle. Bane sends his followers to conquer and pillage, using war for the sake of unjust gain, wanton violence, or sheer blood-lust. Kord's way is one of accepting challenges as they come and using mastered talents to overcome them. His dogma is one of bravery, strength, and skill. No test of mortal mettle is stronger than the crucible of battle. The glory and fame that Kord admonishes his followers to seek involves striving to win the respect of their fellows for upholding their duty and facing danger with their heads held high.

Warriors and warlords of all sorts esteem Kord. Those who know that fighting is sometimes necessary pray to Kord for favor, rather than to Bane. Such warriors know that it is the fate of a few to stand against senseless destruction and oppression. Kord's followers do so without flinching. They uphold the right to independence that Kord's wild nature demands. When battle is done, revelry, boasting, and toasting—celebrating life and health—are all that Kord requires as thanks.

Numerous schools of military thought use Kord's dogma as part of their philosophy. Leaders must be strong and courageous. They must hone their talents to assure victory and survival in bloody days. Renown should be earned through bold and decisive action that serves as an example to one's comrades. A valiant warlord protects his fellow soldiers by leading from the front and luring in the enemy, as Kord did in older days.

You are a leader who reveres Kord's ways. As such, you have shaped your skills by leading your comrades against many dangers. With a war cry, you fearlessly engage your enemies. You stride among your adversaries, seeking the greatest among them and challenging them with your amazing exploits. Your brashness inspires your allies to decisive action and helps create the opportunities in which triumph can be secured.

BATTLELORD OF KORD PATH FEATURES

Mighty Action (11th level): When you spend an action point to take an extra action, any ally who can see and hear you gains a +1 bonus to attack rolls and damage rolls until the start of your next turn.

Tempestuous Inspiration (11th level): When you use your *inspiring word* power, you can give the target of the power a +2 bonus to attack rolls and a bonus to damage rolls equal to your Charisma modifier that lasts until the end of your next turn. If the target's first attack during that time misses, the target grants combat advantage to attackers until the end of your next turn.

Kord's Focus (16th level): Whenever you are marked, you can immediately make a saving throw against the condition. If you save, the condition ends. Also, you gain a +5 bonus to saving throws against fear effects.

BATTLELORD OF KORD EXPLOITS

Tempest of Triumph	Battlelord of Kord Attack 11

Your killing blow sets off a chain reaction of inspired attacks, potentially laying low all your foes.

Encounter ✦ Martial, Weapon
Standard Action — Melee weapon
Target: One creature
Attack: Strength vs. AC

Hit: 1[W] + Strength modifier + Charisma modifier damage. If this attack reduces the target to 0 hit points, an ally within 5 squares of you can make a basic attack against a different target as an immediate reaction, adding your Charisma modifier to the damage roll. If that ally's attack reduces its target to 0 hit points, a different ally within 5 squares of you gains the same benefit. Repeat until an attack fails to reduce a target to 0 hit points or until you run out of allies within 5 squares.

Blood-Tested Inspiration	Battlelord of Kord Utility 12

Faith in Kord leads you to amazing exploits during the glory of battle.

Daily ✦ Martial
Minor Action — Personal

Effect: Expend one use of *inspiring word* to regain the use of an encounter attack power you have used during this encounter.

Path of the Storm	Battlelord of Kord Attack 20

You roam the field like a rogue thunderhead, striking foes as Kord strikes the earth with lightning.

Daily ✦ Martial, Weapon
Standard Action — Melee weapon

Effect: You can shift a number of squares equal to your Charisma modifier. During this movement, you can make a number of melee basic attacks equal to your Charisma modifier against any enemies within reach. You can use as many of these attacks as you wish against any of the possible targets.

BORDERLANDS MARSHAL

"We are as wolves. Evil is our prey."

Prerequisites: Warlord and ranger

On the bloody frontier, no system of honorable engagement holds. Evil and savage creatures view adherence to principles as weakness, and have no patience for complex plans. Monstrous beasts eat anything they can catch, with no chance for reason or mercy. Indeed, the wilderness as a whole has no respect for the conventions of society. In the wild, you act or you die.

This situation has always been true, even when great empires made portions of the land safe. It is doubly true now that no vast empire holds sway. No unified army stands ready to secure the borders and push back monsters, and few are willing to defend strangers. On the borderlands, far even from independent towns and their militias, people have to make do against the gathering darkness. That darkness grows each passing year as creatures, malevolent or merely hungry, gnaw away at the edges of civilized lands.

You know the wilds. Your experience on the borderlands has pushed you to pragmatism that other leaders lack. You strike first when you can, taking any advantage possible. If your approach fails, you do what is necessary to survive, and then try another tactic. When you attack, you make sure that you and your comrades are as efficient as any pack of predators.

BORDERLANDS MARSHAL FEATURES

Reinforcing Action (11th level): When you spend an action point to take an extra action, each ally who can see and hear you gains a +4 bonus to his or her lowest defense until the start of your next turn. If multiple defenses are tied for lowest, the ally chooses which one gains the bonus.

Grim Satisfaction (11th level): Allies gain a +1 bonus to attack rolls against your quarry.

Open Quarry (16th level): When you or an ally uses the Hunter's Quarry class feature, you or the ally can designate any enemy you can see as the quarry (rather than the nearest enemy).

BORDERLANDS MARSHAL EXPLOITS

Tag Quarry — Borderlands Marshal Attack 11

Your attack shows all who the hunted is.

Encounter ✦ Martial, Weapon
Standard Action   Melee or Ranged weapon
Requirement: You must be wielding a heavy thrown weapon to use this power at range.
Target: One creature
Attack: Strength vs. AC
Hit: 2[W] + Strength modifier, and you can designate the target as your quarry as if you had used the Hunter's Quarry class feature.

Pack Hunter Stance — Borderlands Marshal Utility 12

You fight your chosen foe with a rhythm that shows your comrades how to form up during the assault.

Daily ✦ Martial, Stance
Minor Action   Personal
Effect: Until the stance ends, whenever you hit your quarry, you or one ally within 5 squares of you can shift as a free action.

New Victim — Borderlands Marshal Attack 20

You brutally choose a new quarry by making a swift attack.

Daily ✦ Martial, Weapon
Free Action   Melee or Ranged weapon
Trigger: Your quarry is reduced to 0 hit points
Requirement: You must be wielding a heavy thrown weapon to use this power at range.
Target: One creature
Attack: Strength vs. AC
Hit: 3[W] + Strength modifier.
Miss: Half damage.
Effect: You can designate the target as your quarry as if you had used the Hunter's Quarry class feature.

COMMANDO CAPTAIN

"These roughnecks bow to no king, but they do follow me. Under my command, they can go anywhere and do anything. What do you need?"

Prerequisite: Warlord

Sometimes a small squad of specially trained or highly skilled people can do what an army can't. A precise strike or a cunning raid can turn the tide in many dangerous situations. Numerous nobles and mercantile interests keep or patronize assault teams such as these for situations that call for decisive offensive action. A unit of such specialists can instead become its own employer, attacking and looting monster lairs on the borderlands and becoming rich in the process. Another such group might itself become a menace, turning superior combat prowess toward banditry or tyranny.

The world is in a dark age. Desperate times favor resourceful people. But even bold and venturesome folk need wily leadership to thrive. Such a leader helps a team hit hard and stay mobile, avoiding obstacles, overcoming foes, and keeping one step ahead of the enemy. In fact, precision command and an eye toward stealth can make all the difference in small-squad engagements.

You are such a leader, whether through formal training in elite unit command or as a result of direct experience, or both. Those who observe you might say you're the team's commander, but you see yourself as an expert facilitator among able peers. You know the skills of those with whom you work, and you always have the right trick to keep the whole party in fighting shape. The cohesion you have created among your comrades has seen you through much in the past, and it speaks of your future success.

COMMANDO CAPTAIN PATH FEATURES

Commando Action (11th level): When you spend an action point to take an extra action, an enemy of your choice within 10 squares of you grants combat advantage to you until the end of your next turn.

Camouflaging Command (11th level): When you use a warlord power that grants movement to an ally, that ally gains concealment until the end of your next turn.

Mobility Tactics (16th level): Whenever an adjacent ally shifts, the ally can shift 1 additional square.

COMMANDO CAPTAIN EXPLOITS

Blindside Assault — Commando Captain Attack 11

Your ally makes a sly sidelong attack, which opens up your foe to your surprise attack.

Encounter ✦ Martial, Weapon
Standard Action — **Melee** weapon
Target: One creature
Effect: Before the attack, you slide one ally 6 squares to a space adjacent to the target. The ally can then make a melee basic attack against the target as a free action.
Attack: Strength vs. AC
Hit: 2[W] + Strength modifier damage.

Commando Maneuver — Commando Captain Utility 12

You call on two allies to move watchfully into new positions.

Encounter ✦ Martial
Move Action — **Close** burst 10
Targets: One or two allies in burst
Effect: The targets can shift 3 squares.

Morale-Shaking Strike — Commando Captain Attack 20

Your attack causes your enemy to reel with indecision, which one of your allies can exploit.

Daily ✦ Martial, Weapon
Standard Action — **Melee** weapon
Target: One creature
Attack: Strength vs. AC
Hit: 3[W] + Strength modifier damage.
Miss: Half damage.
Effect: Until the end of the encounter, the target grants combat advantage to an ally of your choice.

CONCORDANT LEADER

"The elements blend together favorably within my soul and on any battlefield where I have command."

Prerequisites: Genasi, warlord

Within the Elemental Chaos, disparate elements battle for supremacy. In numerous places, the land, sky, and sea roil in a never-ending clash of lightning and fire, poison gas and rolling earth, biting water and tearing wind. The chaos is much like a worldly battlefield on which no leader exerts control. Where one element dominates, the will of a mighty force of nature is often what makes it so.

The unrestrained chaos is much like a worldly battlefield on which no skilled leader exerts control. In such a combat zone, forces clash without clear direction. The tide of battle is all too often determined merely by fate. Clear advantage on one side or the other can rarely be overcome. One side overwhelms the other by happenstance or because of uneven odds. Victory is won at too heavy a cost.

A mythological genasi general of the ancient world, Vyn-kazi, knew the price of warfare's chaos all too well. She had witnessed it. Like the entropic realm from which they sprang, the great Primordials warred with the gods with no common purpose and no organization—no plan at all. Most of these mighty beings were fractious and grasping loners with armies of fierce slaves. They all but allowed the gods to coordinate against them. One by one, each and its armies succumbed to the gods and their legions.

Vyn-kazi survived a disastrous battle in which her master, Nekal of the Glowing Deep, fell against a host that included Pelor, Kord, Bane, Ioun, and Sehanine. The watersoul genasi went on to swear fealty to Pelor and to take on a fire-soul aspect in his name. She then led her people against other Primordials in service to the god of the sun, taking the calm blending of two elements in her spirit and what she had witnessed in Nekal's defeat as models for her command style.

Similar to celebrated Vyn-kazi, you have learned to mingle and control the elements that cavort in your body and spirit. Your military training has taught you how to guide a combat to triumph by blending the skills of your allies with the needs and variables of the challenge. You have applied your life's lessons to your teaching, acknowledging that every clash is a meeting of contrasting elements. By carefully mixing those forces, you need not rely on fortune for your success.

CONCORDANT LEADER PATH FEATURES

Concordant Action (11th level): When you spend an action point to take an extra action, you can also change your elemental manifestation to any other you are capable of manifesting. When you do, you also regain the use of the power associated with the new manifestation if you have used it during this encounter.

Extra Manifestation (11th level): You gain the Extra Manifestation feat (*Forgotten Realms Player's Guide*). If you already have the feat, you instead select any other feat for which you meet the prerequisites.

Concordant Resistance (16th level): You gain resist 5 to cold, fire, and lightning. While any ally is adjacent to you, he or she gains the same resistances. These resistances are not cumulative with any other resistance you or your allies possess.

CONCORDANT LEADER EXPLOITS

Borrowed Protection — Concordant Leader Attack 11

Your elemental soul allows you to tap into your enemy's resistance to protect another.

Encounter ✦ Martial, Weapon
Standard Action — Melee weapon
Target: One creature
Attack: Strength vs. AC
Hit: 3[W] + Strength modifier damage. If the target has any resistances, you grant the same resistances to yourself or an ally within 10 squares of you until the end of your next turn.

Shared Manifestation — Concordant Leader Utility 12

You call upon the elemental power within you, imbuing a temporary fragment of it into a nearby ally.

Daily ✦ Martial
Minor Action — Close burst 5
Target: One ally in burst
Effect: The target shares one elemental manifestation you are currently manifesting. The target can use the associated racial power of that manifestation, even if you have used that power during this encounter. If the target already has an elemental manifestation, the new manifestation replaces the previous one for the duration of this effect. The effect lasts until the end of the encounter or until you take a minor action to end it.

Elemental-Heart Strike — Concordant Leader Attack 20

You channel your energy resistance into a potent melee attack, briefly leaving yourself unprotected.

Daily ✦ Martial, Weapon; Cold, Fire, or Lightning
Standard Action — Melee weapon
Target: One creature
Attack: Strength vs. AC
Hit: 3[W] + Strength modifier damage. You lose your resistance to cold, fire, or lightning until the start of your next turn—whichever resistance is highest—and the attack deals extra damage equal to that resistance and of the damage type opposed by the resistance.
Miss: Half damage, and no extra damage.

Dujun of Erathis

"When diplomacy and philosophy fail, war brings advancement to the benighted."

Prerequisite: Warlord

Progress, taming of the wilds for the good of all, innovation, collaboration, and the rule of law—these are the values Erathis has set before mortals. Yet the nature of the world opposes her. Empires rise like beacons only to be shattered within a few centuries, leaving flickering shards of civilization behind. Still, in each age, a mighty and ambitious few rise to beat back the shadows and create a safe haven for common folk.

Those who follow Erathis's edicts range from plucky adventurers who rid the wilderness of dangers to would-be lords who subdue untamed lands to call their own. The god of civilization delights in the expansion of organized habitation. She blesses those who boldly make way for progress, as well as those who defend existing societies against fell beasts.

To truly and fully take Erathis's dogma to heart is to embrace both cooperation and leadership. You must be educated in the ways of governance and regulation, as well as be cognizant of the follies of history that ravaged the cultures of old. You must look outside the confines of secure walls and take Erathis's banner to new territory. To sit idly within the halls of established civilized edifices simply won't do.

So far, you have proven to be one of the few who can undertake this mission. You know that a true leader must be an authority in combat and in peace, but also be a guide who elicits the help of capable collaborators. You cultivate camaraderie, planning a meaningful role for all in battle and outside it. You have polished your party into the perfect cohesive unit, proven by the extraordinary heights at which it performs under your guidance. Now, it's time to move onward to broader conquest and, perhaps, your own dominion.

Dujun of Erathis Path Features

Organizing Action (11th level): You can spend an action point to grant each ally who can see and hear you an extra move action on his or her next turn, instead of taking an extra action yourself.

Communal Aid (11th level): When you use *inspiring word*, the target can spend one of your healing surges instead of his or her own, but still using his or her healing surge value.

Solidarity's Virtue (16th level): You and allies within 10 squares of you gain an extra +1 bonus when flanking or aiding another.

Dujun of Erathis Exploits

Graded Assault — Dujun of Erathis Attack 11

Your strike sends the enemy reeling, and it opens the way for a series of attacks from your comrades.

Encounter ✦ Martial, Weapon
Standard Action Melee weapon
Target: One creature
Attack: Strength vs. Will
Hit: Deal your Strength modifier in damage. Until the start of your next turn, the target is dazed, and any ally within 5 squares of you who attacks the target with an at-will attack power can determine his or her attack result as if the result of the roll was a 10, instead of rolling the die.

Unification Stance — Dujun of Erathis Utility 12

Your very presence, symbolizing the unity of your allies, aids in their recovery.

Daily ✦ Martial, Stance
Minor Action Personal
Effect: Until the stance ends, at the end of each of your turns, each ally within 5 squares of you can make a saving throw.

Diplomacy of Steel — Dujun of Erathis Attack 20

Each of your movements buttresses the impression of overwhelming force and perfect coordination among your allies.

Daily ✦ Martial, Weapon
Standard Action Melee weapon
Target: One creature
Attack: Strength vs. Will. Gain a bonus to the attack roll equal to the number of allies within 2 squares of you (maximum bonus of +4).
Hit: 3[W] + Strength modifier damage.
Effect: After the first attack, you can make a melee basic attack against the target. If the first attack reduced the target to 0 hit points, you instead gain temporary hit points equal to 10 + your Intelligence modifier, and then you can shift 2 squares and make a melee basic attack against another target.

LUCIO PARRILLO

EARTHFAST BRIGADIER

"Like Bergrom Earthfast, I endure."

Prerequisite: Warlord

A connection to the earth defines dwarves as a connection to woodlands defines elves. All dwarves intuitively heed the earth's example, from the sustenance and riches it provides to the inexorable might of the landslide it spawns. Dwarf bodies are durable; more than once they've been compared to the dirt and stone that dwarves treasure. Any would be dwarf hero does well to take advantage of this natural sturdiness.

Innate toughness is a hallmark of dwarf soldiers and their leaders. Vigor makes for a soldier who can outlast the enemy by withstanding hardship and injury. A robust officer pushes troops onward not only with words, but also by determined example. Dwarf warriors are renowned for their endurance.

Bergrom Earthfast, a dwarf general of legend, exemplifies the ideal dwarf warlord. Mighty in body and mind, Bergrom led his troops against giants before dwarves became free from the slavery of the titans. He endured supernatural elements, fell magic, and the treacherous wilds of old to help bring freedom to his people. His legacy endures in a martial tradition that values a sturdy body and the ability to get one's allies to make the most of their own endurance, as much as it does tactical acumen. Although Bergrom was a dwarf and relied on dwarven resilience, his techniques have spread to other peoples. Anyone who values toughness and spirit in a soldier might learn these ancient methods.

You are such a leader. Even if you didn't acquire formal training in Bergrom's leadership approach—or aren't a dwarf—your talents have led you in a similar direction. Relying on a hardy constitution and heavy weapons as tools, you help your allies push the limits of mortal endurance. Your enemies are hard pressed to keep up.

EARTHFAST BRIGADIER FEATURES

Enduring Action (11th level): When you spend an action point to take an extra action, you and each ally within 5 squares of you can make a saving throw as a free action.

Earthfast Recovery (11th level): When you or any ally within 5 squares of you uses second wind while bloodied, that character regains additional hit points equal to one-half your level + your Constitution modifier.

Dwarven Payback (16th level): Whenever an enemy misses you with a melee or a ranged attack, you can choose one ally you can see as a free action. Until the end of the ally's next turn, the ally gains a power bonus to damage rolls equal to your Constitution modifier against the triggering enemy.

EARTHFAST BRIGADIER EXPLOITS

Earthfast Assault — Earthfast Brigadier Attack 11

Battering your foe mercilessly, you render it unable to move carefully.

Encounter ✦ Martial, Weapon
Standard Action — Melee weapon
Requirement: You must be using a shield.
Target: One creature
Attack: Strength vs. Fortitude
Hit: 2[W] + Strength modifier damage. If the enemy moves before the end of your next turn, it grants combat advantage to you and your allies until the end of your next turn.
Weapon: If you're wielding an axe or a hammer, the attack deals extra damage equal to your Constitution modifier.

Press the Advantage — Earthfast Brigadier Utility 12

You know how to pressure an enemy so that its faltering is inevitable.

Encounter ✦ Martial
Free Action — Melee 1
Target: One creature
Effect: The target takes a penalty to its next saving throw equal to your Constitution modifier.

Stonechannel Strike — Earthfast Brigadier Attack 20

With this powerful strike, you can turn the tide of battle.

Daily ✦ Healing, Martial, Weapon
Standard Action — Melee weapon
Target: One creature
Attack: Strength vs. AC
Hit: 4[W] + Strength modifier damage, and each ally within 5 squares of you regains hit points equal to 5 + your Constitution modifier.
Weapon: If you're wielding an axe or a hammer, the attack deals extra damage equal to your Constitution modifier.
Effect: You and each ally who can see you regain the use of second wind.

FLAMEBROW COMMANDER

"You've awakened the dragon. Now you face the fire."

Prerequisites: Warlord, Bravura Presence class feature

A dragon driven to wrath is a terrifying foe. It stops at nothing to quench its fury in the blood of those who wronged it. Only the desire to protect its young can drive a dragon to even greater heights of recklessness. A dragonborn warrior is little different, and a dragonborn officer displays parental loyalty to those alongside whom he fights. Such is the dragonborn warrior ideal.

An exemplar of this standard was Dhuryan Flamebrow, an audacious but beloved dragonborn mercenary from the fringes of the empire of Arkhosia. Dhuryan was noble born, but upon him fell the consequences of his father's dark deeds. Without title or property in the empire, and living under the shadow of family history, he made his way as a soldier and leader. He made a habit of leading from the front with a brashness born of being indifferent to death. Glory and the erasing of the past was his overriding aim, yet he was unwilling to sacrifice his fellow fighters for his own gain.

Dhuryan succeeded in reshaping the armies of a border province known for its barbarism and monster problems. Eventually, that province and its dragon lord became the most prominent in Arkhosia, although only Dhuryan's name is widely remembered to this day. At long last, Dhuryan had cleansed his family name. He rose then to prominence as a military advisor and became a general in the wars that eventually destroyed Arkhosia. During this time, he penned the military manifesto titled *Flamebrow*, in honor of his clan. Myths from many cultures say that Dhuryan fought in numerous wars in this world and beyond, and that he fell but returned to life more than once. Tales say that he stands now beyond the touch of time, alongside other legendary generals, awaiting the world's need.

Flamebrow still exists, copied into many languages. It is a treatise for the commander who wishes to defeat enemies head-on. Although it speaks of deceptive planning and long-term strategies, it also talks of brutal efficiency and courageous leadership when battle is joined.

Whether through influence, reading and practice, or direct training, your path has been influenced by *Flamebrow*. Boldness of action fails to fully describe your methods. You act decisively, willing to lay your own survival on the line to get the job done and protect your allies.

FLAMEBROW COMMANDER PATH FEATURES

Relentless Action (11th level): When you spend an action point to take an extra action, you can use your Bravura Presence class feature as if you were your own ally.

Flamebrow Revival (11th level): When you are dying, you add your Charisma modifier to any hit points you regain, and you gain a bonus to death saving throws equal to your Charisma modifier.

Roaring Recovery (16th level): Each time you regain hit points when you are bloodied, you gain a +2 bonus to attack rolls until the end of your next turn.

FLAMEBROW COMMANDER EXPLOITS

Flamebrow Assault	Flamebrow Commander Attack 11

On your cue, your comrade attacks. You build on his or her success to land your own strike.

Encounter ✦ Martial, Weapon
Standard Action   **Melee** weapon
Target: One creature
Effect: Before the attack, one bloodied ally within 5 squares of you can make a basic attack as a free action, with a bonus to the attack roll equal to your Charisma modifier. If that attack hits, you gain a +2 bonus to your attack roll; if it misses, you take a –2 penalty to your attack roll.
Attack: Strength vs. AC
Hit: 3[W] + Strength modifier damage.

Rallying Lure	Flamebrow Commander Utility 12

Paying more attention to the welfare of your flagging friends than to your own safety, you shout heartening words.

Daily ✦ Healing, Martial, Stance
Minor Action   **Personal**
Effect: Until the stance ends, you grant combat advantage to all enemies. At the start of your turn, each bloodied ally within 5 squares of you regains hit points equal to your Charisma modifier. If no bloodied allies are within 5 squares of you at the start of your turn, the stance ends.

Renewal Smite	Flamebrow Commander Attack 20

An ally pushes to greater heights, urged on by your dauntless attack.

Daily ✦ Martial, Reliable, Weapon
Standard Action   **Melee** weapon
Target: One creature
Attack: Strength vs. AC
Hit: 4[W] + Strength modifier damage, and one bloodied ally you can see regains the use of an encounter attack power he or she has used during this encounter.

Infernal Strategist

"No pact binds me to a single strategy."

Prerequisites: Warlord, Resourceful Presence class feature

Bael Turath's armies were warlike beyond mortal measure. Backed by the power of the Nine Hells, the leaders of the tiefling empire thought their forces could overcome any challenge. And in fact the legions of Bael Turath were often victorious, a testament to their officers as much as their supernatural might.

The most infamous of Bael Turath's generals was a tiefling known today as Malachi. As a lower-ranking officer in campaigns of conquest, Malachi proved to be a disciplined and innovative commander, renowned for being able to adapt to any situation. He watched and learned from his enemies, changed tactics at pivotal moments, and regularly used what he knew of his enemies against them. Malachi never knew defeat until he faced forces under the command of Dhuryan Flamebrow of Arkhosia.

Stories differ on what happened next. Some say Arkhosia's leaders put Malachi to death. Others claim that he retired alongside Dhuryan, whom he befriended. A few claim that Malachi now marshals the forces of the Nine Hells.

Whatever his fate, Malachi's brilliance is the root of a tradition of battlefield leadership that has spread across the world. A collection of writings from Bael Turath known as *The Hellpath Tome* supposedly preserves a portion of Malachi's own writings. You might have benefited from such education. Perhaps your leanings led you on a crafty path much like Malachi's. Whatever your background, you know how to conjure victory from situations most dire.

Infernal Strategist Path Features

Felling Action (11th level): You can spend an action point as a free action to allow an ally who can see and hear you to reroll an attack roll.

Infernal Pincer (11th level): When you and an ally are both flanking an enemy, you and that ally gain a bonus to melee damage rolls against that enemy equal to your Intelligence or Charisma modifier.

Pliable Command (16th level): You gain a second warlord Commanding Presence. You can apply only one Commanding Presence benefit for each action point spent.

Infernal Strategist Exploits

Deceiver's Ploy — Infernal Strategist Attack 11

You feint, then lunge, setting your foe off balance.

Encounter ✦ Martial, Weapon
Standard Action   Melee weapon
Target: One creature
Attack: Strength vs. Will. If you are using a shield, you gain combat advantage for this attack.
Hit: 2[W] + Strength modifier damage, and the target takes a –2 penalty to attack rolls until the end of your next turn.

Flexible Authority — Infernal Strategist Utility 12

You have the answer for any desperate situation.

Encounter ✦ Healing, Martial
Immediate Reaction   Close burst 10
Trigger: One ally within 10 squares of you spends an action point to take an extra action
Target: The triggering ally in burst
Effect: You choose for the target to gain one of the following benefits: regain hit points equal to one-half your level + your Charisma modifier; gain a bonus to the extra action's attack rolls equal to one-half your Intelligence modifier; gain a bonus to the extra action's damage rolls equal to one-half your level + your Intelligence modifier; or make a basic attack or take a move action as a free action but grant combat advantage to all enemies until the end of his or her next turn.

Smite of Devil's Luck — Infernal Strategist Attack 20

Your intrepid attack lands, setting up the opportunity for greater daring.

Daily ✦ Martial, Reliable, Weapon
Standard Action   Melee weapon
Target: One creature
Attack: Strength vs. AC
Hit: 4[W] + Strength modifier damage. You gain an action point, which must be spent before the end of the encounter or it is lost. Spending this action point doesn't count against the normal limit of action points spent per encounter.

LONGARM MARSHAL

"I prefer my foes on the end of a spear."

Prerequisite: Warlord

The spear and its cousins have existed almost as long as creation. It was the first weapon ever made, and it and its variants are still the most common arms in use. Simple spears are designed heavy for melee or light for throwing. A melee spear can be used with one hand or two. Specialized variations of the spear such as the longspear, the tratnyr (described in *Adventurer's Vault*), and various polearms were specifically designed for war. Such weapons provide a huge boon in the form of reach, allowing a wielder to strike from relative safety and to control the melee. Others, the tratnyr in particular, are multipurpose.

Spears are the perfect weapon choice for small-unit commanders who like flexibility. Javelins and other thrown spears enable their wielders to loose volleys at a closing enemy, or make a viable option against a foe that prefers to stay at a distance. With a single spear, a warrior can choose to fight with a shield or without. Longspears and polearms allow an officer to contribute to combat while leading from behind the front line, where the clash can be better observed and directed.

Cognizant of the benefits of the spear, you chose to specialize in this multifaceted weapon. You trained to make long lunges and quick jabs with your weapon. A spear's haft is a defensive tool for you, and you have learned how to hedge in your foes or open deep wounds. Your skill is a blessing to your allies, who have seen that your mastery makes you a more reliable leader.

LONGARM MARSHAL PATH FEATURES

Accurate Thrust (11th level): You gain a +1 bonus to attack rolls when wielding a spear.

Longarm Action (11th level): When you spend an action point to take an extra action, you increase your melee reach by 1 square when wielding a spear until the end of your next turn.

Bristling Reach (16th level): Whenever an enemy within your melee reach moves without shifting or makes a ranged attack, you can deal damage equal to your Intelligence modifier to that enemy as an opportunity action.

LONGARM MARSHAL EXPLOITS

Driving Spear — Longarm Marshal Attack 11

You force your foe away with a pointed thrust.

Encounter ✦ Martial, Weapon
Standard Action   **Melee** or **Ranged** weapon
Requirement: You must be wielding a spear.
Target: One creature
Attack: Strength vs. Fortitude
Hit: 2[W] + Strength modifier damage, and you push the target a number of squares equal to your Intelligence modifier.

Whirling Spear — Longarm Marshal Utility 12

Using your spear's haft like a staff, you deftly parry incoming attacks.

Daily ✦ Martial, Stance
Minor Action   **Personal**
Requirement: You must be wielding a spear.
Effect: Until the stance ends, you gain a +1 bonus to AC, or a +2 bonus to AC when wielding a spear with two hands.

Vital Rend — Longarm Marshal Attack 20

With a stab and a twist, you tear a wound that saps vitality, weakening the enemy's resistance to subsequent blows.

Daily ✦ Martial, Weapon
Standard Action   **Melee** or **Ranged** weapon
Requirement: You must be wielding a spear.
Target: One creature
Attack: Strength vs. AC
Hit: 2[W] + Strength modifier damage.
Effect: The target takes ongoing damage equal to 5 + your Intelligence modifier (save ends). Until the ongoing damage ends, each melee or ranged attack that hits the target deals extra damage equal to the ongoing damage.

PLATINUM WARLORD

"Those who favor peace at all costs are noble, but misguided. Sometimes battle is the only righteous choice."

Prerequisites: Warlord, good or lawful good

Bahamut requires his devotees to protect the innocent and the weak. Those who revere the Platinum Dragon are ever watchful for the rise of evil, and in particular the followers of Tiamat. Negotiation with Tiamat's forces is rarely useful and often fatal. The tenets of justice also require adherents of Bahamut's faith to oppose injustice and despotism. Although the metallic dragon god is a lover of peace, his laws regularly require battles and crusades.

Many valiant folk who serve Bahamut are paladins or clerics. But Bahamut spurns no noble soul's offer of service. Even those without divine investiture have a place in the effort to bring Bahamut's light to the world's gloomy places. Secular leaders who venerate Bahamut lend power to the Platinum Dragon's cause by ensuring order, honor, and justice in worldly institutions.

Temples dedicated to honorable battle invariably include Bahamut among the gods respected. Such places teach techniques and values aimed at bringing virtue to the world by example rather than by exhortation. Those sent to learn are often warriors or nobles bound for a nation's military.

Perhaps you came to Bahamut through such schooling. Other good-hearted people find the Platinum Dragon's ways through personal devotion or study, or even providence. Bahamut willingly instills a small measure of divine grace in those who show true commitment. Your heroic deeds and pure heart have proven you to be worthy of Bahamut's blessing. So you carry Bahamut's mark, using his minor gifts to protect, heal, and shine forth as a model of justice.

PLATINUM WARLORD PATH FEATURES

Protector's Action (11th level): When you spend an action point to take an extra action, each ally who can see and hear you gains a +1 bonus to all defenses until the start of your next turn. If that ally is bloodied, the bonus is +2 instead.

Platinum Scales (11th level): You gain the Armor Proficiency (Scale) feat, even if you don't meet the prerequisites.

Righteous Inspiration (16th level): When you use *inspiring word* on a bloodied ally, all enemies adjacent to the target take radiant damage equal to your Charisma modifier and are marked by you until the end of your next turn.

PLATINUM WARLORD EXPLOITS

Platinum Blood Smite — Platinum Warlord Attack 11

Although you waver, your conviction lends you strength to strike and push on.

Encounter ✦ Martial, Weapon
Standard Action — Melee weapon
Target: One creature
Attack: Strength vs. AC
Hit: 3[W] + Strength modifier damage. If you are bloodied, you or an ally within 5 squares of you can use second wind as a free action.

Bahamut's Liberation — Platinum Warlord Utility 12

Your sense of justice, rather than fickle fate, ends your ally's pain.

Encounter ✦ Martial
Minor Action — Close burst 5
Target: One ally in burst
Effect: Negate any ongoing damage affecting the target.

Exemplar's Talon — Platinum Warlord Attack 20

In desperate straits, you strike. Your example as a shining paragon of justice cheers your allies.

Daily ✦ Healing, Martial, Weapon
Standard Action — Melee weapon
Requirement: You must be bloodied.
Target: One creature
Attack: Strength vs. AC
Hit: 4[W] + Strength modifier damage.
Effect: You and each bloodied ally within 5 squares of you regain hit points equal to your armor's armor bonus (including its enhancement bonus) + your Charisma modifier.

SPIRAL TACTICIAN

"The circle of my fey steps encompasses one center—victory."

Prerequisites: Eladrin, warlord, Tactical Presence class feature

The Feywild, home of the eladrin, is a wondrous reflection of the world. Within that plane, beauty thrives that defies the worldly mind, but so too does evil. Eladrin are as prone to wickedness as humans are, and in a bygone age, the drow were also natives of the Feywild.

In a time long before other great empires, eladrin faithful to Corellon fought bitter wars within the Feywild against the followers of Lolth and other evil fey. These wars culminated in what came to be known as the Last Battle of the Spiral Tower. During that clash, the Corellon loyalists finally turned the tide and a hero was born.

Ossandrya was an eladrin squad commander when the Last Battle of the Spiral Tower began. Drow and demons had taken the mythic site during a protracted battle that saw the eladrin fighting on many fronts. Several fruitless assaults on the enemy-held tower cost Ossandrya's superiors their lives. With reinforcements unavailable, the eladrin commander was forced to lead the remaining troops against the drow. She devised a multipronged attack that utilized the eladrin's *fey step*, taking the biggest risks on herself and having no regard for the tower's ultimate fate. In the end, Ossandrya's efforts proved successful. Although the Spiral Tower was reduced to a blackened spindle bereft of magic, the eladrin drove the drow out for good.

In time, the Spiral Tower was rebuilt. Ossandrya, who survived other campaigns that drove the drow out of the Feywild, eventually passed from the mortal realm. She is counted among legendary warlords. Within the ruins of the Spiral Tower, her story is recorded. Eladrin warriors across the Feywild study her brilliant strategies and tactics, many of which require fey powers.

You have studied Ossandrya's story and schemes, or you have intuited similar ploys thanks to your fey nature. It could be that some combination of these possibilities influenced your course in life. You have a strongly tactical mind, a sharp sense of space and timing, and the ability to adapt your powers to tactical needs. These aptitudes serve you well in your battles, leading you toward the acclaim Ossandrya has long possessed.

SPIRAL TACTICIAN PATH FEATURES

Second Step (11th level): When you spend an action point to take an extra action, you regain the use of your *fey step* racial power if you have used it during this encounter.

Spiral Timing (11th level): When you and your allies roll initiative, you can allow one ally you can see to reroll with a bonus equal to your Intelligence modifier. The ally must use the new result.

Fey Tactics (16th level): The attack bonus provided by your Tactical Presence is equal to your Intelligence modifier (instead of one-half your Intelligence modifier).

SPIRAL TACTICIAN EXPLOITS

Fey Step Assault — Spiral Tactician Attack 11

You step through the Feywild to deliver a significant strike from an unexpected angle.

Encounter ✦ Martial, Weapon
Standard Action — Melee weapon
Target: One creature
Attack: Strength vs. Reflex. If you used *fey step* to move adjacent to the target during this turn, you gain combat advantage for this attack and it deals 1[W] extra damage.
Hit: 2[W] + Strength modifier damage.

Convey Ally — Spiral Tactician Utility 12

With fey sight, you know exactly how and where to place an ally. You can move him or her there through the Feywild.

Encounter ✦ Martial, Teleportation
Move Action — Ranged 20
Target: One ally
Effect: You teleport the target a number of squares equal to your *fey step* distance.

Spiral of Fey Death — Spiral Tactician Attack 20

In a moment of perfect clarity, you teleport to each nearby enemy and deliver a crushing strike.

Daily ✦ Martial, Teleportation, Weapon
Standard Action — Melee weapon
Target: One creature
Attack: Strength + 2 vs. AC
Hit: 3[W] + Strength modifier damage.
Effect: You either slide the target a number of squares equal to your Intelligence modifier or deal ongoing 10 damage (save ends). You can then teleport adjacent to a different target within 3 squares of you and repeat the attack against the new target. Until you have attacked each eligible target once, you can teleport adjacent to a different target within 3 squares of your starting position and repeat the attack against the new target. You then teleport back to your starting position.

TWICEBORN LEADER

"My story will live on. Will yours?"

Prerequisite: Warlord

The folktale of Jarret the Twiceborn is told throughout the lands. Although humans and elves cherish this celebrated figure, many other peoples speak of him with reverence. Tales differ about his actual heritage, human or half-elf. It is known that he was born to common folk outside elf lands in a kingdom that would one day be part of the empire of Nerath.

Jarret's natural charm won him friends above his station, including young nobles with little or no chance of inheritance. As a result, Jarret gained martial training and took to forming groups of do-gooders and fortune seekers. His ability to lead these small bands to success against all odds came to be well documented. He and his comrades traveled widely and are credited with making life safer in many places. Jarret's companions seldom left the adventuring life for any reason other than significant wealth; certainly death was not the primary reason.

Jarret wasn't so lucky. He fell in battle against the mind flayers of Thoon deep within the Underdark. No magic could bring him back.

The story doesn't end there, however. Many believe Jarret was reborn as a lad of the same name who grew up in nearly the same place. This perhaps-reincarnated Jarret became an inspiring leader and hero like his namesake. He performed similar deeds, and never refuted claims that he was the same Jarret. Instead, he used the rumor to his advantage, renewing former ties of friendship and striking fear into old enemies. He became known for taking special interest in opposing aberrant creatures, such as mind flayers. Those who knew and loved him eventually dubbed him Jarret the Twiceborn. Yarns say he lives still in the heavens, alongside great generals from times past.

Jarret's accomplishments and methods are recorded in story, history, and song. From these, many venturesome souls draw inspiration and try to duplicate Jarret's feats. Some successful imitators even claim to teach his methods.

Maybe your natural talents led you on a road similar to Jarret's. You've taken what you could from folktales and, perhaps, teachers. In your travails, you carry on Jarret's folk-hero tradition. In doing so, perhaps you'll become even greater than the Twiceborn.

TWICEBORN LEADER PATH FEATURES

Twiceborn Recovery (11th level): When you use *inspiring word*, you can choose two targets instead of one. Each target can spend a healing surge but doesn't gain extra dice of healing normally granted by the power. When you use this path feature, you can't choose yourself as a target.

Assault Action (11th level): When you spend an action point to take an extra action, each ally within 10 squares of you gains a +2 power bonus to attack rolls until the start of your next turn.

Twofold Defense (16th level): Each ally who can see and hear you when he or she uses second wind gains a +4 bonus to all defenses (instead of the usual +2) until the end of his or her next turn.

TWICEBORN LEADER EXPLOITS

Reminiscent Assault   Twiceborn Leader Attack 11

You attack in the name of Jarret, taking the action to new heights if you strike your enemy down.

Encounter ✦ Martial, Weapon
Standard Action   Melee weapon
Target: One creature
Attack: Strength vs. AC
Hit: 2[W] + Strength modifier damage. If the target is an aberrant creature, you and your allies gain a +4 power bonus to attack rolls against the target until the end of your next turn. If this attack reduces the target to 0 hit points, you or one ally within 10 squares of you can make a basic attack as a free action.

Twinning Ploy   Twiceborn Leader Utility 12

You and a chosen ally engage in a complex maneuver that distracts your enemies enough to assure the success of your attacks.

Daily ✦ Martial, Stance
Minor Action   Personal
Effect: Choose an ally within 5 squares of you. Both you and the ally, on your own turns, can roll an extra d20 and choose the higher result for one attack roll each turn. Until the stance ends, this effect applies only when you are both conscious and within 5 squares of each other.

Seconded Smite   Twiceborn Leader Attack 20

When the going is rough, you are at your best, allowing an ally to mirror your ruinous attack.

Daily ✦ Martial, Weapon
Standard Action   Melee weapon
Target: One creature
Attack: Strength vs. AC. You gain a bonus to the attack roll equal to the number of conscious allies within 10 squares of you who have already used second wind during this encounter (maximum bonus of +4).
Hit: 4[W] + Strength modifier damage.
Miss: Half damage.
Effect: One ally within 10 squares of you who has already used second wind during this encounter can shift a number of squares equal to your Charisma modifier and then make a melee basic attack as a free action.

4

CHAPTER 5

MARTIAL OPTIONS

IN THE DUNGEONS & DRAGONS game, more options mean more fun. This chapter focuses on expanding the choices that allow you to customize your martial character. With few exceptions (such as the multiclass feats), the options here are solely for such PCs.

✦ **New Feats:** As in the *Player's Handbook*, this chapter presents feats by tier. Whether you're a warlord who wants to improve your *inspiring word*, a rogue who wants to complement the new Ruthless Ruffian tactic, or any martial character who wants a bit of flavor from your race, scores of new possibilities reside here.

✦ **Multiclass Feats:** If you have your eye on expanding your capabilities by dabbling in a martial class, this section of the chapter is for you. Even if your primary class isn't martial, you might find something of interest. In doing so, you also open access to the paragon paths elsewhere in this book.

✦ **Epic Destinies:** The mythic warrior takes many forms. These new epic destinies expand your (and your DM's) options for defining your ascent to legendary status.

GENASI AND DROW FEATS

A few of the feats in this chapter are designed for genasi or drow characters. (Those two races are described in the *FORGOTTEN REALMS® Player's Guide*.) If your campaign doesn't include characters of these races, you can disregard those feats.

JEREMY JARVIS

Feats offer a remarkable opportunity to customize your character. These feats focus on martial activity and providing interesting options for martial characters.

You must meet a feat's prerequisites, if any, to take the feat. If you ever lose a prerequisite for a feat (for example, if you use the retraining system to replace training in a prerequisite skill with training in a different skill), you can't use that feat thereafter. A feat that has a class as a prerequisite is available only to members of that class, including characters who have joined the class through a class-specific multiclass feat.

HEROIC TIER FEATS

Any feat in this section is available to a character of any level who meets the prerequisites. Heroic tier feats and multiclass feats are the only feats you can take if you are 10th level or lower.

AGGRESSIVE ASSAULT

Prerequisites: Rogue, Brutal Scoundrel class feature, First Strike class feature

Benefit: At the beginning of an encounter, whenever you hit a target that has not acted, you slide that target 1 square.

ANKLE CUTTER

Prerequisites: Halfling, rogue, Sneak Attack class feature

Benefit: When you hit a Large or larger enemy and would deal Sneak Attack damage against that target, you can forgo rolling Sneak Attack damage and instead cause the target to be slowed until the end of your next turn. Using this option counts as using Sneak Attack for the round.

BEAST GUIDANCE

Prerequisites: Ranger, Beast Mastery class feature

Benefit: Your beast companion gains a +2 feat bonus to any skill in which you are trained.

BEAST PROTECTOR

Prerequisites: Ranger, Beast Mastery class feature

Benefit: If an enemy makes a melee attack against your beast companion, doing so provokes an opportunity attack from you. If you are adjacent to your beast companion, you can make this attack even if you can't reach the attacker (you attack the attacker's reaching limb, for instance).

BEAST TRAINING

Prerequisites: Ranger, Beast Mastery class feature

Benefit: Your beast companion gains training in a skill. If you change beast companions, you can also change the skill that this feat grants to your beast companion.

Special: You can take this feat more than once. Each time you select this feat, your beast companion gains training in a skill.

BLOODIED INVIGORATION

Prerequisites: Con 13, dragonborn, fighter

Benefit: When you hit with a power that has the invigorating keyword while you are bloodied, you gain an additional 2 temporary hit points.

BOLD COMMAND

Prerequisites: Halfling, warlord, Bravura Presence class feature

Benefit: If an enemy that has combat advantage against you misses with a melee attack, your allies gain a +1 bonus to attack rolls against that enemy until the start of your next turn.

BOLSTERING INSPIRATION

Prerequisites: Dwarf, warlord

Benefit: When you use *inspiring word* on an adjacent ally, that ally either regains additional hit points equal to your Wisdom modifier or can make a saving throw.

BRACING BREATH

Prerequisites: Con 13, dragonborn, fighter

Benefit: When you use your *dragon breath* racial power, you gain a +1 bonus to attack rolls for powers that have the invigorating keyword until the end of your next turn.

BRAVURA SPIRIT

Prerequisites: Dragonborn, warlord, Bravura Presence class feature

Benefit: When a bloodied ally uses your Bravura Presence, that ally gains either a +2 bonus to the attack roll or a +2 bonus to speed for the move action (the ally's choice).

BREATH-RESISTANT BEAST

Prerequisites: Dragonborn, ranger, Beast Mastery class feature

Benefit: Your beast companion gains resist 5 + one-half your level to the damage type of your *dragon breath* racial power.

Brutal Accuracy

Prerequisites: Elf, ranger, Hunter's Quarry class feature

Benefit: If the rerolled attack granted by your *elven accuracy* racial power hits your quarry, the attack deals extra damage equal to 1d6 + your Wisdom modifier.

Brutal Teamwork

Prerequisites: Str 15, dragonborn, rogue

Benefit: You gain a +2 bonus to damage rolls when you are adjacent to at least one ally.

Brutal Wound

Prerequisites: Rogue, Brutal Scoundrel class feature, Sneak Attack class feature

Benefit: When your attack deals ongoing damage and you deal Sneak Attack damage to the target, add 1 to the ongoing damage for every die of Sneak Attack damage dealt.

Camouflage

Prerequisites: Ranger, trained in Stealth

Benefit: When you have any cover or concealment outdoors, you gain a +5 feat bonus to Stealth checks.

Command the Darkness

Prerequisites: Drow, warlord

Benefit: When you use your *cloud of darkness* racial power, you can choose for it to lightly or heavily obscure its area, instead of totally obscuring it. If you reduce the darkness in this way, creatures inside the cloud are not blinded.

Coordinated Opportunity

Prerequisites: Ranger, Beast Mastery class feature

Benefit: If your beast companion is adjacent to the target of your opportunity attack, you gain a +2 bonus to the damage roll.

Cunning Ambusher

Prerequisites: Tiefling, rogue

Benefit: If you use *infernal wrath* when you have combat advantage against the attack's target, you gain a bonus to the attack and damage rolls equal to your Intelligence modifier.

Darkfire Targeting

Prerequisites: Drow ranger or drow rogue

Benefit: Whenever you deal Sneak Attack or Hunter's Quarry damage to the target of your *darkfire* power, the attack deals extra damage equal to your Wisdom modifier.

Deep Gash

Prerequisites: Con 15, fighter

Benefit: When you deal ongoing damage that has no damage type to a target as a result of an attack that uses an axe or a pick, the target takes a –2 penalty to saving throws against the ongoing damage.

Defensive Resilience

Prerequisites: Con 13, Wis 13, fighter

Benefit: When you use second wind while you are bloodied, you gain a +1 bonus to all defenses, in addition to the normal bonus for second wind, until the end of your next turn.

Devoted Challenge

Prerequisites: Dwarf, fighter, Combat Challenge class feature

Benefit: When you make a melee basic attack granted by Combat Challenge, you gain a bonus to the attack and damage rolls equal to your Wisdom modifier.

Dirty Fighting

Prerequisite: Fighter or rogue

Benefit: You gain a +4 bonus to melee weapon damage rolls against surprised enemies.

Dragging Flail

Prerequisites: Dex 15, fighter

Benefit: Whenever you use a flail to knock an enemy prone, you can also slide that enemy 1 square.

Drow Beast Mastery

Prerequisites: Drow, ranger, Beast Mastery class feature

Benefit: Your beast companion is immune to the effect of your *cloud of darkness* racial power.

Dwarf Stoneblood

Prerequisites: Dwarf, fighter, Battlerager Vigor class feature

Benefit: Add one-half your Constitution modifier to the temporary hit points granted by your Battlerager Vigor.

Dwarf Trapsmith

Prerequisites: Dwarf, rogue

Benefit: You gain a +4 feat bonus to Perception checks to find traps and to Thievery checks to open locks or disable traps.

HEROIC TIER FEATS

Any Martial Class	Prerequisites	Benefit
Martial Alacrity	Dex 15, any martial class	+2 to initiative and shift quickly during your first turn
Martial Freedom	Wis 13, any martial class, trained in Endurance	+5 to saving throws against the slowed and immobilized conditions

Fighter Feat	Prerequisites	Benefit
Bloodied Invigoration	Con 13, dragonborn, fighter	Invigorating powers grant +2 temporary hp when bloodied
Bracing Breath	Con 13, dragonborn, fighter	*Dragon breath* gives +1 to attack with invigorating powers
Deep Gash	Con 15, fighter	Enemy takes -2 to saving throws against ongoing damage
Defensive Resilience	Con 13, Wis 13, fighter	+1 to all defenses with second wind when bloodied
Devoted Challenge	Dwarf, fighter, Combat Challenge	Bonus to melee basic attacks equal to Wis modifier
Dirty Fighting	Fighter or rogue	+4 melee damage against surprised enemies
Dragging Flail	Dex 15, fighter	Using a flail, slide enemy as you knock it prone
Dwarf Stoneblood	Dwarf, fighter, Battlerager Vigor	Add half Con modifier to Battlerager Vigor temporary hp
Fey Blades	Eladrin, fighter, Tempest Technique	+1 damage with longsword in each hand
Group Assault	Half-elf, fighter	Allies gain +1 damage against your marked target
Halfling Stalwart	Halfling, fighter	+1 to attack rolls against Large or larger marked targets
Improved Vigor	Fighter, trained in Endurance	Invigorating powers grant +1 temporary hp
Keeper of Storm	Genasi, fighter, Combat Challenge	Deal thunder or lightning damage when using stormsoul
Lingering Wrath	Tiefling, fighter, Combat Challenge	Bonuses from *infernal wrath* last as long as your mark
Master of Rumbling Earth	Genasi, fighter	Bonuses to attack rolls and damage with *earthshock*
Offensive Resilience	Dex 13, Wis 13, fighter	+1 to attack roll after using second wind when bloodied
Opportunistic Accuracy	Wis 13, elf, fighter	Retain *elven accuracy* when you miss
Polearm Momentum	Dex 15, Wis 15, fighter	Knock pushed or slid enemy prone with polearm
Reaping Blade	Dex 15, fighter	Shift as a minor action when you drop an enemy
Shield Defense	Wis 13, fighter	+1 AC and Reflex when power requiring shield hits
Sideways Defense	Human, fighter, Combat Challenge	Adjacent allies gain +1 defense against marked enemy
Surprising Charge	Dex 17, fighter or rogue	+1[W] damage on charge with light blade or spear
Take Measure	Wis 15, fighter	+2 to all defenses against target with melee critical hit
Thunder Hammer	Con 15, fighter	Enemy takes -2 to saving throws against conditions delivered with hammer or mace
Victor's Confidence	Con 15, fighter	+2 to saving throws after reducing an enemy to 0 hp

Ranger Feat	Prerequisites	Benefit
Beast Guidance	Ranger, Beast Mastery	Beast gains +2 to your trained skills
Beast Protector	Ranger, Beast Mastery	Attack against beast provokes opportunity attack from you
Beast Training	Ranger, Beast Mastery	Beast gains training in a skill
Breath-Resistant Beast	Dragonborn, ranger, Beast Mastery	Beast gains resistance to your *dragon breath*'s damage type
Brutal Accuracy	Elf, ranger, Hunter's Quarry	Hit with *elven accuracy* reroll gains extra damage
Camouflage	Wis 13, ranger, trained in Stealth	+5 to Stealth outdoors when you have concealment
Coordinated Opportunity	Ranger, Beast Mastery	+2 damage to opportunity attack if beast is adjacent
Darkfire Targeting	Drow ranger or drow rogue	Target of your *darkfire* takes extra damage
Drow Beast Mastery	Drow, ranger, Beast Mastery	Beast sees through your *cloud of darkness*
Elven Beast Mastery	Elf, ranger, Beast Mastery	Beast benefits from Wild Step and *elven accuracy*
Expert Tracker	Wis 13, ranger, trained in Perception	+5 to your Perception checks to find tracks and to the DC for others to find your tracks
Feyborn Companion	Eladrin, ranger, Beast Mastery	Beast gains fey origin and other benefits
Fiendish Companion	Tiefling, ranger, Beast Mastery	Beast gains resist fire
Group Quarry	Half-elf, ranger	Allies gain +1 damage against your quarry
Human Beast Mastery	Human, ranger, Beast Mastery	Beast gains +1 to all defenses
Hunter of Wind and Wave	Genasi, ranger	+2 to movement with *swiftcurrent* or *windwalker*
Hunter's Aim	Ranger, Hunter's Quarry	Ignore quarry's cover or concealment
Lucky Skirmisher	Halfling ranger or halfling rogue	Enemies find you harder to hit when you run
Nimble Companion	Halfling, ranger, Beast Mastery	Beast gains +2 AC against opportunity attacks
Predatory Action	Ranger, Hunter's Quarry	Deal Hunter's Quarry damage again with an action point

HEROIC TIER FEATS (CONTINUED)

Ranger Feat	Prerequisites	Benefit
Prime Strike	Ranger	+1 to melee attack rolls when no others are near your target
Secure Encampment	Wis 13, ranger, trained in Nature, Perception, and Stealth	Allies gain bonus to Perception and Stealth during extended rest
Thundertusk Companion	Dwarf, ranger, Beast Mastery	Your boar's hp increase by your level
Vengeful Beast	Ranger, Beast Mastery, Hunter's Quarry	Beast gains +1 to attack and damage rolls against quarry

Rogue Feat	Prerequisites	Benefit
Aggressive Assault	Rogue, Brutal Scoundrel, First Strike	Slide targets that have not yet acted 1 square
Ankle Cutter	Halfling, rogue, Sneak Attack	Cause Large or larger Sneak Attack target to be slowed
Brutal Teamwork	Str 15, dragonborn, rogue	+2 damage when adjacent to any ally
Brutal Wound	Rogue, Brutal Scoundrel, Sneak Attack	Deal additional ongoing damage with Sneak Attack
Cunning Ambusher	Tiefling, rogue	Combine *infernal wrath* with combat advantage for bonus to attack and damage rolls
Darkfire Targeting	Drow ranger or drow rogue	Target of your *darkfire* takes extra damage
Dirty Fighting	Fighter or rogue	+4 to melee damage against surprised enemies
Dwarf Trapsmith	Dwarf, rogue	+4 to Perception and Thievery for traps and locks
Group Rattling	Half-elf, rogue, trained in Intimidate	Allies gain +1 to attack rolls against your enemy affected by rattling power
Into the Fray	Rogue, First Strike	+1 to speed and to melee attack rolls in surprise round
Longsword Finesse	Eladrin, rogue	Treat longsword as light blade
Lucky Skirmisher	Halfling ranger or halfling rogue	You are harder to hit when you run
Rash Sneak Attack	Human, rogue, Sneak Attack	Grant combat advantage for extra Sneak Attack damage
Rattling Wrath	Cha 15, tiefling, rogue	Combine rattling power with *infernal wrath* to increase rattling penalty to –4
Reckless Scramble	Rogue, Artful Dodger	Move farther instead of shifting
Ruthless Injury	Rogue, Ruthless Ruffian, Sneak Attack	Enemy takes –2 to saving throws against conditions delivered with club or mace
Slaying Action	Rogue, Sneak Attack	Deal Sneak Attack damage again with an action point
Sneaky Accuracy	Elf, rogue, Sneak Attack	Retain *elven accuracy* on an enemy's miss
Speedy Response	Dex 15, rogue	Gain speed when hit by an opportunity attack
Street Thug	Str 13, Con 13, rogue	Treat mace as light blade
Surprising Charge	Dex 17, fighter or rogue	+1[W] damage when charging with light blade or spear
Trap Sense	Wis 13, rogue	+2 to all defenses against traps, +2 to find traps
Tunnel Stalker	Str 13, Con 13, dwarf, rogue	Treat one-handed axes, hammers, and picks as light blades
Two-Fisted Shooter	Rogue	Treat hand crossbow as off-hand weapon, reload free action
Wielder of Piercing Flame	Genasi, rogue	*Firepulse* ignores target's resistance or immunity when you have combat advantage

ELVEN BEAST MASTERY

Prerequisites: Elf, ranger, Beast Mastery class feature

Benefit: Your beast companion ignores difficult terrain when it shifts.

You can use your *elven accuracy* racial power to reroll an attack roll you made or one your beast companion made.

FEY BLADES

Eladrin weaponers often make bladed weapons in matched pairs. Whether two identical blades, one heavy and one light, or a double sword, the weapons are made to look good together. More important, they are balanced together so that they seem to fit perfectly in the wielder's hands.

EXPERT TRACKER

Prerequisites: Wis 13, ranger, trained in Nature

Benefit: You gain a +5 feat bonus to Perception checks to find tracks.

Add 5 to the Perception DC for other creatures to find your tracks. You can extend this benefit to up to ten allies traveling with you.

FEY BLADES

Prerequisites: Eladrin, fighter, Tempest Technique class feature

Benefit: When you're wielding two light blades, two heavy blades, or a heavy blade and a light blade, you gain a +1 bonus to damage rolls.

FEY COMMAND

Prerequisites: Eladrin, warlord, Tactical Presence class feature

Benefit: When an ally you can see spends an action point to make an attack, the ally can teleport 1 square before or after the attack.

FEYBORN COMPANION

Prerequisites: Eladrin, ranger, Beast Mastery class feature

Benefit: Your beast companion gains the fey origin, instead of the natural origin, and a +5 bonus to saving throws against charm effects.

When you use your *fey step* racial power, your beast companion can teleport the same distance that you teleport.

FIENDISH COMPANION

Prerequisites: Tiefling, ranger, Beast Mastery class feature

Benefit: Your beast companion gains resistance to fire equal to 5 + one-half your level.

GROUP ASSAULT

Prerequisites: Half-elf, fighter

Benefit: Allies gain a +1 bonus to damage rolls against targets marked by you.

GROUP QUARRY

Prerequisites: Half-elf, ranger, Hunter's Quarry class feature

Benefit: Allies gain a +1 bonus to damage rolls against your quarry.

GROUP RATTLING

Prerequisites: Half-elf, rogue, trained in Intimidate

Benefit: Allies gain a +1 bonus to attack rolls against enemies that have a penalty to attack rolls as a result of your successful attack with a power that has the rattling keyword.

HALFLING STALWART

Prerequisites: Halfling, fighter

Benefit: You gain a +1 bonus to attack rolls against Large or larger creatures marked by you.

HUMAN BEAST MASTERY

Prerequisites: Human, ranger, Beast Mastery class feature

Benefit: Your beast companion gains a +1 bonus to all defenses.

HUNTER OF WIND AND WAVE

Prerequisites: Genasi, ranger

Benefit: When you use your *swiftcurrent* or *windwalker* racial power, add 2 squares to the distance the power allows you to move.

HUNTER'S AIM

Prerequisites: Ranger, Hunter's Quarry class feature

Benefit: You don't take the normal –2 penalty to attack rolls against your quarry if it has cover or concealment.

IMPROVED BRAVURA

Prerequisites: Warlord, Bravura Presence class feature

Benefit: When an ally uses your Bravura Presence, that ally gains either a +1 bonus to the attack roll or a +1 bonus to speed for the move action (the ally's choice).

IMPROVED INSPIRATION

Prerequisites: Warlord, Inspiring Presence class feature

Benefit: Your Inspiring Presence restores an additional 2 hit points.

IMPROVED INSPIRING WORD

Prerequisite: Warlord

Benefit: Add your Charisma modifier to the hit points restored by your *inspiring word*.

IMPROVED RESOURCES

Prerequisites: Warlord, Resourceful Presence class feature

Benefit: Add 2 to the damage bonus and the temporary hit points granted by your Resourceful Presence.

IMPROVED TACTICS

Prerequisites: Warlord, Tactical Presence class feature

Benefit: Add 1 to the attack roll bonus granted by your Tactical Presence.

IMPROVED VIGOR

Prerequisites: Fighter, trained in Endurance

Benefit: You gain 1 additional temporary hit point each time you gain temporary hit points from a power that has the invigorating keyword.

If you have the Battlerager Vigor class feature, this benefit also applies to the temporary hit points gained from it.

At 11th level, this bonus increases to 2 additional temporary hit points. At 21st level, this bonus increases to 3 additional temporary hit points.

INSPIRED DEFENSE

Prerequisites: Human, warlord

Benefit: When you use *inspiring word*, the target also gains a +1 power bonus to all defenses until the start of your next turn.

HEROIC TIER FEATS (CONTINUED)

Warlord Feat	Prerequisites	Benefit
Bold Command	Halfling, warlord, Bravura Presence	Allies gain +1 to attack rolls against enemy that misses you
Bolstering Inspiration	Dwarf, warlord	Saving throw or additional hp for *inspiring word* target
Bravura Spirit	Dragonborn, warlord, Bravura Presence	Bloodied ally gains additional bonus from Bravura Presence
Command the Darkness	Drow, warlord	Change how much *cloud of darkness* obscures its area
Fey Command	Eladrin, warlord, Tactical Presence	Ally can teleport before or after attacking
Improved Bravura	Warlord, Bravura Presence	Ally gains +1 to attack rolls or speed with Bravura Presence
Improved Inspiration	Warlord, Inspiring Presence	Ally gains +2 hp with Inspiring Presence
Improved Inspiring Word	Warlord	Add Cha modifier to *inspiring word* hp restored
Improved Resources	Warlord, Resourceful Presence	Ally gains +2 damage and temporary hp from Resourceful Presence
Improved Tactics	Warlord, Tactical Presence	Ally gains +1 to attack rolls with Tactical Presence
Inspired Defense	Human, warlord	Ally gains +1 to all defenses with *inspiring word*
Inspired Tactics	Half-elf, warlord, Inspiring Presence	Ally gains +1 to attack rolls when spending action point
Leading Fire	Elf, warlord, Combat Leader	Allies gain +1 to ranged attack rolls against target
Lend Might	Warlord	+1 to attack rolls of attacks you grant
Saving Inspiration	Warlord	Ally gains saving throw with *inspiring word*
Tactical Inspiration	Eladrin, warlord	Add Int modifier to *inspiring word* hp restored
Unbalancing Wrath	Tiefling, warlord	*Infernal wrath* target grants combat advantage

INSPIRED TACTICS

Prerequisites: Half-elf, warlord, Inspiring Presence class feature

Benefit: When an ally who can see you spends an action point to make an attack, that ally gains a +1 bonus to the attack roll.

INTO THE FRAY

Prerequisites: Rogue, First Strike class feature

Benefit: During the surprise round and the first round of an encounter, you gain a +1 bonus to your speed and to your melee attack rolls.

KEEPER OF STORM

Prerequisites: Genasi, fighter, Combat Challenge class feature

Benefit: If you are manifesting stormsoul when you make a melee basic attack granted by Combat Challenge, you can choose for the attack to deal thunder damage or lightning damage instead of its normal damage type.

LEADING FIRE

Prerequisites: Elf, warlord, Combat Leader class feature

Benefit: When you hit an enemy with a bow attack, each ally within 10 squares of you who can see and hear you gains a +1 bonus to ranged attack rolls against the attack's target until the start of your next turn.

LEND MIGHT

Prerequisite: Warlord

Benefit: When an ally makes an attack granted by one of your warlord powers to attack an enemy adjacent to you, that ally gains a +1 bonus to the attack roll.

LINGERING WRATH

Prerequisites: Tiefling, fighter, Combat Challenge class feature

Benefit: When you use the *infernal wrath* racial power against an enemy marked by you, you gain the bonuses from *infernal wrath* against that enemy until it is no longer marked by you.

LONGSWORD FINESSE

Prerequisites: Eladrin, rogue

Benefit: You can wield a longsword to deal Sneak Attack damage and to use rogue powers that require a light blade (you still cannot throw the longsword). You reduce Sneak Attack damage by one die when using a longsword.

LUCKY SKIRMISHER

Prerequisites: Halfling ranger or halfling rogue

Benefit: When you run, enemies making opportunity attacks against you during that movement must roll twice and take the lower result.

MARTIAL ALACRITY

Prerequisites: Dex 15, any martial class

Benefit: You gain a +2 feat bonus to initiative checks. Also, during your first turn in an encounter, you can shift as a minor action.

Martial Freedom
Prerequisites: Wis 13, any martial class, trained in Endurance
Benefit: You gain a +5 bonus to saving throws against the slowed and immobilized conditions.

Master of Rumbling Earth
Prerequisites: Genasi, fighter
Benefit: You gain a +1 bonus to attack rolls with your *earthshock* racial power, and you deal damage equal to your Strength modifier to enemies knocked prone by the power.

Nimble Companion
Prerequisites: Halfling, ranger, Beast Mastery class feature
Benefit: Your beast companion gains a +2 bonus to AC against opportunity attacks.

When an attack hits your beast companion, you can use your *second chance* racial power on the beast's behalf.

Offensive Resilience
Prerequisites: Dex 13, Wis 13, fighter
Benefit: When you are bloodied and use second wind, you gain a +1 bonus to attack rolls until the end of your next turn.

Opportunistic Accuracy
Prerequisites: Wis 13, elf, fighter
Benefit: If you use your *elven accuracy* racial power to reroll an opportunity attack and the second roll misses, you do not expend the power.

Polearm Momentum
Prerequisites: Dex 15, Wis 15, fighter
Benefit: Whenever you use a polearm or a spear attack to push or slide a target 2 or more squares, you can also knock that target prone at the end of the forced movement.

Predatory Action
Prerequisites: Ranger, Hunter's Quarry class feature
Benefit: If you spend an action point to take an extra action and have already dealt Hunter's Quarry damage during this round, you can deal the extra damage a second time during this turn.

Prime Strike
Prerequisite: Ranger
Benefit: You gain a +1 bonus to melee attack rolls against a target if no other creatures are within 3 squares of it.

Rash Sneak Attack
Prerequisites: Human, rogue, Sneak Attack class feature
Benefit: When you deal Sneak Attack damage, you can choose to gain a +2 bonus to the damage roll. If you do so, you grant combat advantage to all enemies until the end of your next turn.

Rattling Wrath
Prerequisites: Cha 15, tiefling, rogue
Benefit: When you use your *infernal wrath* racial power in conjunction with a power that has the rattling keyword, the penalty to the target's attack rolls from the rattling keyword changes to -4.

If you score a critical hit with this attack, you do not expend *infernal wrath*.

Reaping Blade
Prerequisites: Dex 15, fighter
Benefit: If you reduce an enemy to 0 hit points with an attack using a heavy blade, you can shift as a minor action until the end of your current turn.

Reckless Scramble
Prerequisites: Rogue, Artful Dodger class feature
Benefit: When a power lets you shift, you can instead choose to move that distance + 2 squares.

RUTHLESS INJURY

Prerequisites: Rogue, Ruthless Ruffian class feature, Sneak Attack class feature

Benefit: When you use a club or a mace to make a sneak attack that causes the target to become blinded, immobilized, slowed, or weakened, that target takes a –2 penalty to saving throws against any of those conditions.

SAVING INSPIRATION

Prerequisite: Warlord

Benefit: When you use *inspiring word*, you can forgo any extra dice of healing granted by the power to instead grant the target a saving throw.

SECURE ENCAMPMENT

Prerequisites: Wis 13, ranger, trained in Nature, Perception, and Stealth

Benefit: If you are conscious when you and your allies begin an extended rest, your allies gain a bonus to Perception checks and Stealth checks during that rest equal to your Wisdom modifier. This bonus lasts until the end of the extended rest.

SHIELD DEFENSE

Prerequisites: Wis 13, fighter

Benefit: When you hit with a power that requires a shield, you gain a +1 bonus to AC and Reflex until the end of your next turn or until you stop using the shield.

SIDEWAYS DEFENSE

Prerequisites: Human, fighter, Combat Challenge class feature

Benefit: Allies adjacent to you gain a +1 bonus to all defenses against any creature marked by you.

SLAYING ACTION

Prerequisites: Rogue, Sneak Attack class feature

Benefit: If you spend an action point to take an extra action and have already dealt Sneak Attack damage during this round, you can deal the extra damage a second time during this turn.

SNEAKY ACCURACY

Prerequisites: Elf, rogue, Sneak Attack class feature

Benefit: If you use your *elven accuracy* racial power to reroll an attack against an enemy granting you combat advantage and the second roll misses, you do not expend *elven accuracy*.

SPEEDY RESPONSE

Prerequisites: Dex 15, rogue

Benefit: If you are hit by an opportunity attack while moving, you gain a +1 bonus to speed for that move. This benefit is cumulative if you are hit multiple times.

STREET THUG

Prerequisites: Str 13, Con 13, rogue

Benefit: You can wield a mace with any rogue power that requires a light blade. You reduce Sneak Attack damage by one die when wielding a mace.

SURPRISING CHARGE

Prerequisites: Dex 17, fighter or rogue

Benefit: When you make a charge attack against a target that is granting combat advantage to you, the attack deals 1[W] extra damage if you hit with a light blade or a spear.

TACTICAL INSPIRATION

Prerequisites: Eladrin, warlord

Benefit: Add your Intelligence modifier to the hit points restored by your *inspiring word*.

TAKE MEASURE

Prerequisites: Wis 15, fighter

Benefit: When you score a critical hit against a target with a melee attack, you gain a +2 bonus to all defenses against that target's attacks until the end of your next turn.

Thunder Hammer

Prerequisites: Con 15, fighter

Benefit: When you make an attack using a hammer or a mace that causes the target to become dazed, immobilized, slowed, or stunned, that target takes a –2 penalty to saving throws against any of those conditions.

Thundertusk Companion

Prerequisites: Dwarf, ranger, Beast Mastery class feature

Benefit: If you select a boar as your beast companion, its maximum hit points increase by an amount equal to your level.

Trap Sense

Prerequisites: Wis 13, rogue

Benefit: You gain a +2 feat bonus to all defenses against attacks by traps and to Perception checks to find traps.

Tunnel Stalker

Prerequisites: Str 13, Con 13, dwarf, rogue

Benefit: You can use any rogue power that requires a light blade while wielding an axe, a hammer, or a pick with one hand. You reduce Sneak Attack damage by one die when wielding one of these other weapons.

Two-Fisted Shooter

Prerequisite: Rogue

Benefit: You can treat the hand crossbow as an off-hand weapon, and you can reload it one-handed as a free action. When you score a critical hit and have a hand crossbow in your off hand, you can make a ranged basic attack with that weapon.

Unbalancing Wrath

Prerequisites: Tiefling, warlord

Benefit: The target of an attack benefiting from your *infernal wrath* racial power grants combat advantage to your allies until the start of your next turn.

Vengeful Beast

Prerequisites: Ranger, Beast Mastery class feature, Hunter's Quarry class feature

Benefit: When your quarry damages you with an attack, your beast companion gains a +1 bonus to attack rolls and damage rolls against that creature until the end of your next turn.

Victor's Confidence

Prerequisites: Con 15, fighter

Benefit: When you reduce an enemy to 0 hit points with a melee attack, you gain a +1 bonus to saving throws until the end of the encounter.

Wielder of Piercing Flame

Prerequisites: Genasi, rogue

Benefit: When you have combat advantage against the target of your *firepulse* racial power, that power ignores any fire resistance or immunity possessed by the target.

Paragon Tier Feats

Any feat in this section is available to a character of 11th level or higher who meets the feat's other prerequisites.

Agile Tempest

Prerequisites: 11th level, Dex 15, fighter, Tempest Technique class feature

Benefit: The damage bonus granted by your Tempest Technique when you wear chainmail or light armor increases by 1. At 21st level, it increases by 2.

Avandra's Gift

Prerequisites: 11th level, halfling, rogue

Benefit: When you use your *second chance* racial power and the enemy's attack misses, you gain combat advantage for the next attack roll you make against that enemy before the end of your next turn.

Avenging Spirit

Prerequisites: 11th level, human fighter or human warlord

Benefit: When an ally of your level or higher is reduced to 0 hit points or fewer, you gain an action point that you must use before the end of your next turn or the action point is lost. You must see or hear the ally when he or she is reduced to 0 hit points or fewer to gain this feat's benefit.

Bleeding Backstab

Prerequisites: 11th level, rogue, Sneak Attack class feature

Benefit: Whenever you deal Sneak Attack damage to a target with a rogue daily attack power, the target takes ongoing 5 damage (save ends). If the power already deals ongoing damage that has no damage type, instead increase that ongoing damage by 5.

Bleeding Precision

Prerequisites: 11th level, ranger, Hunter's Quarry class feature

Benefit: Whenever you hit your quarry with a ranger daily attack power, the target takes ongoing 5 damage (save ends). If the power already deals ongoing damage that has no damage type, instead increase that ongoing damage by 5.

BLOODY INSPIRATION

Prerequisites: 11th level, dragonborn, warlord

Benefit: If you use *inspiring word* while you are bloodied and do not target yourself, a second ally within the power's range gains temporary hit points equal to twice your Constitution modifier.

BLOODY TENACITY

Prerequisites: 11th level, human, any martial class

Benefit: When you are bloodied for the first time in an encounter, you gain a +2 bonus to all defenses until the end of your next turn.

CHAINMAIL AGILITY

Prerequisites: 11th level, Dex 15, fighter

Benefit: You ignore the speed penalty normally incurred by wearing chainmail.

COMBAT OPENING

Prerequisites: 11th level, half-elf, fighter, Combat Challenge class feature

Benefit: When you can make a melee basic attack against a target because of Combat Challenge, you can instead choose to let an ally make a melee basic attack against that target as a free action.

CULL THE WEAK

Prerequisites: 11th level, Cha 15, rogue

Benefit: When you have combat advantage against a bloodied or a weakened target, you gain a +2 bonus to melee weapon damage rolls against the target.

DARKHUNTER

Prerequisites: 11th level, drow, ranger, Hunter's Quarry class feature

Benefit: When you use the *cloud of darkness* racial power, each enemy within the cloud is designated as your quarry until it is no longer within the cloud. These quarries don't count toward the normal limit of one quarry, and any other creature designated as your quarry remains so. You can deal Hunter's Quarry damage against each quarry that you hit in the cloud.

DARKJUMPER

Prerequisites: 11th level, drow, rogue

Benefit: On the turn when you use the *cloud of darkness* racial power, you can teleport once to any unoccupied square within the cloud as a free action.

DAUNTING CHALLENGE

Prerequisites: 11th level, fighter, Combat Challenge class feature

Benefit: Creatures marked by you take a -3 penalty to attack rolls for any attack that doesn't include you as a target (rather than a -2 penalty).

DEFENSIVE SURGE

Prerequisites: 11th level, Con 15, warlord

Benefit: When you use your second wind, you can grant the +2 bonus to all defenses to an adjacent ally, in addition to gaining the bonus yourself.

DISTRACTING COMPANION

Prerequisites: 11th level, ranger, Beast Mastery class feature, Hunter's Quarry class feature

Benefit: If your quarry is adjacent to your beast companion when you hit your quarry with an attack, your quarry takes a -2 penalty to attack rolls against you and your beast companion until the start of your next turn.

DRACONIC ARROGANCE

Prerequisites: 11th level, dragonborn, fighter

Benefit: Whenever you push an enemy or knock an enemy prone, you deal damage to that enemy equal to your Strength modifier.

DRAGONBREATH WARRIOR

Prerequisites: 11th level, dragonborn, any martial class

Benefit: When you use your *dragon breath* racial power, your next melee weapon attack deals 1[W] extra damage on a hit. The damage type is the same as your *dragon breath*.

PARAGON TIER FEATS

Any Martial Class	Prerequisites	Benefit
Bloody Tenacity	Human, any martial class	+2 to all defenses when first bloodied
Dragonbreath Warrior	Dragonborn, any martial class	Extra damage on melee attack after *dragon breath*

Fighter Feat	Prerequisites	Benefit
Agile Tempest	Dex 15, fighter, Tempest Technique	+1 damage with Tempest Technique
Avenging Spirit	Human fighter or human warlord	Gain action point when ally is reduced to 0 or fewer hp
Chainmail Agility	Dex 15, fighter	Ignore speed penalty for chainmail
Combat Opening	Half-elf, fighter, Combat Challenge	Enable ally to attack your enemy
Daunting Challenge	Fighter, Combat Challenge	Marked creatures –3 to attack anyone other than you
Draconic Arrogance	Dragonborn, fighter	Deal damage to enemies you push or knock prone
Elemental Guardian	Con 15, genasi, fighter	Racial trait improves when you are adjacent to an ally
Enduring Wallop	Dwarf, fighter	Deal ongoing 5 damage with fighter daily power
Fey Charge	Eladrin, fighter	Use reliable *fey step* with charge
Fiendish Defender	Tiefling, fighter, Combat Challenge	Apply *infernal wrath* to enemy that hits your ally
Grit	Con 17, fighter	Gain temporary hp when you spend healing surge
Marked Scourge	Fighter, Combat Challenge	Add Wis modifier to damage against marked enemy
Mighty Battlerage	Con 15, fighter, Battlerager Vigor	Gain increase to Battlerager Vigor damage
Opportunistic Archer	Elf, fighter, Combat Challenge	Use a bow for attacks granted by Combat Challenge
Phalanx Warrior	Fighter or warlord, proficiency with light or heavy shields	Adjacent allies gain +1 AC when you wield shield
Reckless Attacker	Fighter	Make a follow-up basic attack after critical hit
Stonefoot Reprisal	Dwarf, fighter	Enemy that pushes or slides you provokes opportunity attack

Ranger Feat	Prerequisites	Benefit
Bleeding Precision	Ranger, Hunter's Quarry	Deal ongoing 5 damage with daily ranger power
Darkhunter	Drow, ranger, Hunter's Quarry	Each enemy in *cloud of darkness* is designated as your quarry
Distracting Companion	Ranger, Beast Mastery, Hunter's Quarry	Quarry –2 to attack and damage you and your beast
Halfling Beast Mastery	Halfling, ranger, Beast Mastery	Beast companion gains *second chance* once per encounter
Hunter's Advantage	Elf, ranger, Hunter's Quarry	Deal +2 damage against quarry with combat advantage
Hunter's Resurgence	Ranger, Hunter's Quarry	Use your second wind when you drop an enemy
Preternatural Senses	Wis 15, ranger, trained in Perception	Roll twice for Perception checks
Prime Quarry	Wis 15, ranger, Hunter's Quarry, Prime Shot	Prime Shot bonus to attack rolls increases if target is also your quarry
Protective Beast	Ranger, Beast Mastery	You gain +1 AC if adjacent to beast companion
Sturdy Beast	Ranger, Beast Mastery	Your beast companion gains healing surge and hp
Wrathful Hunter	Tiefling, ranger, Hunter's Quarry	Use *infernal wrath* against quarry for bonus to attack rolls

Rogue Feat	Prerequisites	Benefit
Avandra's Gift	Halfling, rogue	Gain combat advantage with *second chance*
Bleeding Backstab	Rogue, Sneak Attack	Deal ongoing 5 damage with daily rogue power
Cull the Weak	Cha 15, rogue	Deal +2 damage in melee to bloodied or weakened enemies
Darkjumper	Drow, rogue	Teleport as free action within your *cloud of darkness*
Evasive Footwork	Dex 17, Cha 15, rogue	+1 to AC and Reflex when you shift 2 or more squares
Fey Gambit	Eladrin, rogue	Gain combat advantage against enemy you *fey step* next to
Group Flanking	Half-elf, rogue	Allies gain combat advantage against enemy you flank
Infernal Sneak Attack	Tiefling, rogue, Sneak Attack	Combine Sneak Attack with *infernal wrath* for extra damage
Opportunistic Sneak Attack	Rogue, Sneak Attack	Sneak Attack with opportunity attack slows target
Prime Slayer	Elf, rogue	Deal +2 damage if you are closest to target
Rogue Weapon Mastery	Rogue, Rogue Weapon Talent	Treat daggers and shuriken as high crit weapons
Roundabout Charge	Rogue, trained in Acrobatics	End your charge in any square adjacent to target

PARAGON TIER FEATS (CONTINUED)

Warlord Feat	Prerequisites	Benefit
Avenging Spirit	Human fighter or human warlord	Gain action point when ally is reduced to 0 or fewer hp
Bloody Inspiration	Dragonborn, warlord	Second ally benefits from your *inspiring word*
Defensive Surge	Con 15, warlord	Ally gains defensive bonuses from your second wind
Elemental Companions	Genasi, warlord	Adjacent allies share your racial energy resistance
Fey Tactics	Eladrin, warlord	Nearby ally can use *fey step* when you do
Impetuous Charger	Cha 15, warlord	Allies gain combat advantage against enemy you charge
Phalanx Warrior	Fighter or warlord, proficiency with light or heavy shields	Adjacent allies gain +1 AC when you wield shield
Reliable Resources	Warlord, Resourceful Presence	Ally gains temporary hp from your Resourceful Presence
Steadfast Tactics	Dwarf, warlord	*Inspiring word* reduces effect of push, pull, or slide
Vital Inspiration	Half-elf, warlord	Allies regain more hp with second wind
Warlord's Formation	Int 17, warlord	Aid two allies simultaneously

ELEMENTAL COMPANIONS

Prerequisites: 11th level, genasi, warlord

Benefit: Adjacent allies benefit from any resistance or saving throw bonus you have because of your current elemental manifestation.

ELEMENTAL GUARDIAN

Prerequisites: 11th level, Con 15, genasi, fighter

Benefit: While you are adjacent to any ally, your innate racial defensive talent improves. Apply the benefit for your current elemental manifestation.

Earthsoul: Increase racial bonus to saving throws to +2.

Firesoul, Stormsoul, or Windsoul: Increase resist value by 5.

Watersoul: Increase racial bonus to saving throws against ongoing damage to +4.

ENDURING WALLOP

Prerequisites: 11th level, dwarf, fighter

Benefit: When you hit an enemy with a fighter daily attack power while wielding an axe, a hammer, or a pick, that enemy takes ongoing damage equal to your Constitution modifier (save ends). If the power already deals ongoing damage that has no damage type, instead increase that ongoing damage by an amount equal to your Constution modifier.

EVASIVE FOOTWORK

Prerequisites: 11th level, Dex 17, Cha 15, rogue

Benefit: When you shift 2 or more squares on your turn, you gain a +1 bonus to AC and Reflex until the start of your next turn.

FEY CHARGE

Prerequisites: 11th level, eladrin, fighter

Benefit: When you charge, you can use your *fey step* racial power as a free action to replace up to 5 squares of your charge movement with teleportation.

If the charge attack hits, you do not expend *fey step*.

FEY GAMBIT

Prerequisites: 11th level, eladrin, rogue

Benefit: When you use your *fey step* racial power to move adjacent to an enemy, you gain combat advantage against that enemy until the end of your turn.

FEY TACTICS

Prerequisites: 11th level, eladrin, warlord

Benefit: When you use your *fey step* racial power, you can also teleport one ally within 5 squares of your starting position a distance equal to your *fey step* distance.

FIENDISH DEFENDER

Prerequisites: 11th level, tiefling, fighter, Combat Challenge class feature

Benefit: Your *infernal wrath* racial power can also be applied to any enemy marked by you that hit an ally since your last turn.

GRIT

Prerequisites: 11th level, Con 17, fighter

Benefit: When you spend a healing surge to regain hit points, you also gain temporary hit points equal to your Constitution modifier.

GROUP FLANKING

Prerequisites: 11th level, half-elf, rogue

Benefit: While you're flanking an enemy, all allies gain combat advantage against that enemy.

HALFLING BEAST MASTERY

Prerequisites: 11th level, halfling, ranger, Beast Mastery class feature

Benefit: Your beast companion can use the *second chance* racial power as an encounter power. This use doesn't count against your use of the power, and vice versa.

HUNTER'S ADVANTAGE

Prerequisites: 11th level, elf, ranger, Hunter's Quarry class feature

Benefit: You deal 2 extra damage with Hunter's Quarry when you have combat advantage against your quarry.

HUNTER'S RESURGENCE

Prerequisites: 11th level, ranger, Hunter's Quarry class feature

Benefit: When you reduce your quarry to 0 hit points, you can use your second wind as a free action. You do not gain the normal bonus to defenses if you do so.

IMPETUOUS CHARGER

Prerequisites: 11th level, Cha 15, warlord

Benefit: When you charge an enemy, your allies gain combat advantage against that enemy until the end of your next turn.

INFERNAL SNEAK ATTACK

Prerequisites: 11th level, tiefling, rogue, Sneak Attack class feature

Benefit: If you deal Sneak Attack damage with an attack benefiting from your *infernal wrath* racial power, you deal an extra die of Sneak Attack damage.

MARKED SCOURGE

Prerequisites: 11th level, fighter, Combat Challenge class feature

Benefit: Add your Wisdom modifier to damage rolls you make against enemies marked by you.

MIGHTY BATTLERAGE

Prerequisites: 11th level, Con 15, fighter, Battlerager Vigor class feature

Benefit: The damage bonus granted by your Battlerager Vigor increases by 1. At 21st level, it increases by 2.

OPPORTUNISTIC ARCHER

Prerequisites: 11th level, elf, fighter, Combat Challenge class feature

Benefit: When you can make a melee basic attack against a target because of Combat Challenge, you can instead make a ranged basic attack with a bow against the target. The ranged basic attack does not provoke opportunity attacks.

OPPORTUNISTIC SNEAK ATTACK

Prerequisites: 11th level, rogue, Sneak Attack class feature

Benefit: When you hit with an opportunity attack and deal Sneak Attack damage, the target is slowed until the end of your next turn.

PHALANX WARRIOR

Prerequisites: 11th level, fighter or warlord, proficiency with light or heavy shields

Benefit: When you are using a shield, adjacent allies gain a +1 shield bonus to AC.

PRETERNATURAL SENSES

Prerequisites: 11th level, Wis 15, ranger, trained in Perception

Benefit: Whenever you make a Perception check, roll twice and use the higher result.

PRIME QUARRY

Prerequisites: 11th level, Wis 15, ranger, Hunter's Quarry class feature, Prime Shot class feature

Benefit: The bonus to attack rolls granted by Prime Shot increases to +2 if the target is also your quarry.

PRIME SLAYER

Prerequisites: 11th level, elf, rogue

Benefit: While none of your allies are closer to your target than you are, you gain a +2 bonus to damage rolls for ranged attacks against that target.

PROTECTIVE BEAST

Prerequisites: 11th level, ranger, Beast Mastery class feature

Benefit: Whenever your beast companion is adjacent to you, you gain a +1 bonus to AC.

RECKLESS ATTACKER

Prerequisites: 11th level, fighter

Benefit: When you score a critical hit with a fighter attack power, you can make a melee basic attack as a free action. If you do so, you take a –2 penalty to AC until the end of your next turn.

RELIABLE RESOURCES

Prerequisites: 11th level, warlord, Resourceful Presence class feature

Benefit: When an ally who can see you spends an action point to take an extra action and doesn't use that action to make an attack, the ally gains temporary hit points equal to your Charisma modifier.

ROGUE WEAPON MASTERY

Prerequisites: 11th level, rogue, Rogue Weapon Talent class feature

Benefit: When you wield a dagger or a shuriken, the weapon gains the high crit property.

ROUNDABOUT CHARGE

Prerequisites: 11th level, rogue, trained in Acrobatics

Benefit: When you charge, you can end your movement in any square adjacent to the target from which you can attack it.

STEADFAST TACTICS

Prerequisites: 11th level, dwarf, warlord

Benefit: When you use *inspiring word* on an ally, that ally can reduce pull, push, and slide effects against him or her by 1 square until the end of the encounter.

STONEFOOT REPRISAL

Prerequisites: 11th level, dwarf, fighter

Benefit: If an adjacent enemy pushes or slides you, you can make an opportunity attack against that enemy before the forced movement. If the attack hits, you can negate the forced movement.

STURDY BEAST

Prerequisites: 11th level, ranger, Beast Mastery class feature

Benefit: Your beast companion gains one additional healing surge as well as additional hit points equal to 5 + your Wisdom modifier.

VITAL INSPIRATION

Prerequisites: 11th level, half-elf, warlord

Benefit: Any ally who can see and hear you adds your Charisma modifier to the hit points regained by using second wind.

WARLORD'S FORMATION

Prerequisites: 11th level, Int 17, warlord

Benefit: When you use the aid another action, you can aid up to two allies. You must provide the same aid to both allies (for instance, you can't aid one ally's attack roll and another ally's defenses, and you can't aid attack rolls against different targets).

WRATHFUL HUNTER

Prerequisites: 11th level, tiefling, ranger, Hunter's Quarry class feature

Benefit: If you use your *infernal wrath* racial power against your quarry, you gain a +3 power bonus to your next attack against the target (instead of +1).

EPIC TIER FEATS

Any feat in this section is available to a character of 21st level or higher who meets the feat's other prerequisites.

ACTION GRANT

Prerequisites: 21st level, Int 15, Cha 15, warlord, Resourceful Presence class feature

Benefit: When you roll initiative at the start of an encounter, you can give one of your action points to an ally you can see. That action point must be spent during the encounter or it is lost.

AGGRESSIVE LEADERSHIP

Prerequisites: 21st level, Cha 19, warlord

Benefit: While you are conscious, bloodied allies who can see and hear you gain a +2 bonus to damage rolls.

ARTFUL PROVOCATION

Prerequisites: 21st level, Cha 17, rogue, Artful Dodger class feature

Benefit: When you are missed by an opportunity attack, you gain combat advantage against the attacker until the end of your next turn.

BOLD SPIRIT

Prerequisites: 21st level, warlord, Bravura Presence class feature

Benefit: When you are hit by a melee attack while you are bloodied or granting combat advantage to the attacker, you gain temporary hit points equal to your Charisma modifier after the attack is resolved.

BRUTAL ADVANTAGE

Prerequisites: 21st level, Str 17, rogue, Brutal Scoundrel class feature

Benefit: When you have combat advantage against a target but don't use Sneak Attack against it, add your Strength modifier to the damage roll.

CALL TO GLORY

Prerequisites: 21st level, Cha 17, warlord

Benefit: Whenever you grant an ally an attack by using a warlord power, that ally gains temporary hit points equal to one-half your level if the attack hits.

CHANNELED BATTLERAGE

Prerequisites: 21st level, Con 17, fighter, Battlerager Vigor class feature

Benefit: When you hit with a melee attack, you can choose to lose all temporary hit points you have to reroll the attack's damage and use the better result.

CORRECTING AIM

Prerequisites: 21st level, ranger, Hunter's Quarry class feature

Benefit: If you miss your quarry with an attack, you gain a +2 bonus to your next attack roll against it.

DARKFIRE WARRIOR

Prerequisites: 21st level, drow, any martial class

Benefit: When you reduce the target of your *darkfire* racial power to 0 hit points with a weapon attack, you regain the use of *darkfire*.

EPIC TIER FEATS

Any Martial Class	Prerequisites	Benefit
Darkfire Warrior	Drow, any martial class	Regain use of *darkfire* after reducing target to 0 hp
Dragon Warrior	Con 17, dragonborn, any martial class	Regain *dragon breath* when first bloodied
Elemental Warrior	Genasi, any martial class	Regain use of racial power after scoring critical hit
Epic Recovery	Con 19, any martial class	Use second wind twice per encounter
Feywild Warrior	Dex 17, eladrin, any martial class	Teleport yourself and your target after using daily power
Fortune's Warrior	Dex 17, halfling, any martial class	Gain combat advantage after using *second chance*
Hawkeye Warrior	Wis 17, elf, any martial class	+1 to attack rolls after using *elven accuracy*
Infernal Warrior	Cha 17, tiefling, any martial class	Retaliate against a critical hit with *infernal wrath*
Invigorating Exploit	Any martial class	Martial attack power becomes invigorating
Martial Mastery	Any martial class	Regain encounter power when spending action point
Martial Resolve	Wis 15, any martial class, trained in Endurance	Make saving throws against certain conditions at both start and end of turn
Rattling Exploit	Any martial class	Martial attack power becomes rattling
Stoneheart Warrior	Con 17, dwarf, any martial class	Use second wind as free action
Timely Revival	Human, any martial class	Make death saving throws at the start of your turn

Fighter Feat	Prerequisites	Benefit
Channeled Battlerage	Con 17, fighter, Battlerager Vigor	Lose temporary hp to reroll damage
Knock-Back Swing	Con 17, fighter	Attacks with certain weapons push target 1 square
Mobile Warrior	Dex 17, fighter	Shift 1 square after attacking with certain weapons
Practiced Reliability	Fighter	Add reliable keyword to fighter encounter power
Reaching Whirlwind	Dex 15, Wis 15, fighter	Expand fighter power burst size with reach weapon
Rending Tempest	Dex 17, fighter or ranger	Hit with both weapons to deal extra damage
Tactical Insight	Half-elf, fighter	Allies gain +2 damage against marked enemy
Unstoppable Charge	Str 21, Con 17, fighter	Your turn does not automatically end after a charge

Ranger Feat	Prerequisites	Benefit
Correcting Aim	Ranger, Hunter's Quarry	+2 to attack rolls against your quarry when you miss
Improved Prime Shot	Wis 17, ranger, Prime Shot	Prime Shot attack roll bonus increases to +2
Peerless Hunter	Wis 17, ranger, Hunter's Quarry	Designate two targets as your quarry
Prime Hunter	Ranger	+1 to melee attack rolls against isolated enemies
Quick Beast Command	Wis 17, ranger, Beast Mastery	Command beast to attack as minor action
Rending Tempest	Dex 17, fighter or ranger	Hit with both weapons to deal extra damage
Staggering Shot	Ranger, Hunter's Quarry	Slow quarry instead of dealing Hunter's Quarry damage
Surprise Action	Wis 17, ranger	Full round of actions during surprise round

Rogue Feat	Prerequisites	Benefit
Artful Provocation	Cha 17, rogue, Artful Dodger	Missed opportunity attack grants combat advantage against attacker
Brutal Advantage	Str 17, rogue, Brutal Scoundrel	Add Str modifier to damage when you have combat advantage
Lasting Advantage	Rogue	Target grants combat advantage to you after a critical hit
One with Shadow	Rogue	Move through enemies' spaces while hidden
Ruthless Terror	Str 17, rogue, Ruthless Ruffian, trained in Intimidate	Rattling attacks apply -1 penalty on a miss
Whirlwind Sneak Attack	Rogue, Sneak Attack	Deal Sneak Attack damage to all targets of a rogue encounter attack power

DRAGON WARRIOR

Prerequisites: 21st level, Con 17, dragonborn, any martial class

Benefit: When you are first bloodied in an encounter, you regain the use of the *dragon breath* racial power if you have used it during this encounter.

ELEMENTAL WARRIOR

Prerequisites: 21st level, genasi, any martial class

Benefit: When you score a critical hit with a melee weapon, you can regain the use of a genasi racial power you have used during this encounter. You can gain this benefit once per encounter.

EPIC TIER FEATS (CONTINUED)

Warlord Feat	Prerequisites	Benefit
Action Grant	Int 15, Cha 15, warlord, Resourceful Presence	Ally gains one of your action points
Aggressive Leadership	Cha 19, warlord	Bloodied allies gain +2 damage
Bold Spirit	Warlord, Bravura Presence	Temporary hp when bloodied or granting combat advantage
Call to Glory	Cha 17, warlord	Ally gains temporary hp when you grant attack
Protective Leadership	Int 19, warlord	Bloodied allies gain +1 to all defenses
Supreme Inspiration	Cha 19, warlord	Heal one extra target with *inspiring word*
Tactical Cunning	Int 17, warlord	Allies you slide gain +2 to AC

EPIC RECOVERY

Prerequisites: 21st level, Con 19, any martial class

Benefit: You can use your second wind twice per encounter.

FEYWILD WARRIOR

Prerequisites: 21st level, Dex 17, eladrin, any martial class

Benefit: When you hit a target with a martial daily attack power, you can teleport yourself and the target 5 squares after you resolve the attack.

FORTUNE'S WARRIOR

Prerequisites: 21st level, Dex 17, halfling, any martial class

Benefit: When you use the *second chance* racial power against an attacker, you gain combat advantage with martial attack powers against that attacker until the end of your next turn.

HAWKEYE WARRIOR

Prerequisites: 21st level, Wis 17, elf, any martial class

Benefit: When you use the *elven accuracy* racial power, you gain a +1 bonus to attack rolls against the target of the attack until the end of the encounter.

IMPROVED PRIME SHOT

Prerequisites: 21st level, Wis 17, ranger, Prime Shot class feature

Benefit: The bonus to ranged attack rolls granted by your Prime Shot is +2 instead of +1.

INFERNAL WARRIOR

Prerequisites: 21st level, Cha 17, tiefling, any martial class

Benefit: When an enemy scores a critical hit against you, you can use your *infernal wrath* racial power against that enemy as a free action, even if you have already used the power this encounter.

INVIGORATING EXPLOIT

Prerequisites: 21st level, any martial class

Benefit: Choose a martial encounter attack power that you know. That power gains the invigorating keyword.

Special: Each time you gain a level, you can choose to assign this feat's benefit to a different power and remove it from the power to which it currently applies.

KNOCK-BACK SWING

Prerequisites: 21st level, Con 17, fighter

Benefit: When you make an opportunity attack with an axe, a hammer, a mace, or a pick, you push the target 1 square, whether or not the attack hits.

LASTING ADVANTAGE

Prerequisites: 21st level, rogue

Benefit: Whenever you score a critical hit with a rogue attack power, the target of the attack grants combat advantage to you until the end of your next turn.

MARTIAL MASTERY

Prerequisites: 21st level, any martial class

Benefit: When you spend an action point to take an extra action, you also regain the use of a martial encounter power you have used during this encounter.

MARTIAL RESOLVE

Prerequisites: 21st level, Wis 15, any martial class, trained in Endurance

Benefit: You can make saving throws against the dazed, slowed, stunned, weakened, and immobilized conditions at both the start and the end of your turn.

MOBILE WARRIOR

Prerequisites: 21st level, Dex 17, fighter

Benefit: When you make an attack with a flail, a heavy blade, a light blade, or a spear, you can shift 1 square after resolving the attack, whether or not it hits.

One with Shadow

Prerequisites: 21st level, rogue

Benefit: While you are hidden from an enemy, you can move through that enemy's space and remain hidden.

Peerless Hunter

Prerequisites: 21st level, Wis 17, ranger, Hunter's Quarry class feature

Benefit: When designating a target as your quarry, you can designate a second target within 5 squares of the first target as your quarry as well. When you designate a third target as your quarry, you decide which of the previous two quarries is no longer your quarry.

Practiced Reliability

Prerequisites: 21st level, fighter

Benefit: Choose a fighter encounter attack power that you know and that has a single target and a single attack roll. That power gains the reliable keyword.

Special: Each time you gain a level, you can choose to remove this feat's benefit from the power and assign it to a different power.

Prime Hunter

Prerequisites: 21st level, ranger

Benefit: You gain a +1 bonus to melee attack rolls against any target that is adjacent to no creature other than you.

Protective Leadership

Prerequisites: 21st level, Int 19, warlord

Benefit: While you are conscious, bloodied allies who can see and hear you gain a +1 bonus to all defenses.

Quick Beast Command

Prerequisites: 21st level, Wis 17, ranger, Beast Mastery class feature

Benefit: On your turn, you can use a minor action to command your beast companion to make a melee basic attack.

Rattling Exploit

Prerequisites: 21st level, any martial class

Benefit: Choose a martial encounter attack power that you know. That power gains the rattling keyword.

Special: Whenever you gain a level, you can choose to assign this feat's benefit to a different power and remove it from the power to which it currently applies.

Reaching Whirlwind

Prerequisites: 21st level, Dex 15, Wis 15, fighter

Benefit: While wielding a reach weapon, you can treat any fighter attack power that has the weapon keyword and that is a close burst 1 as a close burst 2 instead.

Rending Tempest

Prerequisites: 21st level, Dex 17, fighter or ranger

Benefit: When you hit a target with a melee attack using two weapons during your turn, your subsequent melee attacks against the target deal 1[W] extra damage on a hit during the same turn.

Ruthless Terror

Prerequisites: 21st level, Str 17, rogue, trained in Intimidate

Benefit: When you miss with a rattling attack, the target takes a -1 penalty to attack rolls against you until the end of your next turn.

Staggering Shot

Prerequisites: 21st level, ranger, Hunter's Quarry class feature

Benefit: When you hit your quarry with a ranged attack, you can forgo dealing Hunter's Quarry damage to instead cause the target to become slowed until the end of your next turn.

Stoneheart Warrior

Prerequisites: 21st level, Con 17, dwarf, any martial class

Benefit: You can use your second wind as a free action.

SUPREME INSPIRATION

Prerequisites: 21st level, Cha 19, warlord
Benefit: Whenever you use *inspiring word*, you can heal two targets instead of one (either two allies or one ally and yourself).

SURPRISE ACTION

Prerequisites: 21st level, Wis 17, ranger
Benefit: During the surprise round, you can take a standard action, a move action, and a minor action if you aren't surprised.

TACTICAL CUNNING

Prerequisites: 21st level, Int 17, warlord
Benefit: Whenever you use a warlord power to slide an ally, that ally gains a +2 bonus to AC until the end of your next turn.

TACTICAL INSIGHT

Prerequisites: 21st level, half-elf, fighter
Benefit: Allies gain a +2 bonus to damage rolls against enemies marked by you.

TIMELY REVIVAL

Prerequisites: 21st level, human, any martial class
Benefit: You make death saving throws at the start of your turn rather than at the end. If you succeed on a death saving throw and have not used your second wind this encounter, you can use your second wind. You then take the rest of your turn as normal.

UNSTOPPABLE CHARGE

Prerequisites: 21st level, Str 21, Con 17, fighter
Benefit: Your turn does not automatically end after you charge; you can take further actions.

WHIRLWIND SNEAK ATTACK

Prerequisites: 21st level, rogue, Sneak Attack class feature
Benefit: Choose a rogue encounter attack power that you know. You can deal Sneak Attack damage to every target you hit with that power, and doing so counts as one use of Sneak Attack. You still must have combat advantage against a target to deal the extra damage to it, and you can't deal the extra damage more than once to any target, even if the power attacks that target multiple times.
Special: Whenever you gain a level, you can choose to assign this feat's benefit to a different power and remove it from the power to which it currently applies.

MULTICLASS FEATS

Some of these feats have paragon multiclassing in a particular class as a prerequisite. To qualify for such a feat, you must have chosen paragon multiclassing (*Player's Handbook*, page 209) in that class rather than taking a paragon path.

BATTLE ACUMEN [MULTICLASS FIGHTER]

Prerequisites: Any multiclass fighter feat, paragon multiclassing as a fighter
Benefit: You gain the fighter's Combat Superiority class feature.

BATTLE AWARENESS [MULTICLASS FIGHTER]

Prerequisites: Str 13, Wis 13
Benefit: You gain training in one skill from the fighter's class skill list.

Once per encounter, whenever an enemy that is adjacent to you shifts or makes an attack that does not include you as a target, you can make a melee basic attack against that enemy as an immediate interrupt.

BATTLE INSTRUCTOR [MULTICLASS WARLORD]

Prerequisites: Any multiclass warlord feat, paragon multiclassing as a warlord
Benefit: You gain the warlord's Combat Leader class feature.

COURAGEOUS SHOOTER [MULTICLASS RANGER]

Prerequisites: Any multiclass ranger feat, paragon multiclassing as a ranger
Benefit: You gain the ranger's Prime Shot class feature.

FIRST IN [MULTICLASS ROGUE]

Prerequisites: Any multiclass rogue feat, paragon multiclassing as a rogue
Benefit: You gain the rogue's First Strike class feature.

MARTIAL MULTICLASSING

What might lead your character to take a multiclass feat to dabble in the abilities of a martial class? Whether you're a fighter looking to improve your abilities with a warlord's leadership or a rogue's high damage, or a paladin looking to broaden your defender's arsenal with a fighter feat, it's easy to imagine that, as part of the teamwork of your adventuring party, you pick up some tricks from another character in your group. You might even seek out specialized training when you're in town or figure out on your own how you can add something extra to the powers your class gives you.

MULTICLASS FEATS

Name	Prerequisites	Benefit
Battle Acumen	Any multiclass fighter feat, paragon multiclassing as a fighter	Fighter: Combat Superiority
Battle Awareness	Str 13, Wis 13	Fighter: training in one skill, immediate interrupt basic attack once per encounter
Battle Instructor	Any multiclass warlord feat, paragon multiclassing as a warlord	Warlord: Combat Leader
Courageous Shooter	Any multiclass ranger feat, paragon multiclassing as a ranger	Ranger: Prime Shot
First In	Any multiclass rogue feat, paragon multiclassing as a rogue	Rogue: First Strike
Inspiring Leader	Str 13, Cha 13	Warlord: training in one skill, ally gains action point benefit once per encounter
Ruthless Efficiency	Str 13, Dex 13	Rogue: training in Stealth skill, Ruthless Ruffian
Sly Dodge	Dex 13, Cha 13	Rogue: training in Bluff skill or Intimidate skill, add Cha modifier to AC once per encounter
Tactical Leader	Str 13, Int 13	Warlord: training in one skill, ally gains +1 to attack roll once per encounter
Two-Blade Warrior	Str 13, Dex 13	Ranger: training in one skill, wield one-handed weapon as off-hand weapon

INSPIRING LEADER [MULTICLASS WARLORD]

Prerequisites: Str 13, Cha 13

Benefit: You gain training in one skill from the warlord's class skill list.

Once per encounter, when an ally who can see you spends an action point to take an extra action, that ally also gains temporary hit points equal to 1 + one-half your level.

RUTHLESS EFFICIENCY [MULTICLASS ROGUE]

Prerequisites: Str 13, Dex 13

Benefit: You gain training in the Stealth skill. You gain the Ruthless Ruffian class feature.

SLY DODGE [MULTICLASS ROGUE]

Prerequisites: Dex 13, Cha 13

Benefit: You gain training in the Bluff skill or the Intimidate skill.

Once per encounter, when an enemy makes an opportunity attack against you, you can add your Charisma modifier to your AC against that attack.

TACTICAL LEADER [MULTICLASS WARLORD]

Prerequisites: Str 13, Int 13

Benefit: You gain training in one skill from the warlord's class skill list.

Once per encounter, when an ally you can see spends an action point to make an attack, that ally gains a +1 bonus to the attack roll.

TWO-BLADE WARRIOR [MULTICLASS RANGER]

Prerequisites: Str 13, Dex 13

Benefit: You gain training in one skill from the ranger's class skill list.

You can wield a one-handed weapon in your off hand as though it were an off-hand weapon.

EPIC DESTINIES

These epic destinies are forged with armor, sword, or claw. Pursue a path of martial excellence and gain acclaim as an unstoppable combat force.

ADAMANTINE SOLDIER

You are as solid as the foundations of the world. Nothing can break you—ever.

Prerequisites: 21st level, fighter or warlord

Throughout your career, you have been an unstoppable force in heavy armor. In your coat of metal, you have stood against the weapons and powers of creatures that could lay waste to cities. In the end, your armor might have been a little worse for wear, and maybe you were, too. But still you stood unbowed.

You know that armor is more than just a piece of equipment. It's a second skin, and it's the face you show the world. You've made it a hallmark of your legend. When your helmed silhouette appears on the horizon, your admirers take hope and your enemies quail. Those same folk might fail to recognize your face, but they easily identify your superhuman shell.

IMMORTALITY?

The adamantine warrior must prove the hardest of fighters. Your saga might make you an eternal symbol, your armor's distinctive shape and markings burned into the world's iconography. Already, people hold you up as the exemplar of the soldier who is unbreakable in body and spirit.

Armored Icon: When you complete your final quest, you stand as an immaculate example of the knight in shining armor. All armored warriors throughout time recall your story. Your armored form is the ultimate gauge by which all other armored juggernauts measure themselves.

To become this icon of indestructibility, you must stand fast in your last battle. You cannot fall, give in to pain, or break in any way. Prove that your armor is like your skin, and your skin is like your armor. It can't slow you down; instead, it holds you up; Unbreakable, you carry each other into fable. Perhaps your armor even takes you to the side of a deity, such as Kord, who forever holds you up as an exarch of glorious and fearless battle. You then become the patron saint of all such warriors.

Your name becomes synonymous with toughness and resilience. It develops into a word with which fighters compliment one another for bold exploits in heavy armor. When you hear echoes of your name spoken in the world, you pound your gauntlet-clad fist to your breastplate. You know that those who aspire to be like you hear the ringing sound with spiritual ears and take heart.

ADAMANTINE SOLDIER FEATURES

Armor Supremacy (21st level): You gain a +2 bonus to AC while wearing heavy armor. You also ignore any check penalty or speed penalty normally imposed by heavy armor.

Unbreakable Skin (24th level): While wearing heavy armor, you gain resistance to all damage equal to your Constitution modifier.

Hard to Kill (30th level): Once per day, you can treat any saving throw you just rolled as if you had rolled a natural 20.

ADAMANTINE SOLDIER POWER

Inexorable Advance	Adamantine Soldier Utility 26

Nothing can hold you back.

Daily ✦ Martial, Stance
Minor Action   **Personal**
Effect: Until the stance ends, you can shift 1 square into an adjacent enemy's space and then push the enemy 1 square as a move action.

BEASTLORD

You and your beast companion are like twin aspects of one being, acting in perfect accord. Any separateness is an illusion of space and time—a seeming that might one day be erased.

Prerequisites: 21st level, ranger, Beast Mastery class feature

Your valiant allies fought alongside you and, in time, triumphed. In their midst, you have known friendship and an interdependence that few people can even imagine. With these treasures, you might have even saved the world you love. But even this seemingly perfect camaraderie, this example of flawless alliance, pales in comparison to your relationship with your beast companion.

You, like no other among your epic peers, know true companionship and trust. The beast at your side is more than a friend and ally. It forms an extension of your own soul.

IMMORTALITY?

Some Beastlords remain apart from their beast companions, and they wander the cosmos in service to a higher entity or ideals. Others pass into the mists of death, as is natural, believing that they'll one day be reborn when the world has need. A few go on to attain a form of unity, in body and consciousness, as described here.

5

Beastlord Apotheosis: When your final task is complete, you have proven that humanoid and beast are not separate. You and your companion act as a single being split into two bodies. Those who tell your story give an account of how the two of you illustrated this truth by becoming one. In fact, they whisper that what became apparent in the end was always so.

You manifest a spirit that encompasses the values your beast companion symbolizes, and you merge with the beast exemplified by your nature. In so doing, you take the shape of a great spirit of nature, pristine and immortal. Your shape is thereafter as you wish it to be—person, beast, two at one time, or an amalgam thereof. Forever, you endure in the wild places of the world as a guardian and an inspiration. Perhaps you'll be an exarch of Melora, or you'll remain distinct from any deity, an example of a creature unique to the world.

Those who follow your model hold you in mind when they travel and fight alongside their own beast companions. They, and others who revere nature and its creatures, look to you as an archetype and a guide.

BEASTLORD FEATURES

Ultimate Understanding (21st level): Once per round, you can take a minor action to command your beast companion to take a standard action, a move action, or a minor action.

Fused Fate (24th level): Whenever an effect targets you, you can choose for it to target your beast companion in addition to you or instead of you, as long as the beast is within 20 squares of you and you can see it.

Shared Life (30th level): As long as either you or your beast companion has at least 1 hit point, the other can't be killed, regardless of negative hit points or failed death saving throws. Keep track of negative hit points and failed death saving throws as normal; if you both are reduced to 0 hit points or fewer, the negative hit points and failed death saving throws immediately take effect.

BEASTLORD POWER

Quickened Companion	Beastlord Utility 26

Your beast companion understands your desire before you finish thinking it.

Encounter ✦ Beast, Martial
Free Action   **Close** burst 20
Target: Your beast companion in burst
Effect: The target takes a standard action, a move action, or a minor action of your choice.

DARK WANDERER

You stride the eerie paths of fate. Until destiny meets you on this road, you'll roam forever.

Prerequisites: 21st level, ranger or rogue

You left home ages ago, saying goodbye to the comforts that a simpler life might have held. Following an unspoken yearning, you took to the road with other vagabonds. Your way led along sinister paths and to fateful deeds. In time, perhaps you and your companions came to be called heroes. Still, dark strands of fortune draw you onward to an unknown end.

Until that end comes, you wander the world as a shadowy presence, turning up where you're least expected or most needed.

IMMORTALITY?

Providence saved you for the final struggle. When you reach that doom, who knows where it might carry you?

Roaming Wyrd: Your wandering days are not at an end just because you've caught up to your predestined future. From a young age, you have been a cat's-paw of fate, an unwitting agent of luck and ruin. You followed your calling where it led you and did what was required, and now you've finished what dark kismet has set before you. Those who know your story see you as fate personified.

The tapestry of your exploits in life follows you, colored by your final act. If, ultimately, you brought good to the world, your legend is one of how fortune favors the bold. However, your story might have a darker hue from the inescapable pull of grim destiny.

You wander the cosmos, held as a patron or intercessor by those seeking or avoiding fate. You could be the agent of a power related to luck or predestination, such as Avandra or the Raven Queen. More likely, though, you have cut the threads of the inevitable and transcended the snares of chance.

Now, you drift free, straying wherever you wish for once in your life. In so doing, you serve as an example to those who wish to make their own way free of the ensnaring strands of fate and destiny.

DARK WANDERER FEATURES

Not My Destiny (21st level): Any creature of your level or lower that hits you takes a –4 penalty to attack rolls against you until the end of the encounter.

Dark Road (24th level): You can walk to any destination you desire in a single, uninterrupted 24-hour period of walking. No matter how distant the location, or how many planes separate you from it, you reach the destination 24 hours after you begin, finding shortcuts, portals, or other modes of transport previously unknown to you. You do not require any rest, food, or water during this travel, except to

recharge powers and regain healing surges. During your journey, you are safe from hazards, attacks, and other dangers.

When choosing a destination, you must be specific. If your destination is within a structure, such as a particular room within a castle, the long walk leads you to the structure's main entrance, not inside the structure.

You can choose to be accompanied by a number of characters equal to 5 + your Wisdom modifier, all of whom share the benefit of this class feature.

Long Walk Back (30th level): If you die and are not returned to life within 12 hours, your body and possessions disappear. Twelve hours after that—24 hours after your death—you arrive, equipped as you were when you died, having just walked back from wherever it is you and your DM decided you awoke after you were slain. Your condition is the same as if you had been subject to a Raise Dead ritual, but without any death penalty.

You can choose to arrive at the place of your death, at the location of any of your allies, or at any location you consider home. There's a final purpose in your existence, and it's not random death.

Dark Wanderer Power

Never at a Loss	Dark Wanderer Utility 26

You are an endless well of resourcefulness.

Daily ✦ Martial
Minor Action   **Personal**
Effect: You regain the use of a daily utility power you have used today.

Eternal Defender

You stand in the path of those who would rend the defenseless world. That world is safe behind your ever-vigilant shield.

Prerequisites: 21st level, fighter

You have taken the defender ideal to heart. This devotion might have started at childhood, when you stood up for those weaker than you. Perhaps the ideal of the mighty protecting the weak was culturally instilled in you, as it is in all good-hearted dwarves. Whatever the case, rather than using your strength and power solely for personal gain, you willingly placed yourself in harm's way to make sure that others had a chance to survive and thrive.

At the core of your personal morals and beliefs is the certainty that it is your job to protect your allies. When among them, you stand in the forefront in times of danger, no matter how dire the foe. Your skill and courage ever prove an anchor for your companions during the tumult of battle.

Immortality?

Bravery and immovability define you as a champion to your friends and the people you have saved over the course of your chronicle. To many, you are the mountain holding back the onrush of a monstrous tide.

Everlasting Bulwark: You have laid low your final and greatest adversary. During the fight you, as always, formed the steady center around which your allies could operate, taking the brunt of the punishment without bending or complaining. Ever more will you be the supreme standard for those on the front line of any battle.

The world always needs someone of your strength and stature at the ready to come to its defense. Those wishing to take up sword or hammer to defend others refer to you as if you were a saint. Although your name might be spoken as a universally recognized synonym for the ultimate guardian, you're not ready to just lay down your shield and axe.

Perhaps, then, you take a place in divine dominions, next to or in service to a godly stalwart such as Moradin. Building a post somewhere in the cosmos, you might take it upon yourself to stand vigil over a primordial threat or against the machinations of evil deities. If something stirs or threatens, you herald the coming danger and stand the first to face it. Perhaps instead some power helps you eternally watch over a chosen people, infusing your watchful spirit into the land. Or you might make a pact to pass away but instill your defender's heart into your folk, awakening a new profusion of heroes.

5

WES LOUIE

ETERNAL DEFENDER FEATURES

Unending Strength (21st level): Increase your Strength score by 2. Your normal load, heavy load, and maximum drag load are twice their normal values (Strength × 20, Strength × 40, and Strength × 100 pounds, respectively). Once per day, you gain a +10 bonus to a Strength ability check or a Strength-based skill check of your choice.

Godlike Stature (24th level): Your size doesn't change, but your height and weight increase to 25 percent and 100 percent above the normal range for your race, respectively. You can wield weapons as if you were one size larger, and if you are normally Medium or larger, your melee reach increases by 1 square.

Great Power (30th level): Once per day, you can treat any successful melee attack roll you just made as if it were a natural 20, or you can treat any unsuccessful melee attack roll you just made as if it were a hit.

ETERNAL DEFENDER POWER

Implacable Destruction	Eternal Defender Utility 26

You take on a defiant aspect that makes it impossible for your enemies to avoid your attacks completely.

Daily ✦ Martial, Stance
Minor Action   **Personal**
Effect: Until the stance ends, every time you miss with a melee or a close weapon attack, you deal damage to the target equal to your Strength modifier.

GODHUNTER

If it bleeds, you can kill it. If it doesn't bleed, you can make it bleed. Then you can kill it.

Prerequisites: 21st level, ranger or rogue

Face it—you're a killer. That doesn't necessarily make you a bad person. Some creatures need killing. It's better for everyone in the end, and you're especially good at endings.

Not only are you an ace slayer, but you have also developed a reputation for taking out the tough marks. No matter how formidable a foe, you always find a way—by blade or bow—to send it to its doom. Destiny chose you to be the one who has what it takes to kill those tougher than you.

Your allies rely on you for your deadly art. Wary opponents maneuver to avoid giving you an advantage. Common folk and planar denizens equate your name with quick death.

IMMORTALITY?

Already legendary, your name, along with accounts of your remorseless fighting style, shall live forever. Few of your opponents survive past their fateful meeting with you, but you might just live on past your own meeting with fate.

Keen Motivation: You met your utmost challenge, and look who's dead and who isn't. The proof is in the grave. Among those that have a similar mortal origin, you are the greatest slayer in the universe. Maybe a god or two has skills that compare. Maybe.

Sticking around to stir up the cosmos isn't a bad idea. Powerful mortals, deities, demon lords, and primordials can get complacent or uppity. The worst rest in their own realms in smug satisfaction, and either cease doing what they should do or start doing something they shouldn't. No one rests easy with you nearby.

Mortal terror has a way of inspiring decisive change, and you have a pointed way of rousing just such a fear. It's not that you need to threaten anyone in particular. It could just be made known that you have a particular agenda. Working as a free agent, you leave no entity safe from the prospect of your lethal prompting.

Even a little prodding is bound to be a boon to progress. You could be just the wild card the world needs to keep power in the right balance and affairs moving along smoothly.

GODHUNTER FEATURES

Peerless Predator (21st level): Once per encounter, you can reroll an attack roll against a creature that is higher level than you.

Deific Agony (24th level): When you score a critical hit against a creature that is higher level than you, the creature takes a –5 penalty to saving throws and cannot regain hit points or recharge any powers until the end of your next turn.

Blasphemous Recovery (30th level): Once per day, when you are hit by an attack from a creature that is higher level than you, you can choose to treat that attack as a miss and then regain the use of second wind and the use of one encounter power you have used during this encounter.

GODHUNTER POWER

Deicidal Eye	Godhunter Utility 26

Your merciless perspective reveals every weakness, no matter how insignificant.

Daily ✦ Martial
Minor Action   **Close** burst 10
Target: One creature in burst
Effect: Your attacks ignore any resistance or immunity possessed by the target, and the target gains vulnerable 5 to your attacks. This effect lasts until you are reduced to 0 hit points or until you use the power on a new target.
Special: Increase the vulnerability by 5 if the target is higher level than you or if the target is a solo monster. Increase the vulnerability by 10 if the target is both.

LEGENDARY GENERAL

You stand above the famous leaders of history, an inspiration to any being that follows your word.

Prerequisites: 21st level, warlord

Dhuryan Flamebrow, Malachi of Bael Turath, Ossandrya of the Spiral Tower, Jarret the Twiceborn, and Bergrom Earthfast—these names live on in the annals of time because names of mighty leaders always do. Few leaders are more respected than those who have proven themselves on the field of battle and in the nightmare of war. It's no surprise that history remembers those who lead others through mortal danger. These figures have influenced entire military traditions the world over.

Long have you stood among such illustrious company, a celebrated captain. You have led your fellows in battle against uncountable foes and emerged victorious. Your leadership and encouragement inspired your allies and brought them home safely again and again. Perhaps you're the best commander the world has ever known.

IMMORTALITY?

In taking responsibility for leading your comrades on the long and terrifying road you have traveled, you have displayed cunning, resolve, and courage. Now that you've arrived, you might receive an even higher calling.

Battle Everlasting: Upon the accomplishment of your last epic quest, your soul is tugged at by a call to duty. More than one creature of godlike power is bound to offer you immortality, along with a position of power. The only question is whose side you'll take.

The battle between the gods and the primordials ended eons ago. Strife among planar agencies is still common, and the balance could tip to spark war across the cosmos yet again. Deities, especially malevolent ones, plot against one another to the detriment of all. Elemental powers still look with vengeful eyes upon the world and the heavens. Fey entities, and those of shadow, occasionally raise armies to shake the pillars of the universe. Hordes of demons threaten the very roots of existence. Until an unforeseen age takes hold in which evil is quelled and want is subdued, peace and stability feel tenuous. The need for a leader of legendary skill remains constant.

Is it your greater destiny to stand at the fore of united angelic legions as they hold back the chaos? Will you lead the gods to victory over their ancient foes? Do you prefer the side of the primordials? Might you command archons and efreets as they seize dominions in the Astral Sea, usurping the usurpers? Or will you choose a middle road, mercenary or enlightened, and pick your battles carefully as each situation calls you to war?

LEGENDARY GENERAL FEATURES

Mythic Inspiration (21st level): When you use your second wind, one ally within 20 squares of you can also spend a healing surge.

Legendary Tactical Action (24th level): Any ally can spend an action point possessed by you or by any other ally whom he or she can see once per encounter. Spending this action point doesn't count against the ally's limit of spending 1 action point per encounter.

Unyielding Company (30th level): While you have at least 1 hit point, allies within 20 squares of you do not fall unconscious at 0 hit points or fewer and cannot die because of negative hit points. Allies at 0 hit points or fewer still make death saving throws as normal, and they can die as a result of failed death saving throws.

LEGENDARY GENERAL POWER

Legendary Exploits	Legendary General Utility 26

Your word is the call of destiny leading your allies into legend.

Daily ✦ Martial
Standard Action   **Close** burst 20
Targets: You and each ally in burst
Effect: Each target regains the use of a power of level 25 or lower, either an encounter power he or she has used during this encounter or a daily power he or she has used today. The power cannot be one that allows the target to regain the use of another power.

MARTIAL ARCHETYPE

You are a vehicle of destruction born from your perfection of the fighting forms. You embody martial power.

Prerequisites: 21st level, any martial class, paragon multiclassing in a martial class

From the moment you could raise a sword, you knew your destiny lay along its keen edge, your future in the hilt and pommel, and your legacy in the mastery of this single piece of steel. You spent your youth training. You honed your technique and studied the martial forms of combat. As you grew and set out from your humble beginning, your adventures exposed you to the exploits of countless combatants. In them, you became sure of a common connection, a link binding all who live and die by the sword.

Try as you might, this fundamental truth of martial power eluded you. For some reason, its perfect truth continued to slip beyond you reach, but remained just visible behind your mastery. You thought that through incomparable discipline, practice, and innovation, you'd find it once more and this time never let it go.

Driven by the vision of your potential, you redoubled your efforts, devoting your attention to the possibility of ultimate fighting prowess. You remain confident that one you will day perfect your maneuvers. When that day comes, you will stand among the greatest warriors who have ever lived.

IMMORTALITY?

Each step on the road to mastering the fighting arts, you draw closer to the realization of your full potential. The dawning understanding brought on with each new revelation impels you further, to seek out and learn more until you attain the heights of true mastery.

Legendary Master: With a practiced strike, you dispatch the last foe, the final obstacle standing between you and the fulfillment of your final quest. With this triumph, something stirs inside your consciousness. It is as if your last exploit unlocked a door in your mind, throwing it open to reveal the secrets you have long sought. The revelation strikes you to the soul, ripping away the last doubts, the last of your reluctance to push further and lay bare the true depth of martial mastery.

With full comprehension of these fundamental truths fixed in your mind and displayed in your incomparable techniques, you set out to teach others. Mysteries you have struggled to master you can now impart to those new to the sword. Through these scions you will live forever. As your fighting techniques are passed down, your memory will grow beyond your legendary exploits. Your martial mysticism shall transcend the mortal coil to become a living part of the power all warriors use.

MARTIAL ARCHETYPE FEATURES

Archetype's Edge (21st level): You gain a 17th-level encounter attack power from any martial class. Also, whenever you score a critical hit, you regain the use of a martial encounter attack power you have used during this encounter.

Reliable Warrior (24th level): Every martial encounter attack power you know gains the reliable keyword as long as the power has only one target and has no effect on a miss.

Warrior's Ascent (26th level): You gain one 22nd-level utility power from any martial class. Also, whenever you score a critical hit with a martial encounter or daily power, you can spend a healing surge as a free action.

Perfect Warrior (30th level): You gain an encounter attack power or a utility power of any level from any martial class. Also, whenever you score a critical hit with a martial encounter or daily power, you can make a melee basic attack against each adjacent enemy as a free action.

PERFECT ASSASSIN

You have become so good at butchery that it has become part of your very being. You are a shade of death.

Prerequisites: 21st level, rogue

Slaying quickly and efficiently is an art, like composing music or painting a masterpiece. Your instruments are weapons, and your medium is enemy flesh. The hands are the true tools of any master. And your hands are sublime in their lethal skill.

You have worked this bloody trade for so long that they say death has suffused your body, spirit, and soul. Rumor has it that you see death hovering over your foes, showing you which one is next. Your enemies sense your connection with quietus, and it unnerves them. Your reputation as a killer has taken on supernatural proportions. Little do those know who hear your legend, but the tales about you are almost entirely true.

IMMORTALITY?

In focusing on your deadliness, you have all but become extinction incarnate. Can death die in turn?

Death Can't Die: By the time you have dealt death to your final adversary, you have perfected death-dealing beyond all mortal bounds. Any who have skill in your chosen art see you as an inspiration—a dark ideal. Some venerate you, and others hope to prove themselves superior to you by carving out their own sinister legends. No doubt you've attracted the attention of entities connected to the greatest forces of life's end.

You might choose to lead such creatures, guiding them along mortality's fickle paths. Instead, you could work as an operative of the Raven Queen, maybe even as a commander above cadres of the sorrowsworn. Perhaps to serve in shadow isn't good enough for you, and as other mortal beings have attempted before, you will challenge the beings of the cosmos that contend for authority over death. Could you be the one that determines who has that final authority?

Like the undying warrior, you might pass on your skills to those who seek you out, guiding them along the path you followed. If you tire of destruction, even the righteous kind, you can instead remove yourself from the cares of the world. You could live on quietly in a secluded part of existence, possibly in the company of your longtime allies.

The choice is yours. You are beyond the Raven Queen's grasp, unless one day you choose to surrender yourself to the final destination of most mortal souls. Perhaps you unravel death's remaining secrets for all mortals, dealing the fear of life's end a deathblow.

PERFECT ASSASSIN FEATURES

Death's Eye (21st level): Whenever you reduce an enemy to 0 hit points, choose another enemy you can see. Until the end of your next turn, you gain combat advantage against the second enemy, and it takes a –2 penalty to attack rolls against you.

Assassin's Advantage (24th level): When you miss with an attack against a target you have combat

advantage against, you deal damage to that target equal to your Dexterity modifier + 1 per die of Sneak Attack damage you normally deal.

Pierce the Weakness (30th level): Once per encounter, you can choose for an attack of yours to be against the target's lowest defense, rather than the defense normally targeted by the attack. You can add your Sneak Attack damage to this attack even if you don't have combat advantage. Doing so doesn't count against the normal limit on Sneak Attack use.

PERFECT ASSASSIN POWER

Spirit of Death — Perfect Assassin Utility 26

No matter what would normally stop you, you flit away from your fallen foe like a ghost.

Encounter
Free Action — **Personal**
Trigger: You reduce an enemy to 0 hit points
Effect: If you are dazed, immobilized, restrained, or slowed, you end any of those conditions. You then turn invisible and insubstantial and can shift your speed. At the end of the shift, you turn visible and are no longer insubstantial.

UNDYING WARRIOR

Your body and soul are one, not beyond the bite of steel but past the reach of death.

Prerequisites: 21st level, fighter

You are the ultimate survivor. Kobold spears, goblin arrows, orc axes, dragon fire, the necrotic touch of a wraith—you've seen it all in your adventures. And you're still alive to tell the tales.

Death has tried to claim you many times, but it failed. You have either survived your wounds or returned from beyond mortality's shroud. Each time you faced death, your soul quickened within your body, attaching itself more deeply to your physical shell.

As you grow in epic power, destiny conspires to keep you breathing. You recover from wounds that would take the life of any lesser mortal. Your reserves appear limitless. Whenever an enemy tries to take you down, your retaliation seems assured.

IMMORTALITY?

On the verge of your climactic confrontation, your body and soul become one. It seems you can't die.

To Live Forever: When you have reached your career's destined end point, your immortality is assured. Simultaneously a being of soul and body, you pass through death's final mystery only if you choose to do so. Until you decide to abandon your body, it is your vehicle to eternity.

You could retire peacefully, perhaps taking up residence with your preferred deity. Fame and skill could serve you well as you live in a remote place in the world or among the planes, perhaps establishing a tradition to pass on your knowledge to younger would-be heroes. Alongside a Legendary General, you might fight the battle everlasting, or you could keep a vigil like that of the Eternal Defender. Perhaps you'll wander without end, or take up a wild card position in the cosmos. One day, you might ascend to literal godhood.

Your options are as limitless as your time now is. In the endless future, you might learn the method of your transfiguration into an undying being or some other form of wisdom the world needs. You choose whether to share this knowledge or to let it pass away if you finally give up everlasting life.

Undying Warrior Features

Wounded Resurgence (21st level): If you are bloodied, you can spend a healing surge as a minor action to restore your current hit points to your bloodied value. Also, you don't take a death penalty when you are returned to life by the Raise Dead ritual.

Undying Stamina (24th level): Each time you reach a milestone, you regain 1d4 healing surges.

Spontaneous Resurrection (30th level): When you die, you can return to life at the start of your next turn. Doing this doesn't require an action. You appear in a space of your choice within 5 squares of where you died and have hit points equal to your bloodied value. You are freed of any temporary effects existing at the time of your death, but permanent conditions remain. Each additional time you are

slain during the same day increases the time until you can rise again.

Second Death: Return to life at the end of the encounter.

Third Death: Return to life 1 hour after the end of the encounter.

Fourth Death: Return to life 12 hours after the end of the encounter.

Fifth Death or More: Return to life 24 hours after the end of the encounter.

If you don't use this ability, you can still be raised from the dead normally.

Undying Warrior Power

Undying Enmity	Undying Warrior Utility 26

You narrow your eyes, and even minor deities know how it feels to be prey.

Encounter ✦ Martial
Free Action   **Personal**
Target: An enemy marked by you or that is marking you
Effect: You roll an extra d20 for the next attack you make and choose which die to use as the attack roll (you cannot reroll any of these attack rolls). If you are bloodied when you use this power, roll two extra d20s instead of one.

Warmaster

History is written by the victorious. Who now living can say how you got where you are, a legend among the military leaders of history?

Prerequisites: 21st level, warlord

Surviving countless battles, endless engagements, you carry memories of faces—foes you have dispatched over your career of waging war. You have won more victories than you can count, defeated more enemies than anyone could hope to remember. Some call you lucky, blessed, or cursed. Others say you're brilliant, possessed of a tactical mind unrivaled in the modern age. The truth is that while you have benefited from uncommon good luck and a superior strategic skill, your successes stand on your unwillingness to give up and to use whatever advantages you had in order to win.

Your victories drew the interest of the great and mighty, from kings to exarchs, angelic lords to demon princes. You have crossed swords and wits with legendary leaders whose talents are every bit as sharp as your own. Each time you have managed to survive. If you didn't emerge with decisive victory, you left all your adversaries with a battle to remember.

Immortality?

Is being clever in war enough? For a time, you thought so. You wore each victory as a badge of honor, and you used these triumphs as a means to validate the death wrought at your order. Yet as each victory became more and more sure, you began to wonder if you would ever face a challenge worthy of your talents.

Eternal War: As you have done countless times before, you set your brilliant mind to the task of defeating your enemies, bringing to a close your final quest. Though you are victorious, a realization crashes upon you as you understand that with this last triumph no mortal mind can outmaneuver you, catch you unawares, or surprise you with some unexpected ploy. Your keen wit and pragmatism have secured your place in the annals of history, your name written in the blood of the vanquished. Who will stand against you now that you have defeated the undefeatable? Wins are wins, to be sure, but you want—you need—a challenge. There will be none here, for who will stand against you? No, you must leave this world to pass into the realm of legend, where you might find a worthy foe.

The legend you see is the Eternal War, the ultimate battlefield that draws the greatest commanders to test their brilliance and cunning against their equals, to fight onward until the end of days when the best of them are chosen to lead the armies of light in one final confrontation against the hordes of darkness. Such a locale might be nothing more than a myth, but if there's a chance that you could find a place among these great warlords, it's a chance worth the risk of failure.

WARMASTER FEATURES

Tactical Awareness (21st level): You and any ally who can see you can act during a surprise round even when surprised and do not grant combat advantage from being surprised. Also, each ally who can see you and is not surprised can take a standard action, a move action, and a minor action on his or her turn during a surprise round.

Shock and Awe (24th level): Whenever you spend an action point to take an extra action, one ally within 5 squares of you can also take an extra action on his or her next turn.

Tactical Genius (30th level): During an encounter, you can spend as many of your action points as you want.

WARMASTER POWER

Spring the Trap	Warmaster Utility 26

You lure your foes into a trap, and at your terse command, your allies spring to action.

Daily ✦ Martial
Standard Action   **Close** burst 5
Targets: You and each ally in burst
Effect: In order of highest initiative to lowest, each target can take a standard action, a move action, or a minor action.

ABOUT THE DESIGNERS

Rob Heinsoo led the design of the 4th Edition DUNGEONS & DRAGONS® Roleplaying Game and currently serves as the Lead Designer for Wizards of the Coast Roleplaying R&D. His 4th Edition design credits include the FORGOTTEN REALMS® Player's Guide. His other designs include the Three-Dragon Ante™ and Inn Fighting™ games.

David Noonan is a game designer for Wizards of the Coast. He contributed to the 4th Edition D&D® core rules and cowrote the Scepter Tower of Spellgard™ adventure. He lives in Washington with his wife and two children.

Robert J. Schwalb works as a freelance designer for Wizards of the Coast. His recent credits include the FORGOTTEN REALMS Player's Guide. Robert lives in Tennessee with his incredibly patient wife Stacee and his pride of fiendish werecats. He is happiest when chained to his desk, toiling for his dark masters in Seattle.

Chris Sims works as a game designer for Wizards of the Coast. His recent credits include the 4th Edition Monster Manual® and Dungeon Master's Guide®, as well as the FORGOTTEN REALMS® Campaign Guide.

HOWARD LYON

LEVEL UP YOUR GAME.

Bring more to the gaming table, and make every session even better—D&D® accessories are an indispensable addition to any game. Pick 'em up at the same place you got this book.

Dungeon Master's Screen
Conceal your secrets without blocking your view. Quick reference to common tables helps you keep your game moving.

D&D™ Dungeon Tiles
Define dungeons and add details to every encounter quickly and easily, and help your game come to life.

D&D® Miniatures
Know where everyone, and every thing, is at all times to keep your combats under control.

Character Record Sheets
Keep up with your character and use Power Cards to stay out of the books and in the fight.

D&D® Premium Dic
Everyone needs dice. And som
need more than others. Keep '
in a D&D logo-embroidered di

GET MORE INFORMATION AT: DNDINSIDER.COM

DUNGEONS & DRAGONS